PENGUIN BOOKS

INVESTING FROM SCRA

James Lowell is the editor of America Online's Mutual Fund Resource Center, as well as the editor-in-chief of FundWorks (his AOL site, which provides live fund-manager interviews, fund features, and investment insights). He has written extensively on investing and personal finance for national magazines such as *Worth* and *Your Money*, radio, TV, and the new on-line media. Lowell is often quoted on money and investing matters for those aged twenty-five to thirty-five in such prominent publications as the *Wall Street Journal* and *Fortune* magazine. In addition to his written work, Lowell also works for the Boston-based investment advisor firm Lowell, Blake & Associates. Prior to his current work, he was the editor of the national mutual fund newsletter *Funds Net Insight.* Lowell was also senior writer for Financial Planning Information, where he produced several major personal financial planning books, including *The New Century Family Money Book, The ABCs of Money Management,* and *1001 Ways to Cut Your Expenses.* He is also the author of *How to Survive in the Real World,* a comprehensive personal finance guide for college grads, which is available from Penguin. Lowell was educated at Vassar Collage, Harvard University, and Trinity College (Dublin, Ireland), where he started a poetry magazine. In addition to his comprehensive financial writings, Lowell is a publishing poet, and lecturer in the Philosophy/Religion Department at Northeastern University College in Boston.

You can reach him directly at Lowellinc@AOL.com.

JAMES LOWELL

INVESTING
— *from* —
SCRATCH

A Handbook for the
Young Investor

PENGUIN BOOKS

PENGUIN BOOKS
Published by the Penguin Group
Penguin Books USA Inc., 375 Hudson Street,
New York, New York 10014, U.S.A.
Penguin Books Ltd, 27 Wrights Lane,
London W8 5TZ, England
Penguin Books Australia Ltd, Ringwood,
Victoria, Australia
Penguin Books Canada Ltd, 10 Alcorn Avenue,
Toronto, Ontario, Canada M4V 3B2
Penguin Books (N.Z.) Ltd, 182–190 Wairau Road,
Auckland 10, New Zealand

Penguin Books Ltd, Registered Offices:
Harmondsworth, Middlesex, England

First published in Penguin Books 1997

1 3 5 7 9 10 8 6 4 2

PUBLISHER'S NOTE
This publication is designed to provide accurate and authoritative information with
regard to the subject matter covered. It is sold with the understanding that the
publisher is not engaged in rendering financial, accounting, or other professional
service. If financial advice or other expert assistance is required, the service of a
competent professional person should be sought.

Charts on pages xi, 70, 128, 183 reproduced by permission of
Morningstar (800-735-0700).

LIBRARY OF CONGRESS CATALOGING IN PUBLICATION DATA
Lowell, James
Investing from scratch: a handbook for the young investor/James
Lowell.
p.   cm.
Includes index.
ISBN 0 14 02.5511 7
1. Investments—United States—Handbooks, manuals, etc.
I. Title.
HG4921.L69   1997
332.6—dc20   96–8966

Printed in the United States of America
Set in New Baskerville
Designed by Kathryn Parise

ACKNOWLEDGMENTS

This book is the result of many knowing hands helping to lift a boulder of facts in order to unearth particular investment insights. The patience, perseverance, and persistence of my editor, Jane von Mehren, ensured final deliverance, if not ultimate absolution. Her fine editorial work was complemented by several individuals who were directly involved in the production process. In between his trips to Lithuania and beyond, Don Carleton applied his keen eye for financial fact and grounded grammar. David Pittelli cast a cold eye on rhetorical excess, and celebrated short sentences whenever he could find them. A silent partner throughout my thinking and writing of this book was the man who gave me my first job as a financial journalist, John M. Boyd. John's abilities as both editor and publisher are only exceeded by his talent for friendship and the strength of his belief in socially responsible investing. Lawrence "Larz" Dooley, on his way to becoming an exemplary analyst, made my work more seamless through his insights into the markets. Eric M. Kobren encouraged me to achieve more in less time than I thought possible. And Derk Sturgeon helped me to dust myself off and literally lift myself up whenever the going got truly tough.

Throughout my life, my father's passion for sound investment advice stirred an unshakeable interest in investing within me. Throughout the writing of this book, my wife, Terri, made certain that there was a lot of living going on, too. Now my wife and I are busy rebalancing our daily budget and long-term investment objectives to account for a new arrival. I have already wagered a large bet that our child's first words will be, "Buy this book and help support my future!" If I have done my job right, this book should help you achieve a better financial future for yourself as well.

Contents

PART IV
SMART INVESTING MOVES YOU CAN MAKE

PART V
YOUR FUTURE IS IN YOUR HANDS

INTRODUCTION

Investing Works!

O K. It's everywhere. It's inescapable. It's the talk of the town, the burbs, even remote islands in a stream. The word is out. Investing is where it's at. It's the only way to save your money. It's the only way to save yourself—from the fate of a financially insecure life now and, perhaps even worse, in the future. Word is, you can forget about banks; they're out. Wall Street is the only avenue worth pursuing when it comes to putting your money to work for you.

The truth about investing is that, long term, it can be the smartest move you'll ever make (with your money, that is). Investing wisely and well is a time-proven way to make your money work for you. And since you spend so much of your life earning it, why not have your cash return the favor in the best way that it can—by growing. But, growing assets doesn't happen overnight. Success isn't guaranteed. Selecting winning investments isn't as easy as some hipster friend might have you think. And choosing the best types of investments for your specific objectives requires a solid grasp of several investing fundamentals.

SOME INVESTING FUNDAMENTALS

1. Over time, investing in stocks has proven to be the best way to grow your money. True, there are other options, and some (bonds, for example), in conjunction with stock-based investments (i.e., stocks or stock mutual funds), can help you reduce the overall risk associated with investing while helping you achieve a decent return on your money—far more decent than that from a bank Certificate of Deposit (CD). But, unlike a bank CD, no investment, not even a money market mutual fund (not to be confused with a bank money market account), is insured. If you're not careful, you could end up owning a worthless piece of paper instead of your ticket to a financially secure future.

2. Not all investments are created equal—and no investment is right for everyone. There's a lot you should know about investing before you invest a single dollar in any one type of investment. For example, if you had invested $1,000 back in January 1989 in a bank CD, it would have been worth more than $1,500 in February 1996. If, instead, you had invested that same $1,000 in a stock mutual fund which invested in large-cap stocks (well-established companies with a market capitalization of more than $3 billion as represented by the S&P 500 Index), it would have become a sizeable $8,400. But if you think that would have been your best move, think again. If you had put that $1,000 in a small-cap value fund (smaller, less well established companies with a market capitalization of less than $1 billion as represented by the Wilshire SmallCap Value Fund Index), your small sum would have turned into a tidy $15,800 in the same time period.

3. There are no foolproof investment strategies—but there are several strategies that have proven to be reliable and successful. This book will tell you not only which strategies are worth your time and effort, it will also spotlight some of the more common scams that lead too many unwitting investors (and their money) down a dead road. One of the best strategies? Diversification. The bottom line is that diversification can work in your favor. What is it? Simply put, it's the distribution of your assets among several different types of investments, the theory being that when one investment is slipping from favor, another is often gaining ground.

4. A little knowledge can go a long way. You don't need a Ph.D. in economics to invest wisely and well. But you will need to bring yourself up to speed on some of the most prevalent themes that

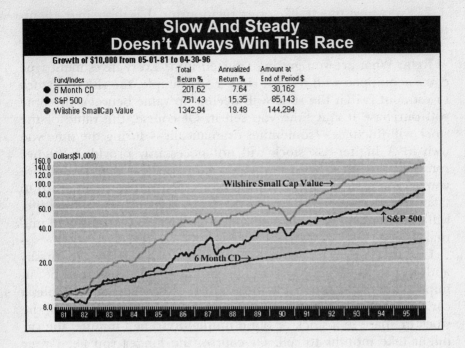

Slow And Steady
Doesn't Always Win This Race

Growth of $10,000 from 05-01-81 to 04-30-96

Fund/Index	Total Return %	Annualized Return %	Amount at End of Period $
● 6 Month CD	201.62	7.64	30,162
● S&P 500	751.43	15.35	85,143
◉ Wilshire SmallCap Value	1342.94	19.48	144,294

shape the markets you're investing in. Doing so requires a basic understanding of how economies work to shape the various markets where investment opportunities lurk.

5. The more rapidly you want your assets to grow, chances are the more risks you'll have to take. Some of the risks are definitely worth taking. Others you should absolutely avoid. For example, the risks of small-cap value stocks have been well rewarded, whereas the risks of holding gold bullion have not.

6. Stocks, bonds, and real estate are the three main categories of investments. Of these three, real estate requires the most money to get started, is the least liquid, and has a history of disappointing those who thought they could rely on property as their primary source of retirement savings. Most bonds also require a lot of up-front capital (although bond funds are a less expensive way to participate). And bonds historically have performed less well than stocks over the long run, and are not as safe as many people believe. Stocks require the least amount of money to get started and provide the greatest potential for profit, and are therefore the most appropriate area of the market for you to concentrate your money in— once you know what you're doing!

7. Every investment, like every relationship, has three ingredients that you need to have prior knowledge of:

RISK: What are you getting yourself into? Every investment type comes equipped with its own risks. For example, the risk of a stock investment is that the stock will decline in value between the time you purchase it and time you sell it. Of course, the value of the stock will fluctuate—sometimes dramatically—during the time you own it. A higher-risk stock will not necessarily provide a higher return, although it often will, while a lower-risk stock may not give you an adequate return. Knowing how much risk you can afford to take, and keeping your eye on the prize of a self-determined life, will help you create a balanced portfolio of stocks, bonds, and mutual funds.

LIQUIDITY: How easily can you get out if you have to? How easily and quickly you can convert your investment to cash may be an important consideration for those just starting out. For example, a car is a less liquid investment than a stock because you can sell the stock or share in a stock or bond mutual fund in a minute; the car might take months to sell. Of course, the longer you keep your money in a good investment, the better off you will be—at least up to a point. When it comes to a return on your investment, a car won't get you very far, but stock investing will.

RETURN: What's in it for you? The total amount of interest or dividends your investment generates, plus its rise (or fall) in value is known as its "total return." A healthy return is your reward for selecting top-performing investments.

BASIC STEPS TO INVESTING SUCCESS

Make no mistake, investing is the best way to build a better life for yourself. There's no real mystery to investing—just the simple truth that you need to do so, now. The following 11-step plan will help you put investing in perspective right from the start.

1. The crowd isn't always wrong, it seldom makes sense to follow the herd. More investors begin to invest when the market is at or nearing the top (the least optimal time to do so, since they're paying a higher purchase price) than buy at the bottom. Think of it this way: Most investors are like Christmas shoppers; those who purchase wrapping paper for their December 1997 presents in January 1997 will pay about half as much as those who buy their wrapping paper at the height of the holiday season. Same paper. Same function. But you can obtain greater value by purchasing at a lower price.

2. *You can make your own investment decisions.* And it won't take you two years and a degree to do it. Making your own investment decisions doesn't have to mean spending hours in front of CNBC watching the ticker run on all the exchanges. In fact, such daily nail biting will probably get you into more trouble than it's worth. This book will help you focus on the best ways to build a portfolio that can last, with some modifications, for the rest of your life.

3. *You know what's in your best interest—a broker rarely does.* Successful investing, whether you invest yourself or use an investment advisor in tandem with your own research, will always be measured in proportion to your achievement of your objectives. (Do not trust a broker, who could typically care less if you meet your objectives, since he or she is busy trying to fulfill their own—namely, selling you products from their shelf—with your money). In Part I, you'll find several strategies for developing objectives—and achieving them. Why is it so important to decide what your objectives are? Your objectives will dictate what your investments need to accomplish.

4. *The ultimate objective is to reach retirement with all the sources of income you'll ever need*—no matter what happens in the meantime. Of course, like a sailor who aims to go around the world, you can plan only for so many unforeseen circumstances, together with the foreseen ones. Looking ahead, anticipating obstacles, preparing now to overcome them—that's what you need to do. No one else can or will do it for you.

5. *Typically, the best investments aren't the hyped stocks or mutual funds that everyone is talking about.* This month's top performer is seldom the next month's. And while it is true that, in some rare instances, a hot performer can stay hot for several months, rarely does it do so for long. Look beyond the hype. There are plenty of stocks and funds that have delivered solid results over the long term, far surpassing the spectacular gain of a short-lived darling.

6. *Good investments are rarely cloaked.* By and large, the best investments are in name brands, known industries, and services and products that have a clear business or consumer demand. Occasionally, a technological revolution and the products (like software for the Internet) that attend it will become profitable. Mostly, however, the

best are solid and sober, not the kinds of investments that you have to buy and sell all the time.

7. *Always consider the toll inflation and taxes may take.* Many investors forget to benchmark the returns they get on their investments to inflation. Others forget to take into consideration the fact that they will pay taxes on their portfolios sooner or later.

8. *Use automatic investing and dollar-cost averaging* to achieve your goals—both your immediate one of being a more disciplined and regular investor, and your longer-term goal of financial security.

9. *Don't confuse saving with investing.* In terms of discipline and chicken-and-egg logic, you have to save to invest, but that's where the relationship between the two ends. A savings account may play a role in your overall investment program, but it should be a specific one—such as being an emergency account. The lion's share of your "savings" should be invested in order to ensure that your net worth grows sufficiently to help you achieve your financial goals.

10. *Patience brings lasting rewards.* Always take a long-term view of your investments. Overreacting to current market moves can have devastating consequences to your overall portfolio.

11. *Forget slacking.* Financial independence is actually getting harder to achieve. That's one reason why *investing is more important today than ever before.*

GETTING STARTED

To begin with, you need to get your overall financial house in order, and develop some clear-cut immediate, intermediate-, and long-term objectives. *Your ultimate objective should be to increase your investment know-how and maximize your actual investing.*

Part I will help you review your current financial condition to ensure that you have the right balance between what is immediately due and payable (from your rent or mortgage to your credit cards), and what you hope to achieve longer term—for example, home ownership, college funding for any little ones (real or imagined), and, yes, a financially secure retirement. After all, if you can't afford to pay this month's bills, you're not going to be doing yourself any favor by investing in some hot stock tip with the hope of striking it rich (which rarely happens). Instead, focus on a slow and steady pace to win the race.

Part II will bring you up to speed on some basic economic and investment themes and strategies. After reading this section, you'll be able to understand why Federal Reserve Board Chairman Alan Greenspan is among the most important world leaders. You'll no longer be uncertain about just how a leading economic indicator is akin to a prospector's headlamp when it comes to mining for investment "gold." You'll also develop a better understanding of how risk can work in your favor when it comes to selecting some undervalued or overlooked investment opportunities.

Wrapping your mind around the world of investing in general will lead you to Part III, which covers the best types of investments for your particular objectives. Some of what you read there may surprise you. While the "experts" will tell you that there are three main categories of investments—stocks, bonds, and real estate—they seldom tell you which category is most appropriate for you. Each category does present numerous types of investment opportunities, but the fact is that some are more appropriate for younger, less moneyed investors. The upshot is that most expert advice is generic, canned, and unfocused when it comes to you and your goals.

Part IV will help you become an investment detective. You'll learn about clues that will help you solve the mystery of what is (and isn't) a profitable investment. You'll also learn about several ways to manage your investments—from hiring someone to do the work for you to controlling your own investment decisions—as well as how to invest in (and on-) line with your financial objectives and your ethical intentions.

Part V provides the scoop on the best ways to reach your ultimate investment objective—a financially secure future. Doing so requires that you learn how to select one or more of the several tax-advantaged investment opportunities that are ready and waiting for you. In this section, you'll learn how to put your investment knowledge to work for you in such plans—whether they're offered by your employer in the form of a 401(k) or 403(b) plan or whether you offer them to yourself in the form of an Individual Retirement Account (IRA) or Keogh plan. No matter what, you don't want to miss out on the advantages such plans provide.

Part V will also help you understand the tax consequences of investing wisely and well—and how you can benefit from investments that have turned out to be duds. While taxes are hardly on everyone's hit list of things to get psyched about, it's in your best interest to know what investment-related tax moves make the most sense for you and your money.

Each part of the book, and every chapter, is designed to be read alone or in relation to the others. The latter, holistic approach is the better one to take, since investing is part of your overall financial planning process, and selecting particular investments requires that you understand more of the process than the sum of its parts alone. The best way to begin to take control of your financial future is to know which investment moves make the most sense for you—and how to avoid those that don't. Take this book with you to work. Stuff it in your knapsack on your next weekend getaway. Keep it close by. Read it. The more informed you are about investing, the more likely you will be to achieve your financial objectives. The truth is that *Investing* provides you with the basic ingredients you need to make a better life for yourself—*from scratch*.

PART I

A Primer on Your Future Well-Being

CHAPTER ONE

Where Are You Heading?

How can you begin to think about investing before you have paid the rent or mortgage—let alone the $10 you owe your friend for last night's café latte binge? Managing your monthly living expenses will no doubt prove to be an ongoing challenge. But it won't be your first—or last—financial challenge. Instead, it will be one of many that you will encounter from here on out. The trick is to know what you can do to meet the challenge, come out on top, and move on to the next level—one that challenges you to do more for yourself (rather than for your landlord or banker) by investing in and for yourself.

Your future is now. Knowing what financial responsibilities lie ahead can help you avoid costly collisions between your means and your short- and long-term dreams. No doubt many financial responsibilities have already arrived on your doorstep. Most of us are hit with the following mundane monthly expenses:

- Student loan payments
- Grocery bills
- Car payments
- Credit card bills
- Rent/mortgage payments
- Insurance bills

- Child care costs
- Phone bills

In addition to these regular and recurring payments, there are "life experience" events—for example, returning to grad school, purchasing a home, marriage, children, and more—that can be costly and, without advance planning, troublesome. Embarking on a career is perhaps your most important life experience, but, starting or restarting a new career path is a personally and financially exhausting pursuit. Planning for the related expenses of beginning (or changing) your career—from the cost of purchasing matching paper and envelopes for your résumé, to the cost of the infamous "interview suit" and a new pair of shoes—can help you manage your job search with greater personal and financial ease. This ease should translate into greater professional poise. You won't be sitting in an interview wondering whether or not the bubblegum will stay in the hole in the bottom of your shoe or if you can afford the cost of parking your car in that expensive lot.

INVESTING AND YOUR LIFE

The job of your dreams may not enable you to live exactly the lifestyle you most desire. It takes time to acquire a better standard of living, but it also takes planning. For example, knowing the average salary you can expect from your current or future career will help you frame your great expectations within the boundary of financial realism. How can you get to know what the average salary for your chosen job is? *Money* magazine does an annual survey of career-related pay. But you can do your own informal survey by asking your friends what they make. This is an especially good idea if one or more of your friends is in a field that interests you; sure, it's a little embarrassing, but, hey, so is asking your parents to help you meet this month's rent. No friends? Just ask the research librarian at your local library for help in getting your hands on the facts and figures you need. They live for that kind of stuff.

What other life experiences can you count on? Take a look at the following list, and check which experiences you think you have already encountered and are more than likely to encounter in the near future:

[ ] Renting a more expensive apartment
[ ] Buying a car
[ ] Taking out a personal loan
[ ] Paying taxes
[ ] Saving for a down payment on a home
[ ] Starting a retirement plan

These financially important life experiences are but a few of many. To make a more comprehensive list of common financial hurdles that you think you will encounter, get together with your friends and see what you can come up with. Distill from that list a more personalized one which details experiences you think you are most likely to meet. To do so, first divide your list into three sections:

1. Experiences you're likely to encounter within one year (e.g., student loan payments, rent, car loan)
2. Experiences you're likely to encounter in one to five years (student loan payments, car loan, down payment on home, mortgage, retirement-oriented investing, graduate school)
3. Experiences you're likely to encounter in five to ten years (undergraduate and graduate student loan payments, car loan, home mortgage, retirement-oriented investing)

Once done, take a look at your list and ask yourself the following question: What money-management and investment skills will you need to develop and put into practice in order to meet and master the costs of each event?

Chances are you will need to increase your knowledge of most or all of the following:

- Record keeping
- Budgeting
- Spending
- Bill paying
- Saving
- Insuring
- Investing

. . . in order to increase your knowledge and practice of these money-management skills:

- Balancing your checkbook
- Reconciling what you earn with what you owe
- Living a life you can actually afford
- Maintaining a good credit history
- Setting aside some of what you earn so that you can reach your personal goals
- Covering yourself and your assets from uninsured losses
- Investing in order to control your own financial destiny

Think about the best financial moves to make in the short, middle, and long runs. In fact, breaking the next ten years into three distinct parts is a great way to begin to map your goals. The next chapter will go even further in helping you determine your own objectives and goals. Subsequent chapters will show you how to acquire and develop the investment skills you'll need to invest your money so that you can take control of your overall financial life and goals. If you don't do it, no one else will.

BASIC GUIDELINES TO INVESTING

Create an investment plan and stick to it—unless, of course, it isn't working. History has proven that maintaining a relatively stable mix of investments increases your likelihood of succeeding in the stock market. Fables tell us the same thing. Again, think of Aesop's "The Tortoise and the Hare." Slow and steady wins the race, while speed and overconfidence can equal losses. Prepare yourself for the race of your financial life. Here's how.

1. Create an investment plan that relates and responds to your particular objectives and goals. This is crucial to your short- and long-term investment success. Why? Many investments are better suited for shorter and/or longer time frames. For example, if you are planning on returning to graduate school in two years, you don't want to invest in a bond that won't mature until ten years down the road. Instead, you will want to invest in a more liquid (easily sold) investment, like a bond mutual fund. You want to be sure that you are investing in order to meet your goals of a self-determined life.

2. Diversify—invest in a mix of investment types and categories. Diversification is also essential to achieving the best returns on your hard-earned dollars and is one key to investment success. Diversification is based on a down-home notion: never put all your eggs in the same basket. If you do, they might all get scrambled. Instead, spread your investment money around—a portion here, a portion there. Where? Well, you need to decide based on your goals and tolerance for risk. The process of deciding how much money you should place in given kinds and types of investments requires that you first become familiar with them. You can then make the decision that's best for you. The actual process of divvying up your investment dollars and apportioning them to various investments is known as asset allocation. (For more on this, see chapter 14.)

3. Invest regularly and often. Automatic investing combined with dollar-cost averaging is a great way to ensure that you stay on the investment track that will lead you to your goals. (See chapter 15 for details.)

4. Invest in tax-advantaged IRAs and 401(k)s. They're an even smarter way to put your savings to work. Investing in your own retirement may sound like something you should postpone until you near retirement. But consider this: Suppose you opened an IRA at age 23 and deposited $2,000 in your account each year until you reached age 30. You would—assuming you invested your money in mutual funds earning 8 percent—accumulate as much as someone who waited until age 30 to open an IRA and who put $2,000 aside each year until reaching age 65! How can this be? It's the effect of compounding.

Here's another eye-opening demonstration: this table shows what a given annual investment earning 8 percent compounded daily will yield years down the road:

YOU DEPOSIT	YOU WILL HAVE IN		
Per Year	*10 years*	*20 years*	*25 years*
$ 500	$ 8,024	$ 26,081	$ 42,333
$1,000	$16,048	$ 52,162	$ 84,665
$2,000	$32,096	$104,324	$169,330

Two thousand dollars a year?! Where are you going to get that amount of dough? For one thing, you don't have to come up with the lump sum all at once. For example, you could invest $166 each month (which totals to $2,000 in 12 months time). Think of it as a monthly bill that must be paid along with all your other bills—

only this time, you are paying yourself! Or why not get a second job, and invest your paycheck in an IRA? Better yet, if your company offers you the opportunity to invest in a 401(k) or 403(b) plan, take advantage of it. Either way, you give yourself a tax break while at the same time investing in your own future. Good deal. You don't need $1 million to invest in stocks and bonds. You don't even need $100! The fact is that no matter how much or how little you have to invest, the time to start investing is sooner rather than later.

READY RESOURCES

- *Question & Answer Book of Money,* by V. Harper, Adams Publishing.
- *Complete Idiot's Guide to Making Money on Wall Street,* by C. Heady, Macmillan.
- *Securing Your Child's Future,* by W. Conkling, Fawcett.
- *From Cradle to College: A Parent's Guide to Financing Your Child's Life,* by Neale Godfrey with Tad Richards, HarperCollins.
- *Lessons from the Art of Juggling: How to Achieve Your Full Potential in Business, Learning, and Life,* by Michael J. Gelb and Tony Buzan, Crown.

CHAPTER TWO

Creating a Budget You Can Live and Invest With

L ife without a budget is like a plane without a fuel gauge. Life without investing is like a plane without fuel. If you don't balance your spending with your earnings, you will never save enough to invest, which is a sure way to crash-land since you'll never know when you'll run out of juice. Like a good record-keeping system, a budget is the *sine qua non* of solid money management, which, as you now know, is the necessary foundation for building a successful investment program. And since building a successful investment program is the only way to guarantee that you won't be homeless come retirement time, budgeting is a critical step in your overall financial and investment planning process. Yet surprisingly few people take time to create a budget—and even fewer take the time to create a budget that enables their money to do more for them in the present and not-too-distant future.

Creating a budget that works is hardly an exact science. First, you'll need to get used to balancing your earnings with your expenses while ensuring that you have money left to invest. Second, you should revisit your budget on a regular basis so that it reflects changes in your financial situation.

The single greatest hindrance to establishing a successful budget is living on borrowed money (credit cards, loans, friends, etc.). Sooner or later, you will overstep the boundary of reasonable expenditure and end up paying for it by having to scale back your lifestyle drastically or miss out on an opportunity that could change your life—like investing for your future. If you think I'm exaggerating, take a look at your peers. Are most of them happy in their work life? If not, what do you think keeps them bound to the source of their unhappiness? (Freud's *The Economics of Masochism* won't furnish the answer!) Chances are these poor souls are stuck in uninteresting jobs because they are so mired in debt they can't afford the time to find something more satisfying. Profit from their example by avoiding their fate!

There's a good lesson to be learned from your cash-strapped cohorts. Living beyond your budget can get you into financial trouble, if not downright peril. That's because living beyond your budget usually indicates living simultaneously beyond your income and your debt obligations. Many of us wait until the critical moment—a realization that we've run up our charge cards to the max and can't afford to pay even the minimum monthly amounts on each card—before we realize that the budget bell was tolling for us. In this, we aren't alone. As a matter of fact, we're emulating our elders.

If you're looking around and wondering how those older than you achieve a lifestyle that they can't afford, the answer is simple. They do it the new-fashioned way—they charge it. Of course, charging what you can't afford to pay for necessarily entails living a lifestyle that you can't actually afford.

Many people who seem to have it all in reality have very little. This is because they charge everything from the clothes they wear to the VCR and videos they watch. They charge their car. Even their house may be used as a source to charge such unnecessary items as boats, trips to the Caribbean, a sports car, a new deck for the new grill for the new friends. At the end of the day, if you were to add up all the objects that are unpaid for in the stable of what a person claims he or she "owns," you would most likely find that for most, that person should replace the word "own" with "OWE."

Unless you buy your car, stereo, or new wardrobe with cash, you don't own what you're driving, listening to, or wearing—your creditors do. In fact, every time you hear someone say that they would like you to take a look at their new car, why not ask them if they have paid for it in full. If they have, fine and dandy. If they haven't, then perhaps they should come and take a look at what you are doing with your money—i.e., saving it. That's a far more impressive model.

The following "Net Worth" worksheet will help you distinguish between what you own and what you owe. Note that you need to fill in the total outstanding balances (not minimum monthly payments) when it comes to your current liabilities. Don't panic if it's not a rosy picture. You will make it better in short order. To do so, however, you need to know what you're up against.

Your Net Worth Statement

ASSETS		LIABILITIES	
1. Savings	$ _____	1. Rent/Outstanding mortgage	$ _____
2. Investments (market value if sold today)	$ _____	2. Bank loans	$ _____
		3. Car loans/ leases	$ _____
3. Car (sale value if owned)	$ _____	4. Total credit debt	
4. Home Equity (amount owed on mortgage minus original sale value multiplied by 80%)	$ _____	A.	$ _____
		B.	_____
		C.	_____
		D.	_____
		E.	_____
		(Total)	$ _____
5. Other (e.g., trust fund)	$ _____	5. Income taxes	$ _____
		6. Student loans	$ _____
6. Total	$ _____	7. TOTAL	$ _____

NET WORTH
(subtract liabilities from assets): $ _____

Your net worth is a big-picture view of your overall financial condition. From this perspective you can begin to view your particular financial situation through the lens of a practical budget.

CREATING A LIVABLE BUDGET

A budget is a financial reality check—a check of your actual and ongoing financial condition. Your budgeting objective is twofold: to ensure that your expenses do not exceed your earnings, *and to ensure that you can invest regularly.* If your budget is true to your current financial condition, it will always be there to help you see where you have overspent, where you can cut costs, and where you can pat yourself on the back for a job well done.

Budgeting is elemental. There are two basic elements upon which every budget is based: first, the amount of income that you earn and, second, the ways that income will be put to use. When these two elements are combined, they should provide a common-sense, practical, financial frame of reference for living within your means and investing on a regular basis. Knowing what you spend your money on will help you discern the difference between necessary and unnecessary expenditures. Once this is accomplished you will be better able to restore a balance between your earnings and your spending so that, at the end of the month, your income does not fall short of your obligations, your debts don't obligate you to fall short of your goals, and you have enough left over to invest at least 10 percent of your take-home pay.

Budget truthfully, sensibly, practically, and clearly. The more closely your budget reflects your actual income and spending habits, the more helpful it will be to you. In fact, the very act of making a budget helps develop your money-management skills. After all, the more you think about your financial condition, the more likely you will be to make it work to your advantage.

The following monthly budget will help you ensure that your income surpasses your expenses so that you can invest the difference. Once mastered, successful budgeting will put you well on your way to living a self-determined life. Remember that the sample budget is a monthly budget. This means that, unlike the net worth statement above, you need to list the monthly payments due—not the total balance owed.

Your Budget

MONTHLY INCOME:
    Take-home pay $ _____
    Other income $ _____

TOTAL MONTHLY INCOME: $ _____

FIXED MONTHLY EXPENSES:
    [ ] Rent $ _____
    [ ] Food $ _____
    [ ] Utilities $ _____
    [ ] Car loan $ _____
    [ ] Student loan(s) $ _____
    [ ] Bank loan(s) $ _____
    [ ] 5% of pay to your savings account $ _____
    [ ] 5% to 10% of pay to your investment
        accounts: $ _____
           Retirement-oriented $ _____
           Other $ _____
                          SUBTOTAL = $ _____

OTHER FIXED EXPENSES:
    [ ] Health insurance $ _____
    [ ] Car insurance $ _____
    [ ] Renter's insurance $ _____

TOTAL MONTHLY EXPENSES: − $ _____

INCOME FOR IRREGULAR EXPENSES: $ _____

IRREGULAR MONTHLY EXPENSES:
    [ ] Emergency fund $ _____
    [ ] Gas $ _____
    [ ] Telephone $ _____
    [ ] Laundry $ _____
    [ ] Clothing $ _____
    [ ] Car maintenance $ _____
    [ ] Medical/dental $ _____
    [ ] Goals (See chapter 3) $ _____
    [ ] Tuition for continuing education $ _____
    [ ] Club membership dues $ _____

By listing what you make and what you owe, you give yourself the advantage of knowing what you can and can't afford to spend your money on. For example, if you know that you are going to have approximately $150 a month that isn't already taken up by your rent and bills, then you can plan on dividing that sum into the parts of your irregular expenses that you think are most in need. Likewise, if your monthly expenses exceed your monthly income, then you are in a bind unless and until you cut your expenses or increase your income.

STAYING ON TARGET

No matter what you do, don't think that someone else is going to be there to give you the answers to your own financial destiny. Instead, take matters into your own hands. The following should help.

1. Do track your spending. Review your income, spending, saving, and investing patterns monthly. Discern patterns of necessary and unnecessary spending.

2. Don't carry a wad of cash in your pocket. Carrying a lot of money in your pocket is tiresome. Cash weighs so much that it's plumb hard to walk a mile without lightening the load. Who can blame you? Carry only what you intend to spend—and know what you intend to spend it on before you withdraw it.

3. Don't carry your ATM card. Don't? How can I live? How can I be expected to go on? No ATM card? How can I cope? Hey. It's your money. What you spend today you won't have tomorrow. Carrying your ATM card only increases your chances of spending beyond your plans and means. A mini-recipe for financial disaster— that's what an ATM card is.

4. Don't shop retail when discounts are available. While it's tempting to stray from your budget—especially when it comes to clothes and clothing sales—if you must stray, stray into a discount or outlet store. Buying retail (i.e., full price—even at 30 percent off you're likely to be spending more than at a discount or outlet store) is a quick way to make a sinkhole out of a savings account.

5. Do establish a regular investment schedule which coincides with your ability to invest. Typically, setting up an automatic investment account (through your checking account, or via a money market mutual fund) is an excellent way to keep on schedule. Of course, you'll need to be certain that the resources are in the account to begin with.

6. **Do** *participate in a 401(k), 403(b), or IRA tax-advantaged retirement-oriented account.* The benefit of the first two plans is that you may qualify for matching funds and have the investment amount (typically from 2 percent to 10 percent of your pay) automatically deducted. But if no such plan is available to you, there are solid options. (Part V provides the details.)

Remember when you realized that joining the words "now" and "here" spelled "nowhere." That was cool. But no longer. Your future is now, but living in the now, without a budget that accounts for your current income, present debt obligations, and investment needs will get you nowhere fast. On the other hand, living within the guidelines of your budget will enable you to put your finances in order and set to work on achieving your short- and long-term investment goals.

READY RESOURCES

If you want to get a grip on better budgeting, you might try your library or area bookstores for the following books that are chockful of sample budgets.

- *The Budget Kit: The Common Cents Money Management Workbook*, by Judy Lawrence, Dearborn.
- *Bonnie's Household Budget Book*, by Bonnie McCullough, St. Martin's.
- *Making the Most of Your Money*, by Jane Bryant Quinn, Simon & Schuster.
- *The Tightwad Gazette*, by Amy Dacyczyn, Random House.
- *Your Money or Your Life*, by Joe Dominguez and Vicki Robin, Penguin.
- *Make Your Paycheck Last*, Second Edition, by H. Moe, Career Publishers.
- *Penny Pinchers' Almanac Handbook*, by Penny Pinchers, Simon & Schuster.

- *1001 Ways to Cut Your Expenses,* by Jonathan Pond, Dell Trade.
- *Improving Your Credit and Reducing Your Debt,* by Gail Liberman and Alan Lavine, John Wiley.
- *The Way to Save,* by Ginita Wall, Owl/Henry Holt.
- *On Your Own,* by A. Armstrong, Dearborn.

CHAPTER THREE

Plan on Investing

Once you figure out where you stand (financially speaking, that is), the next step is to determine where you want to go. Doing so entails knowing something about the possibilities that lie ahead of you—from graduate school to home ownership to retirement. (Your life in a nutshell.) Thinking about all the possibilities can easily drive you to the funny farm. How can you begin to think about your retirement when you're not even sure that your current job at Kinko's copy center isn't the be-all and end-all of your career advancement? How can you begin to contemplate home ownership when you're still trying to figure out where you want to live? How can you begin to think about investing if you have just bought a home? Can't you put off today what won't happen for many tomorrows?

Let me put it to you this way. When do you think you should start to plan for the mega-events that will happen in your life, let alone for those events which you can't exactly schedule into the calendar year five or thirty-five years hence? If you answered "Today," you can read on. If, however, you answered "Later," you'd better return to the previous chapter for a refresher course on just how little time you have to plan ahead. Remember: If you don't know what you owe, stop here before you go.

Unless you have the perfect job, the perfect place to live, and

17

the perfect all-expenses-paid place to retire to, (in which case, I'd like you to adopt me), then you're like the rest of us. Not exactly dazed and confused, but not at the point where our dreams and reality are in synch. You want to move from where you are to where you most want to be. We all do. And, for the most part, we can all do it.

Personal Goals and Investment Goals Are Directly Related

The good news is that there are many ways in which you can plot a course to achieve short-term, skill-building objectives that will in turn help you reach longer-term, more self-fulfilling goals without sacrificing your current and future financial security. To begin with, you need to be clear about the difference between a goal and an objective.

Determine who you are and who you want to be. Think of a goal as a vision of yourself—who you would most like to be, what you would most like to achieve, what you would most like to do. Your goal might be to rise to the CEO's chair in a major corporation, or to become a tenured professor at a small Midwestern college, or to simply take a backseat to all that pressure and work in a fairly anonymous job. Whatever road you take is fine, so long as you can live within your means and invest enough money to ensure that, 30-odd years from now, you can retire in relative security as opposed to having to start another career—like the guy who picks up the golf balls after the driving range closes, or that grandmotherly woman serving up Happy Meals.

An objective, however, is a practical step that moves you closer to your goal. An objective is a thing that is within your grasp to achieve. Objectives entail specific ends, definite time frames, and achievable targets. You won't be able to achieve your personal goals without concrete personal objectives any more than you will be able to meet your investment goals without concrete investment objectives. Let's take your personal objectives and goals first, and then we'll look at the more essential investment objectives and goals which you need to achieve.

Personal Goals

Even if you are not sure what your ultimate goals are, you can determine specific objectives that can help you on your way to discovering who you want to be and where you want to go. The following are examples of common objectives you ought to set:

- Create a savings account
- Increase your marketable skills
- Pay off as much existing debt as possible
- Apply to graduate school
- Build your current savings
- Invest for your retirement

You should consider adding more specific objectives to this list, ones that will help you get your financial—and personal—house in order. Take a look at the following objectives:

- Save more regularly
- Establish a good record-keeping and investing system
- Ensure adequate health insurance coverage
- Increase your income
- Increase your savings
- Learn to invest
- Invest

Investment Goals

Make your shorter-term objectives work toward your ultimate objective of investing regularly and wisely. In order to get the hang of this, try the following. Pick one of the objectives you just checked from the above list—for example, saving more regularly. Notice that this objective is different from "save more money"—although that's always a wise thing to do, too.

"How do I save more regularly?" you ask. The answer is simple. Create a savings plan. What does a savings plan entail? A schedule for depositing a portion of your earnings into an account that you don't use to rent videos, buy cappuccinos, or debit for groceries and gas. (Determining the best place in which to put that slice from your pay's pie is detailed in chapter 14.)

Try again and again until you design a savings schedule that works for you. Start with a plan that corresponds to your income and expenses. At first, don't worry about how much money you deposit, though 5 percent of your take-home pay is a good place to start. Do focus on the objective of regularly depositing a portion of your pay, all the while keeping the goal of your savings in mind, whether that goal is the discipline of saving itself or the more advanced form of the savings goal—namely, saving for something other than saving itself: investing!

You should say to yourself, I need to save more if I am going to be able to ensure that I can invest more. Why? The last thing you want to do is to have to tap into your investments in order to pay for current obligations. Instead, you should have an emergency savings plans to help you meet the unforeseen circumstance of a forced layoff (for example), or to help you better decide about your financial ability to change career paths, go back to school, or tell your boss to take a hike.

Of course, you'll need to open a savings account—any bank will do as long as it's FDIC insured. (Before you open this emergency savings account, turn to chapter 5, which will teach you the basics of smart banking. If you already have a savings account for this purpose, check out chapter 5 anyway. It might have a tip or two you can use relating to fees that can and so should be avoided.)

Once you have your account, you'll need to figure out what time of the month is best for making your deposit. If you're paid biweekly, the beginning, middle, or end of the month may be appropriate. If you are paid on a monthly basis, the end or beginning of the month will probably prove best. But keep in mind that your bills may not all fall within the same time frame. So, don't let your saving plan collide with your bill paying. Instead, plan ahead. (Also, if you find that you have difficulty paying bills at different times of the month, try asking your creditors to switch the billing date in favor of your system. Many will do so.)

FROM SAVING TO INVESTING

Once you have proven to yourself that you can save more (by building up an emergency savings account which will cover three to six months' worth of your living expenses), then you can really turn up the volume of your ultimate goal—investing more. Determining your investment goals in advance of actually investing will help you achieve them. However, many of us begin investing without a plan (in a company retirement plan, for example) based on the consensus that this is the right thing to do. The truth is that it *is* the right thing to do—but there are better and worse ways to invest. Planning ahead of time—or revisiting your current pattern of investing—will help ensure that the goals you achieve are your own and not generic.

Of course, you'll need to open a investment account. And, as there are several types of banks that are out there waiting for your savings dollars, so are there many places, including banks, that are in the business of vying for your investment dollars. (But, unlike most banks, brokerage firms and mutual fund companies are not FDIC insured.) Before you open your investment account, turn to chapter 14, which will teach you some brokerage basics. If you already have an investment account, check out chapter 14 anyway, since it contains all kinds of cost-cutting moves that you can make to enable more of your investment dollars to go to work for you. If you are already participating in a retirement plan—a 401(k) or pension plan, for example—turn to chapter 21 to maximize your plan's potential to deliver the ultimate reward: a retirement nest egg that won't leave you scrambling for night watchman jobs at age 75. If you aren't participating in a retirement plan, don't miss out on this golden opportunity. (Again, turn to Part V for details.)

Once you have your account, you'll need to figure out whether you'll be investing on a monthly, quarterly, or annual basis—and when. Typically, investing smaller amounts more regularly (e.g., having the money automatically deducted from your paycheck and invested in a mutual fund) is the best way to go since it ensures that you won't spend the money in the here and now. As with setting aside money for your savings account, plan ahead so that your investing plan doesn't collide with your other payment obligations.

Setting objectives can be easy; the hard part is fulfilling them. However, if your objectives move you closer to the ultimate goal of being able to invest a portion of your paycheck, it will be easier to discipline yourself. Why? Because you're doing something for yourself!

For those of you whose financial troubles are threatening your immediate life, let alone your distant future, take heart. There are solutions to almost any problem—and cumbersome debt is no exception. In fact, Part II will explain in detail the ways in which you can increase your current cash flow and boost your investment income while allowing you to pay your debts on a timely basis (Parts II and III will help you accomplish this second feat). No matter what your immediate concerns are, stay focused on the ultimate objective of being able to invest in yourself. In order to accomplish this, you'll need to plan for it.

The following suggestions are to help jump-start your own thinking about investing your way to a better life.

SHORT TERM (within the next six months)

1. Learn more about money management
2. Learn more about investing
3. Establish savings strategy for intermediate-term investing goal

INTERMEDIATE TERM (six months to five years)

1. Select the best tax-advantaged retirement plan for you
2. Select the best type of investments for you and your objectives
3. Open a brokerage (preferably discount) account

LONG TERM (five years and more)

1. Increase retirement-oriented investing amount to at least 10 percent of salary
2. Review portfolio's adequacy for new financial obligations (e.g., college for kids)
3. Assess probability of buying (larger) home within next five years

In addition to stating your goals, you'll want to think about what they will entail and give yourself a deadline.

INVESTMENT GOAL ONE:

Target Date:

Estimated Cost:	*Invested:*	*Need to Invest:*
$ _____	$ _____	$ _____

INVESTMENT GOAL TWO:

Target Date:

| *Estimated Cost:* | *Invested:* | *Need to Invest:* |
| $ _____ | $ _____ | $ _____ |

INVESTMENT GOAL THREE:

Target Date:

| *Estimated Cost:* | *Invested:* | *Need to Invest:* |
| $ _____ | $ _____ | $ _____ |

MONTHLY AMOUNT TOWARD GOAL: $

You will probably need to expand this worksheet to encompass all your goals. And you may want to consider other objectives such as:

OBJECTIVE:	**TURN TO:**
Save more regularly	Part I
Establish an investment record-keeping system	Chapter 4
Buy a stock	Chapters 11, 14
Invest in mutual funds	Chapter 13
Understand investment tax strategies	Part V

BUILD YOUR OWN PYRAMID

Think of investing as building toward a better future. You might start small—but someone had to place the first stone that launched the pyramids.

In the Pyramid Approach to Investing (see page 24), the base of the pyramid represents where most financial experts—from financial planners to investment counselors—suggest you place the money you want to keep safe. It's easily accessible, at a low risk, and shows a predictable return. The middle of the pyramid is comprised

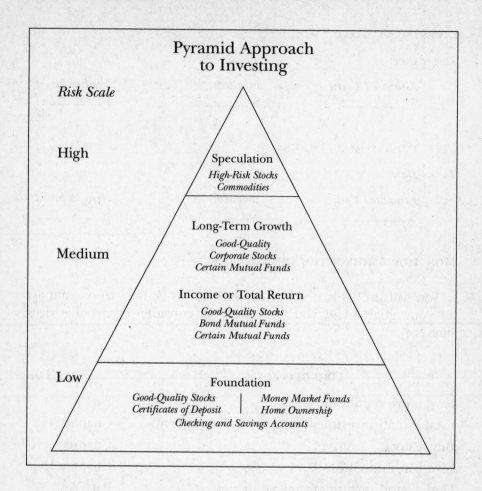

of investments with higher risk and potentially higher return. The greater potential for growth is essential if you want your money to grow fast enough to beat inflation. Mutual funds, high-quality stocks, and bonds are what this part of the pyramid is made of. The peak of the pyramid represents high risk and high potential for loss, but the profits can be extraordinary. Commodities (pork bellies and the like), options, penny stocks and other very risky investments are found here.

The pyramids weren't built in a day. Don't expect that you will change your financial life overnight. In fact, it's a lifelong process.

Keeping track of your investing progress is what the next chapter is all about. If you don't develop a way to track your progress from your immediate objectives to your ultimate goal of a financially secure life, you are working against yourself. On the other hand, establishing a way to track your progress will not only help you get to your ultimate goal faster, it will also help you reduce the potential anxiety that awaits those who have no clear idea of where they are heading—or why.

READY RESOURCES

The following money-management software programs will help you plot your financial course to your ultimate investing-related goals. They will also help you cover most of your bill-paying needs, and some will help you establish a record-keeping system for all your financial concerns—from personal finance to investing.

- Quicken (for DOS, Macintosh, Windows).
- Managing Your Money (for DOS, Macintosh, Windows).
- Microsoft Money (for DOS, Macintosh, Windows).
- Kiplinger's CA—Simply Money (for Windows only).

Chapter Four

Tracking Your Progress

Successful investing relies on a foundation of solid money management. Everything to do with money management relies upon your being fully informed about your current financial condition. A record-keeping system which incorporates your personal finance and investment-related transactions is the best way to keep track of the financial information you need in order to meet the demands of our money-centered culture. Those demands range from paying bills to keeping track of your investments' performance in order to ensure that you're on track in achieving your objectives. If you can't find the bill you need to pay, and if you can't locate the proper documentation to back up your assertion that an error has been made by a mutual fund company, you can find yourself incapable of paying what you owe while earning less than you deserve.

To begin with, a record-keeping system will help you collect and organize the necessary financial information and documentation relating to your current financial obligations, thus enabling you to avoid untimely and potentially costly searches for documentation. A record-keeping system will also help you review and revise your budget. That's all pretty obvious, but a good record-keeping system can help you do much more. Come tax time, for example, your filing system will help you to have all the documents you need at your beck and call. This means you will be able to fill out the forms easily, accurately, and promptly—good news whether the IRS owes you or vice versa. (Either you will get your refund sooner or you will avoid paying a penalty for underestimating your tax bill.)

Organization is half the battle, but organization alone won't do. In fact, you will need to develop a system that is shaped, in part, by your inclination to be disorganized. That's right: one way to ensure that your record-keeping system will work for you is to structure it according to your record-keeping weaknesses (as well as your strengths). In other words, focus on aspects of your money-related record-keeping habits that you are least likely to follow through on. If you're someone who never balances a checkbook, organizing your monthly checks would be the obvious place to start. Address your weaknesses, then move on.

CREATING YOUR OWN SYSTEM

There are many different ways to create a record-keeping system that can work for you. A good system will be divided into two main categories—personal finance and investing—and it will have two main components—an active file and an inactive file. Straightforward enough. But making this system work for you is a more complicated matter. Are you the kind of person who meticulously puts your bills and investment statements away as you receive them? Or do you just toss them in a drawer in your room? Perhaps you scatter them all over the place? Maybe you even throw out bills as soon as you pay them? If there are two of you, this process can be twice as difficult to manage. If you choose to set up an on-line file, the difficulties can surpass the more mundane paper chase, since it's more difficult to enter all the data you need if you aren't organized and disciplined. No matter what record-keeping habits you have (from meticulous to mercurial), the following suggestions should help you develop better record-keeping skills:

- Keep the files easily accessible.
- File away bills and investment statements as they come in—not on a weekly or monthly basis. This is the best way to keep track of what you have spent, what you owe, and when the bill is to be paid, as well as how well you are paying yourself in terms of investing wisely and well.
- Always write the date and amount paid on the bill. Then file it

in its appropriate active file. Writing the date and amount on the bill will help you keep track of your own payment history so that, come the next statement time, you can check and make sure that the company received your payment and recorded it. If you use personal finance software (see the personal finance software resources at the end of chapter 3) to pay your bills, you may think you are off the bill-filing hook. What happens if you lose the program? That's right: it happens. You should print out your bill payments and store the hard copy in your active file.

- Buy a small calendar specifically for bill paying and investing. How many times have you sent in a late payment—or missed a payment altogether? Every time you do, you set yourself back in two ways. First, you are either assessed a late fee or are charged interest on a needlessly high balance, and you may find that your delinquency is reported to credit agencies which, in turn, can make it harder for you to obtain a loan down the road. A bill-paying calendar will help you pay each and every bill on time—warn creditors in advance that you will be unable to do so on time. If you have an automatic investment plan (a smart move), then you have solved one potential problem which many investors fail to overcome—regularly investing a portion of their income. Still, it's a great idea to make a note in your calendar as to the date and amount of your automatic withdrawal so that you don't accidentally overdraw your account. It's also a good idea to mark down significant investment dates—for example, for a quarterly review of your 401(k) portfolio—so that you are prepared to research and make potential trades in due time rather than rushed time.

   Keep the calendar at the front of your active file, and when you receive a bill, open the calendar and mark in red when the payment is due. By the same token, you can use one of the many personal finance software solutions to scheduling and planning your payments and investment statements. Just be sure you keep a backup file.

- Reserve one drawer in one place for your active files. That way, you'll always know where they are so you'll never have to throw your bills on a chair and then forget where you put them. And, perhaps more important, you won't have to wonder about how your investments have been doing—and just what you're in-

vested in. Also, set aside a drawer large enough to accommo-
date what can become sizeable folders.

- Buy an alphabetized accordion folder—or buy loose folders
  and label them, one folder per credit card, bank, or insurance company. Sounds simple—works great! (Cost: $20 max.
  Less than a late payment fee that could have been avoided
  if your records were organized.)
- Keep some extra space set aside for a "research" folder in
  which you can keep information on your investments, or news
  that pertains to them, as well as information on changes in your
  overall personal financial landscape.
- Buy a fireproof box for your most valuable documents—passport, birth certificate, naturalization papers, etc. Also, keep
  copies of your most important papers in your active record-
  keeping system.

Heeding the helpful hints for setting up a record-keeping system
is a good first step. Now you need to take the practical application
plunge. You need to know what documents to file and where to file
them.

Your Active Files

Bank statements (including recently canceled checks); charge card,
credit card, and loan statements; paycheck stubs; and insurance
bills are just some of the items to keep in your active personal
finance file. Investment statements, annual and semiannual reports,
trade documentation, and written memos of any conversations you
have had with your broker, financial advisor, or customer representative are some of the items to keep in your active investment file.

ACTIVE PERSONAL FINANCE FILE
   The following are some categories you might consider:

- Banking
  [ ] Most recent bank statements
  [ ] Deposit/withdrawal/ATM slips
  [ ] Automatic investment slips

• Credit Cards
[ ] Monthly statements

• Food/Entertainment
[ ] Grocery bills
[ ] Liquor bills
[ ] Restaurant/bar tabs

• Insurance
[ ] Health insurance payments
[ ] Car insurance payments
[ ] Renter's/homeowner's insurance payments

• Loans
[ ] Bank loans
[ ] Car loan
[ ] Student loans
[ ] Mortgages

• Receipts/Purchase Slips
[ ] Clothing
[ ] Furniture
[ ] Appliances
[ ] CDs
[ ] Tapes/Videotapes
[ ] Other (like pharmacy bills)

• Rent/Utilities
[ ] Canceled monthly rent check
[ ] Electricity bill
[ ] Phone bill
[ ] Gas bill
[ ] Cable bill
[ ] Gym/Health club bill

• Transportation
[ ] Gas
[ ] Car repairs
[ ] Commuter ticket or monthly card

• Taxes
[ ] Tax statements

ACTIVE INVESTMENT FILE

Following are some categories to consider for your active file of investment activity.

- Investments
[ ] Mutual fund statements
[ ] Brokerage statements
[ ] Retirement plan statements
[ ] Account memos*
[ ] Annual reports
[ ] Most recent semiannual reports on funds and companies you invest in
[ ] Most recent quarterly statements

- Research
[ ] Magazine reports on your stocks, bonds, and mutual funds
[ ] Industry reports relevant to your investments
[ ] New investment ideas

Notice that there is no "temporary" or "to-be-filed" file. Such files all too easily become a permanent pain in the bill-payer's (your) and investor's derriere. As with most events in life, you should never put off doing today what you think you will do tomorrow. Tomorrow comes, chaos remains.

Your Inactive Files

An inactive file is a mini-financial library where you can research your spending, saving, and investing history. Your ability to research your own questions is not only the best way to ensure that you get the answer you are looking for, it's also money saved. If, for example, you call your bank or broker and ask them to research a transaction that you think may have taken place seven months ago, they'll be more than happy to oblige. More than happy, because they're charging you at least twice what they pay the clerk who is researching your account to come up with the noncommittal an-

---

* While the above investment statements are relatively self-explanatory, many investors neglect to keep an accurate record of the time, date, person's name with whom they spoke, transaction request, and response. You should do so every time you call your broker, mutual fund company, or human resource department so that you are certain you have an accurate record to defend your side of the story—should something go wrong.

swer that somehow costs you more money. If, instead, you create an inactive file, you will be able to do most or all of the work yourself.

Another significant advantage of an "inactive" file is that it can easily be activated when needed, particularly as you research how well your investment portfolio has done over time. Many investors become so caught up in the day-to-day performance of their portfolios that they forget to look at the cumulative success (or failure) of their history of investments. You know Santayana's saying "Those who cannot remember the past are condemned to repeat it"? Learn from the history of your own actions. Also, use the history of your investments contained in this file as a sounding board for future investing strategies.

Write the following labels for your inactive file:

• Financial Papers Over Three Months Old
[ ] Bank statements
[ ] Canceled checks
[ ] Past tax returns
[ ] Brokerage/mutual fund slips and statements

• Loans and Other Obligations Over Three Months Old or Paid in Full
[ ] Student loan statements
[ ] Car loan
[ ] Personal loan
[ ] Credit card statements
[ ] Paid credit card/charge card bills

• Copies of Personal Papers
[ ] Adoption papers
[ ] Birth certificate
[ ] Citizenship papers
[ ] College diploma
[ ] Passport
[ ] Social Security card
[ ] Veteran's/R.O.T.C. papers

• Ownership Papers
[ ] Automobile title
[ ] Other:

- Investment statements and reports
- Brokerage statements
- Prospectuses
- Annual reports
- Semiannual reports
- Stock, bond, mutual fund reports
- Economic analyses

Just do it. Once you have created your active and inactive record-keeping files, you will no doubt need to discipline yourself to actually use them. What makes this difficult is easy to understand. It requires no effort not to file a bill or investment statement. It requires some effort to do so. But the effort it requires to file one statement is minimal compared to the effort it will take to file several all at once—or to find the one statement you need in a pile of papers that have been accumulating over the past few months.

You can develop a good record-keeping system for your personal finance and investing areas. You can perfect your own record-keeping skills. If at first you make a mess of things, try and set it right. Just about everything in life requires work, revision, more work, and more revision. Most man-made systems are prone to occasional screwups, so it should come as no surprise that you will need to tinker with your record-keeping system on a regular basis. You will know that you have finally got it right when you don't have to search for bills when you want to pay or question them, or wonder what the total return of your investment portfolio is or what percentage of your investments you have in stocks, bonds, cash, foreign markets, and pork bellies. Practice makes perfect.

READY RESOURCES

- National Center for Financial Education, (619) 232-8811.
- National Consumers League, (202) 835-3323.
- *Kiplinger's Make Your Money Grow,* Revised, by T. Miller, Random House.
- *Kiplinger's Facing 40,* by D. Moreau, Random House.
- *Wall Street Journal Guide to Financial Planning,* by K. Morris, Simon & Schuster.
- *Personal Financial Planning,* Fifth Edition, by G. Hallman, McGraw-Hill.

- *New Century Family Money Book*, by Jonathan Pond, Dell Trade.
- *Price Waterhouse Personal Financial*, by Price Waterhouse, Irwin Press.
- *Time Is Money*, by F. Leonard, Addison.
- *Investing for Good*, by Peter Kinder, Steven Lydenberg, and Amy Domini, Harper Business.
- *Market Movers*, by Nancy Dunnan and Jay Pack, Warner Books.
- *Feathering Your Nest*, by L. Berger, Workman.
- *Great Reckoning—Revised*, by J. Davidson, Simon & Schuster.
- *Can You Afford to Retire?* by B. Doyle, Irwin Press.
- *Money Book of Personal Finance*, by R. Eisenberg, Warner Books.
- *Financial Self-Defense for the Unemployed*, by L. Elkin, Doubleday.

PART II

Five Essential Steps to Your Overall Investment Success

CHAPTER FIVE

Smart Banking

Banks are the traditional cornerstone of your financial house. In fact, for many of us, banks will hold the key (and the right to take it back) to our actual home—typically the single biggest investment we make in our lifetime. That's why, when it comes to growing your money, you need to become as smart about banking as you will become about investing. But banks are no longer the places they once were. For example, not only can you deposit and withdraw money from banks, you can open up an automatic investment account, invest in a bank-related mutual fund, receive investment information, invest in a host of funds from many different fund families, and, when it comes to some banks, you can do it all on-line.

All banks are not created equal. Some are safer than others. Some are more convenient than others. Others offer greater interest on accounts than their competitors do on the same types of accounts. Still others offer a wider range of products and services. All these differences could work to your saving and investing advantage—or, in the event of an uninsured bank closing, the loss of some of your cash.

Most of us have basic banking needs, but the question concerning whether or not we need a bank to fulfill them is getting more interesting these days. For one thing, it's unclear that we will need

37

banks in the near future since, with the advent of mortgage brokers, money market mutual funds with check writing, and debit and credit card privileges, the main staples of a bank's fee-based diet are offered on other menus. Besides, many of us are already used to doing most of our banking automatically with automatic transfers, automatic teller machines (ATMs), and even on-line transactions with a personal computer.

What role should banks play in your life? Before we get ahead of ourselves, perhaps we should review what today's bank can do for you. After all, most of us do have a bank checking account—and should have a savings account (wherein three months of our take-home pay is stashed for emergencies). What's more, a bank is the place many of us will go to get our first mortgage (or refinance the one we've got). And for the lucky few who bought real estate in the early '90s and have seen some appreciation in equity, a second mortgage or equity line of credit is perhaps a worthwhile consideration. Other bank-related services: ATM transactions, new car loans, bill consolidation loans.

Today's banking environment is a jungle of products and services. Many of those products and services are worth considering while others are money pits to be avoided at all costs. In your search for overall financial independence, it's critical that you become an informed banking consumer so that you will know how to shop for the bank that best meets your current and future financial needs.

BANKING BASICS

How did you choose your bank? When it comes to banks, most of us let banks choose us rather than the other way around. Here's how it works. You graduate from college or change your career. You move to a new town. You need to have checks with your name and address on them and you need them now. You look out your window. No bank in sight. You walk one block. There, within walking or easy driving distance to your new digs, is a bank. Your new bank. "How convenient," says a devilishly persuasive voice within your head. "Let's just set up an account here and be done with it. We've got better things to do than fiddle around in bank lobbies all day!" It is a most convincing voice. But is it the voice you should be listening to?

If you ask yourself what should you be looking for in a bank, chances are convenience won't top the list, but with today's on-line banking services, maybe it should—but not at the expense of quality, low-cost service or a wide variety of services. Looking for all the above takes little time and effort and, at the same time, it can actually save you money before you open up a new account. Here's how to start. First, familiarize yourself with the types of banks that are in your area. Second, familiarize yourself with the range of services they offer. Third, choose the one bank which provides the services you need at a cost that is competitive with other banks. Fourth, make sure that the type of bank account you choose enables you to bank on-line and automatically invest. Remember, there are several types of banks. It's not the size that counts; it's the level of savings safety (federally insured), product range, and quality of cost-effective service.

In addition to banks, credit unions are often good places to do business—if you are eligible to join. A credit union is a banking cooperative operated for the benefit of its members. Most credit unions are sponsored by an employer or an association—meaning they aren't open to the general public. Workers' unions—from teamsters to teachers—tend to offer this alternative form of banking. If you have the opportunity to join a credit union you should consider it. Typically, credit unions offer better rates on both savings accounts and consumer loans. One drawback to credit unions, however, is that they're a bit behind the times when it comes to on-line services. While this will no doubt change rapidly in the years ahead, you may find that even your local bank provides greater electronic access.

Above all, be sure that your deposits are federally insured—by the Federal Deposit Insurance Corporation, or FDIC as it's more commonly known. It won't be hard to tell whether or not your bank is FDIC insured. For one thing, if it is, the FDIC logo will likely be posted on every teller window and then some. If you don't see any signs to indicate FDIC insurance, you can ask the branch manager—and ask for positive proof. If you don't make sure your bank is FDIC insured, there's not much to ensure that the money you deposit tonight will still be there come sunup.

How to find a bank that's right for you? *The old-fashioned way:* Get your hands on the Yellow Pages and call several banks that are convenient for you to get to. Call each bank, and ask for the following information:

A. FDIC Insurance: [ ] Yes   [ ] No

B. Types of checking accounts: 1. _____
                                    2. _____
                                    3. _____
                                    4. _____

C. Types of savings accounts: 1. _____
                                    2. _____
                                    3. _____
                                    4. _____

D. Interest rates on B and C: 1. _____   1. _____
                                    2. _____   2. _____
                                    3. _____   3. _____
                                    4. _____   4. _____

E. Fees for B and C: 1. _____   1. _____
                                    2. _____   2. _____
                                    3. _____   3. _____
                                    4. _____   4. _____

F. Location:

The *new way* to select a bank that's best for you? Go on-line. While the details of on-line banking are provided in a special section (pages 53–55), it might surprise you to know that you can actually shop for all your basic and even most of your more complex banking needs without standing up. As long as you're linked to the World Wide Web, the world of banking is literally at your fingertips. True, it's a small world right now. But you can bet that banks will proliferate in virtual reality at a similar speed to their ATM installations during the last decade. Since customers are the driving force of the banking business—and many customers find it increasingly difficult to do their banking during bankers' hours—on-line services make sense, especially since the Web gives them 24 hours a day to catch new customers. Many customers are already banking on-line with services like Quicken and Microsoft Money.

Shopping for a bank which provides all the services you need at a comparably competitive cost has been made considerably easier of late—and not just because banks have gone virtual. Most banks

—big and small—offer a host of service-related incentives to new customers, often waiving monthly fees for new checking and saving accounts. Since average annual service fees can easily cost over $100, this is no small deal. Of course, the deal may be short lived. For example, "No monthly fee for the first year." But that still represents money saved and money in the bank in your account. When it comes to mortgage lending, banks have also become more competitive—some will waive closing costs (all or in part) and many will be less turned off by a spotty credit history. The reason? For one thing, there's more competition from mortgage companies vying for your business. And there are fewer of us, meaning that banks have more to lend—and since lending is their business, it behooves them to find ways to maintain a steady pace. Now, this rosy condition may not last forever. In fact, the next few years are likely to be the best time to buy a home. Mortgage rates are at historical lows, meaning you can buy more house for your buck.

The merits of buying a home versus renting one aren't as straightforward as they used to be, however. The bottom line: think of your house as a home—not as an investment. Chances are you'll qualify for a larger tax break if you own your home, but building equity in your home will take longer, on average, than in previous years (the drawback of a low inflationary environment). Moreover, since you don't really "own" your home (your mortgage lender does), if you are thinking of moving within the next five years, consider renting as an option. Or, consider a two-family home as a possible investment. (For more on real estate investing, turn to chapter 12.)

The bottom line is: select a bank based on services needed, not on services provided. A bank is basically there for putting money in (to your checking and savings accounts), and taking money out (of your checking account, which can also be the base of your automatic investing account, or through loans and mortgages).

To open your bank account you will need the following four items: money, your Social Security number, an address, and some form of positive identification—a driver's license should be just the ticket. Not surprisingly, putting money into the bank is easy. However, deciding which accounts suit your needs likely will prove more difficult.

No matter which bank you select, be sure to stick with the most essential criterion of all—the safety of your money. After you are certain that the bank is federally insured, then you can begin to mix and match your search for cost-effective service and best interest deals with your sense of what constitutes a higher purpose.

ETHICAL CONSIDERATIONS

One of the commonly overlooked aspects of selecting a bank is whether or not your bank practices a business ethic you believe in. Like ethical investing (see chapter 19), there are criteria you can use to rate your bank's social conscience. Not that you have to. Most investors are not concerned with the social responsibility of the companies they invest in. Most banking consumers are, likewise, uninterested. However, we're the new generation of banking consumers and investors. Maybe it's time to become more of an ethical activist and less of a consumer passivist when it comes to where our money is deposited and how it is invested on our behalf by the bank we do business with.

The following criteria may help you rate your bank's social activism:

* Community development: How active is your bank in terms of community development projects? How can you find out? Since 1977, banks have had to file a community reinvestment statement—under the Community Reinvestment Act mandate —in which the bank's distribution of loans among all members of the community is disclosed. Not that numbers tell the whole story—high denial rates among specific minorities may be an indication of an underqualified applicant pool. Nevertheless, requesting a copy of this statement—yours for the asking— from your bank will help you jump-start your thoughtful engagement with the institution that not only holds but invests your money in projects you may or may not agree with.
* Community involvement: Economic commitment to the community as a whole is one thing. Community involvement is another. Use the following criteria to rate a bank's commitment to its community:
    1. Does the bank locate branches in distressed areas? Some banks are opening ATM machines inside area police stations in order to keep banking opportunities open to all, even in high-crime neighborhoods.

2. Are bank officers active in local charities and community organizations?
- Who owns the bank? Minority-owned banks are one way to go. In opening your account at a minority-owned bank, you may be helping to promote lending in less developed areas in your community. It's not, however, a guarantee that you are. To find out if there is a minority-owned, FDIC-insured bank in your area, contact the National Bankers Association, 1802 T Street, NW, Washington, DC 20009, (202) 588-5432.

Aside from questions concerning the merits of the bank you do business with, you'll need to conduct business as usual. For example, remember record keeping. After opening up your account, go home and set up a record-keeping file for it. (If you already have an account, make sure you have an active file for it in your current record-keeping system.) Don't make the common mistake of thinking you don't really need a file for this. An organized file will make such matters as balancing your accounts and checking errors a breeze. Without it, this can become very time-consuming.

Furthermore, if you don't keep accurate and accessible information on your banking accounts, you could be making a costly mistake. Costly? That's right. When it comes to resolving clerical errors, most banks make you foot the research bill. However, if you do go home and set up that file, then you will have the information you need to detect and prove an error. Make your life simple. Keep meticulous records of each of your accounts.

BASIC BANKING ACCOUNTS

SAVINGS ACCOUNTS: Although there are many variations on the savings account theme, there is a basic motif most savings accounts share: You put money into a savings account in order to build up a cash reserve while earning (a modest amount of) interest on it.

Banks calculate interest three different ways. This means the interest you receive on an account may differ from bank to bank depending on how they calculate their savings account's interest. *Day-of-deposit*, which means you earn interest on money from the day it is deposited to the day it's withdrawn, will earn you the most interest; *average daily balance* is less attractive because it pays interest on the average balance in your account; and the *lowest balance* method is the least attractive since it pays interest on the smallest balance in your account during the month or quarter.

Earning interest on your hard-earned money is one advantage of a savings account. Another less obvious benefit is that the act of setting your earnings aside in an account specifically earmarked for savings is, in itself, a positive money-management development. A savings account can also allow you to create an emergency fund—a sum of money set aside for the purpose of providing cash should your monthly resources prove inadequate to meet life's little (but costly) surprises, like a flat tire, or a wisdom tooth.

Is there a downside to a savings account? You bet. Naturally, you assume that the hard-earned money you've deposited in the account will earn enough interest to make it a worthwhile investment. But guess what? Chances are, unless you use your savings account only as a temporary parking place for your cash, the money deposited there will decline in value on an inflation-adjusted basis. This is because the amount of interest earned on a typical savings account is usually lower than the rate of inflation.

Inflation affects the value of each and every dollar you earn, save, and/or spend. If the rate of inflation is 3.5 percent and the rate of interest you're earning on your savings account is 3.25 percent, then your dollar's purchasing power—what it used to be able to buy versus what it can now buy—has lost ground, not gained it. That's why a savings account is strongly recommended for one specific function—the establishment of an emergency reserve fund for life's unexpected surprises. Otherwise, your money can be put to better use earning higher interest.

The one basic type of savings account is the "regular savings" account. There are two subspecies of the regular savings account which differ only in the way your transactions are recorded. In a *passbook account,* all your deposits and withdrawals are recorded in an actual book—a "passbook." In a *statement savings account,* the bank records and stores your transactions in its database and sends you a detailed monthly review of all your account transactions, which can be a handy way to review your savings account's progress. Traditionally, passbook accounts were the standard type of savings account. Thanks to computerization, however, statement savings accounts are now the more common form of regular savings account.

Passbook accounts are easier to use and easier to keep track of. It's there in black and white every time you make a deposit or withdrawal. On the other hand, a passbook can get lost or left behind. If you do not have your passbook with you when you go to deposit or withdraw money, you may be in for some time-consuming hassles. The signature card that most banks require clients to fill out will have to be accessed, and the clerk will have to scrutinize your word against your signature.

A statement savings account will take a bit more effort on your part. You will need to read through the statement when it arrives and match its account history with your own version of the truth. You may, for example, find that it lists an ATM transaction that you don't remember making. If this is so, you will be thankful that you saved your ATM slips for the past month. If you didn't, there's still a chance to reconcile your version with the bank's. You will need to call the bank and request a review of the suspicious item. This request may cost you, so be sure of your doubts before you call.

You have to pay to save. Banks charge you fees for the privilege of depositing your money with them. Fees for similar accounts may differ from bank to bank. That's why it's important to find out whether or not, and how much, you will be charged for each and every type of bank account you open. For example, a basic savings account might run you $4 to $8 per month. Ditto for checking. One way around paying a fee is to open an account that waives fees (as long as you keep a specified, minimum balance). However, if there is a minimum balance required in order to waive the fee, find out what it is, and make sure you're not likely to go below it. Also, check and see whether or not there are withdrawal fees. Some regular savings accounts might assess a withdrawal fee based on an allowable monthly withdrawal limit. In both instances, the fees can easily negate the gain in interest your savings have made—so be sure you know what the fees are, and that you know that you can live within their limits. Moreover, since there's a dramatic difference between interest earned in one bank's savings account as opposed to another's, the fees imposed on the savings account will affect your savings goals to a greater or lesser degree. In fact, an excessive monthly checking account fee could easily negate an attractive rate of interest. Suppose you deposited $250 in Bank A, which paid 3 percent interest but charged a fee of $8.00 per month, and then deposited another $250 in Bank B—where the interest rate was 2.5 percent and the monthly fee was $4.00. At the end of the year, you would have $161.50 on deposit in Bank A and $208.25 at Bank B. As you can see, when your account is small, monthly fees can really hurt.

CHECKING ACCOUNTS: These are the preferred accounts of young people, for good reason. First, like a savings account, a checking account enables you to deposit your earnings. Second, a checking account enables you to avoid carrying a wad of cash on your weekly trip to the supermarket. Third, and perhaps most important, a checking account serves as a convenient and cost-effective way to pay your monthly bills. Having said all that, with the advent of the debit card and electronic bill-paying, you can also access the money in your bank account with the touch of a key-stroke or the insertion of a debit card. Look into the possibility of taking advantage of electronic banking, which gives you the ability to pay your bills using your own personal computer. But be fore-warned: most of these services will cost you money, too. In fact, you may end up paying more for electronic banking in the short run.

Most likely, your bank offers you at least three types of check-ing accounts: regular checking, Negotiable Order of Withdrawal (NOW), and Super-NOW. A regular checking account typically earns no interest and comes with a small monthly fee—$4 to $8—whether or not you write a check. As with savings accounts, there is a way around paying this monthly fee. To do so, you will need to keep enough money in your account (on an ongoing basis) to provide the minimum balance requirements—usually $500 to $5,000—in order to waive the minimum monthly fee.

The NOW and Super-NOW accounts also are potentially fee-free. In addition, both pay interest on your deposits. (A Super-NOW ac-count will pay more interest, but you'll have to keep a higher minimum balance in the account.) Moreover, both NOW and Super-NOW accounts let you write a certain number of checks per month free (some accounts even give you unlimited check-writing privileges). It's important to know how many "free" checks you can write per month. You can easily double or triple your monthly account fee if you write too many checks.

These two types of accounts may also make you eligible for small discounts on same-bank loans, free traveler's checks, and dis-counted or waived fees on bank credit cards. The catch? If you fall below the minimum required balance you'll pay a fee that is higher than the one you would pay on a regular checking account. If you think you will have some trouble keeping the minimum balance required of a NOW or Super-NOW account, stick with a regular checking account. Chances are you will come out ahead of the game if you do since the higher monthly fees of the NOW or Super-

NOW account often outweigh the amount of interest earned plus the small monthly fee for a regular checking account.

There's one surefire way to save money on a checking account, no matter what kind you have. Order your checks from a source other than your bank. It makes sound financial sense to do so since it can cut the cost of getting checks—typically about $9 per 200 from your bank—by about 50 percent. And it's easy to do by ordering your own checks from independent printers right over the phone. Checks in the Mail (800-733-4443) charges $5 for a book of 200 checks (with your name, address, account number, and appropriate bar codes that appear on your current checks). Current, Inc. (800-426-0822), offers similar savings.

BALANCING YOUR CHECKBOOK: A regular checking account is a simple, comprehensive account designed to handle all your day-to-day personal payment needs. Opening one is easy. Writing a check is easy, too. On the other hand, balancing a checkbook—and keeping it balanced—seems to require Herculean efforts beyond the means of mere mortals.

Balancing your checkbook is one of the most important financial moves you can make. If you don't, you run the (expensive) risk of bouncing a check. But even if you don't bounce a check, you will waste valuable time worrying about whether or not you might. Moreover, if you don't balance your checkbook on a regular basis, you'll have no way of knowing if the check you're writing is swinging you over the edge of your budget's precipice. Then there's the matter of keeping track of your checking account ATM usage. It's easy to see why balancing a checkbook can be difficult. But, with a little know-how, it's easy to do.

When you balance your checkbook, you simply subtract each new withdrawal from—or add each new deposit to—your previous balance. You tell yourself that you can subtract and add. The tricky part is actually doing it. This is so tricky that few people ever go through life with a balanced checkbook, and many experience the costly embarrassment of a bounced check. Why is it so tricky? People assume that they can put off balancing their checkbook to the end of the week or month. That's the trap. Here's how you can avoid it.

1. Balance your checkbook every time you write a check.
2. Balance your checkbook every time you make a withdrawal from your checking account with your ATM card.

3. Always subtract the applicable monthly fee, as well as any transaction fees, from your existing balance.
4. Get a "top-stub" checkbook. It may cost you a few pennies more, but it will make keeping your checkbook balanced a whole lot easier. Basically, a top-stub enables you to record your transaction and update your balance each and every time you write a check. The more traditional back-end balance checkbook adds a wrinkle to the process—you have to turn to the back of the checkbook to record transactions and balance your account. That wrinkle turns out to be the tsunami of checkbook balancing. There's no way to ride the wave, so why not opt for a different, more effective checkbook instead.

Following these four steps is the best way to keep your checkbook balanced. It requires minimum effort and brain power—and it can save you a bundle. If that's not enough incentive, consider the major effort it will take to balance your checkbook at the end of the month.

HOW TO BALANCE YOUR UNBALANCED CHECKBOOK: If you are unsure of what your balance is, there are several ways you can find out. But first, don't write another check. Get your hands on your most recent bank statement, your bank's toll-free customer service phone number, a calculator, and a piece of scrap paper. On the piece of scrap paper, create five columns to record the following information:

1. List all the checks accounted for on most recent bank statement
   Check Number: _____   *Check Amount* $ _____
2. List all the checks unaccounted for on most recent bank statement
   Check Number: _____   *Check Amount* $ _____
3. List all the checks unaccounted for since most recent bank statement
   Check Number: _____   *Check Amount* $ _____
4. List all the ATM withdrawals since most recent bank statement:
   Amount $ _____
5. Ending balance on most recent bank statement:

6. Complete (1). Subtract the totals you get for (2), (3), and (4) from (5). You're done.

If you can't locate your most recent bank statement, don't panic. You can call your bank and ask them when your next account statement will be received. If it's only a matter of days, wait it out—unless you are convinced that you have overdrawn your account. In this case, or in the event that the next statement won't be arriving for a week or more, you can contact your bank's customer service department and request the information listed above.

Make sure you have your checkbook, pen, paper, and calculator set up and ready to go. Also, be prepared to have to muscle your request through a reluctant account representative. While most are user-friendly, some suffer from politeness deprivation. If you find yourself up against a snotty clerk, don't feed their Napoleonic urge by letting them know you're aggravated. Simply insist that you speak with their superior. Say it exactly like that, too. "I want to speak to your *superior*." When you get someone you can talk to, let them know that you're having trouble balancing your checkbook and that you'll need the above information to help you out. Once you've gathered all the above information, it will take you under five minutes to balance your checkbook. Go.

If your balance and the bank's balance aren't identical twins, cross-examine yourself. Did you forget to list a check or ATM transaction? Did you remember to subtract the monthly fee owed to the bank? Did you enter a check amount incorrectly—$3 for $30 worth of CDs? Did you include the same check twice—#347 for $23 × 2 = $46? Did you transpose numbers—$34 for $43—when writing a check? If all these questions are answered and you still aren't able to square your account, then call your bank to get help reconciling it.

If you seriously think—or find out—you're overdrawn, place a stop-payment order on each check that has crossed the line. A stop order, or stop-payment order, can be placed on any check that you write—for a fee. If, for example, you write a check and lose it, or write a check and don't want the person or store to whom it was sent to be able to cash it, you can place a stop-payment order on that check for a fee (typically $8 to $15). Since your bank likely will charge you much more for bouncing a check, and since you will also be assessed a processing fee (typically $5) from the merchant to whom you wrote the check, it makes financial sense to place a stop order. It also makes personal sense; you will spare yourself some of the attendant check-bouncing embarrassment.

If the check was written within the past two weeks, you can place the stop-payment order over the phone. To place a stop order, you'll need to know the check number, name of the person to whom the check was written, and/or amount of the check. In most cases, if you don't have the check number, the bank may hem and haw about being able to honor your stop-payment order. This is because it makes it very difficult for them to detect the particular check. Be persistent. In the end, as long as you can tell them the amount of the check and to whom it was written, they will be able to honor your request. After all, you're paying them good money to do so.

Once you balance your checkbook, keep it balanced. As in a game of concentration, you need to be sure that you can match every check that you write with every check that is processed.

MONEY MARKET ACCOUNTS

Instead of a savings account or checking account, you may prefer a money market account. This type of account (not to be confused with a money market mutual fund, discussed on page 160) is a higher-yielding hybrid of a savings account with check-writing privileges. Interest is earned on the amount you have in your account, and you can write checks, sometimes as few as four checks per month, sometimes as many as you wish. However, the minimum balance required to waive the monthly fee is often much higher in this type of savings account—typically over $1,000. Also, the check-writing privilege needs to be viewed for what it is—a fee trap, for most people. This is because the allowable limits usually fall below the average check writer's written checks per month. Think of how many bills you have that you will want to write checks for. Chances are the number exceeds four to six checks per month—and that's not including the checks you write for groceries, or the ATM use for dinner and a movie. The bottom line is that few people write so few checks that they won't trespass the limit boundary of a money market account. The solution is to use a money market account as the place for your emergency money supply. Use a checking account for your check writing. That way you can take advantage of a money market account, and its slightly better interest rate than a savings account, without being taken advantage of —in the form of fees levied for excessive check writing. If you are contemplating the best possible location for immediately accessible emergency money, the money market account is a great way to go.

TOOLS YOU CAN USE

Banks offer a variety of account-related and credit-related services. Consider the following to be some of the most practical and useful banking tools.

OVERDRAFT PROTECTION: If you bounce a check—that is, write a check for more money than you actually have in your checking account—you will not only have to pay hefty fees but may also be placed on a list of bad check writers by the store or bank at which your check bounced. This list may be specific to the establishment where you wrote the check or, worse, a general list of bad check writers that's sent to several retail establishments. In short, you will have trouble writing a check—and you'll always be worried about doing so. The only two surefire ways to avoid such a situation are to always balance your checkbook to the penny or to have overdraft protection for your checking account. This is an automatic line of credit which funds your checking account should you inadvertently overdraw your account. Typically, there's no annual fee for this service; however, there's a finance charge that is assessed on any unpaid credit-line balance. That rate will be high—very high. The result: overdraft protection is an excellent idea so long as it's used to protect you from the expense of bouncing checks. Used incorrectly—i.e., as a source for borrowing money—it's a recipe for debt distress.

ATM CARDS: Chances are you have an Automatic Teller Machine (ATM) card. ATM cards provide you with the convenient benefit of being able to withdraw and deposit money 24 hours a day, in nearly every locale in the country, as well as abroad. To do so, you simply pick and memorize a Personal Identification Number (PIN), then find an ATM machine that is part of (or linked to) your bank's data network. (You will likely be charged a fee for using nonmember banks' machines. You may even be charged a fee for using your own bank's ATMs.) To find the nearest machine you can use, find a phone booth and call the toll-free number on the back of your card. That's it. You're off and running. And, no matter which kind of transaction you're making—deposit, withdrawal, account balance inquiry—you will get a printed readout of your transaction. Don't throw that slip away. Instead, pocket it. Bring it home. Put it in your active banking file. Then, when you receive your statement at the end of the month, you can match your slips to the statement's record of your ATM use. Once it all checks out, you can toss the slips.

SUPER ATMs: You may notice a variation on the ATM theme that extends the uses of a regular ATM card so that it can be used in place of a check or anywhere a major credit card is accepted. In fact, this is a debit card by another name: each purchase you make with it is automatically deducted from your checking account. Both cash withdrawals and debit card purchases will appear on your monthly bank statement, making it easy to keep track of your use —and to target any overuse patterns before they get out of hand.

ATM CARDS: You can now use your ATM card to access mutual fund investment information, and, if you are investing in mutual funds through your bank, you can obtain prices, account balances, and even buy and sell shares. (To buy more shares, you simply authorize a transfer of cash from your savings or checking account.) At the end of your transaction, you will get a printout of what you have done—just the way you do when you make a normal deposit or withdrawal.

SECURED CARDS: This type of card provides the answer to an old riddle—namely, how can you get a credit card if you have no existing credit card history, and how can you get an existing credit card history if you have no credit card? With a secured card, the bank will require you to place a specific sum (typically $500) of money in a secured credit card account. That money then will serve as your secured card's credit limit. Every "charge" you make will be debited from the balance. Every payment you make will be credited to it. This may sound like a loathsome deal—but it's a great way to establish a credit history.

BANKCARDS: A bankcard is a bank-issued credit card. There may be an advantage to taking out a bankcard at your bank as opposed to another. Lower interest rates, and lower or no annual fees top the list. However, you will need to do your homework when comparing the actual cost of a bank-promoted card versus other sources. For one thing, specially promoted low rates may also have a less well promoted short life span, e.g., for the first six months only. The same holds true when comparing the benefits of transferring your existing credit card balances to a bank or other credit card touted to save you money. It may end up costing you in the long run. How? The low-low interest rate for a transferred balance typically applies to that balance only. Additional charges on the card are typically socked with a much higher rate of interest.

LOANS: Banks are often thought of more as a place to take out a loan than as a place to put money into. Nearly every bank on the planet has a host of ways to lend you money.

INVESTMENTS: Banks are now offering a host of investor-related services and products. Bank mutual funds are increasingly common. As with direct-marketed or broker-sold funds, the variety and type of bank-marketed funds can be overwhelming at first. This is especially true if you are unsure about investing basics, let alone facts about mutual fund investing. For more on these topics, turn to Part III. There, you'll find the investment information you will need in order to proceed with the process of selecting the best mutual funds to invest in.

NEW AGE BANKING

There are a number of ways that banks are using new technology to make banking easier for you (and for themselves). Some of these technologies aren't even so new:

DIRECT DEPOSIT: Social security checks, veteran's benefits, and —more relevant to you—paychecks can often be directly deposited into your account. Everyone involved saves time. Just find out if your employer participates in such a plan.

AUTOMATIC INVESTMENT AND WITHDRAWAL: If you invest regularly, you can often design a schedule for automatic transfers from your savings account to your mutual funds or IRAs.

ON-LINE BANKING: Today, you can satisfy most of your banking needs on-line—from opening accounts, looking up your balances, transferring funds between accounts, electronic bill-paying, automatic investing, even shopping and qualifying for a mortgage. What do you need to open up an on-line account? A computer, modem, and access to the Web or one of the on-line services (America Online, CompuServe, Prodigy), for starters. From there, it's a breeze, especially if you are using Quicken or Microsoft Money, which will let you download your bank account information directly into your own personal financial plan.

It's estimated that the number of banks that are accessible on the Web doubles every day. By the time you read this, there should be thousands of banks to choose from. (Right now there are under 500.) In fact, those banks that aren't on-line will be hard-pressed to compete with those that are. Just as banks who bought into the ATM biz in the 1980s took the market by force, so banks on the Internet will be the likely beneficiaries of the New Age banker—you.

Banks on-line offer more than meets the eye. They're not just providing you with a more efficient way to bank, pay your bills, and buy a home—they're providing you with a host of relevant, timely financial information that you can put to good use in your overall financial planning and decision-making processes. A prime example of a "Net" bank is Security First Network Bank—a virtual bank (in that it can only be accessed via the Internet) owned and produced by a small Kentucky-based bank. SFNB can be tapped into at (http://www.sfnb.com). There you'll find a virtual bank which mirrors the one you might find in your hometown. Everything from an information desk and an account rep to a personal finance area and the bank's president are at your disposal.

Currently, some large and small banks are on-line with excellent sites. From the mega Bank of America (http://www.bankamerica.com) to the mini Salem Five Cents Savings Bank (http://www.salemfive.com), services and bargains abound. And while the current level of discounts may fall away, the level of services is likely to continue to increase. In fact, if you tap into Bank of America, you'll find a host of interesting avenues to travel—from loan and budget calculators, home loan rates, mortgage applications, and credit card applications to the more mundane transaction-based services. You will also, no doubt, find more and more banks on the paid on-line services. There, in a simple menu-based format, you can shop for a bank, then open an account which you can visit any time of day or night.

However, you still need to know how to write. Currently, opening an account still requires a signature (for most banks), some paperwork, and a stamp. But once you mail in the necessary items, you can fly on the net bank to your heart's content—for a fee.

There are two types of fees you'll need to note when it comes to on-line banking. The first is the fee you're assessed for accessing the Internet. The second relates to the way the bank charges you for the privilege of doing on-line business with them. Many banks are currently waiving such fees. But don't think this will last too long. Fees are banks' bread and butter. Chances are, you'll be charged real-world rates for your virtual account—perhaps similar to the ones you're currently charged for your use of ATMs. Make sure you know and understand all the fees involved on-line.

There are also security concerns related to on-line banking. First, there's the question of a hacker's ability to explode the code—whether your bank's or yours. Is there a way to ensure that your account is being safeguarded from such an event? Yes. You can be sure that your bank is using one or more of the following services: encryption (which ensures that the data feed between your PC and your bank's server isn't corrupted); private/public key cryptography, which ensures that your data is yours and that its destination is correct; a proprietary authentication method which doublechecks the first two steps. The second area of concern ought to be every banking consumer's primary concern: making sure the on-line bank is FDIC insured.

No matter which browser you use, definitely use it to check out some of the bank sites available. Finally, banking is shedding its boring cloak and donning an interesting, interactive mantle which will provide you with more efficient means to your money's ends.

Ready Resources

- *The Bank Book,* by Edward MinKvicka, HarperCollins.
- *Money, Banking and Credit Made Simple,* by Merle Dowd, Doubleday.
- *Money Is My Friend,* by Philip Laut, Ballantine.

CHAPTER SIX

Useful Economics

Economics? Wasn't that a useless course you took once—together with hundreds of others in an air-conditionless auditorium where the only sounds you could hear were those of your compatriots snoring? What was that professor's name? What was it he said about how one day you would find that you were living the lessons he was droning on about? Chances are that if your Econ professor suddenly appeared at your doorstep today, you'd be far more interested in his theories on supply and demand, not to mention how purchasing power is directly affected by inflation, and how inflation itself can affect your current and future lifestyle and standard of living. Hey—you can always go back and sit in on a class or two (he didn't notice when you weren't there, and it's doubtful he'd notice you there now), but there's a simpler way to refresh yourself on some basic economics. Read on.

Economics, like psychology and many other intellectual disciplines, professes to be a science. But like those '50s sci-fi flicks—where science goes terribly wrong and unleashes ants the size of school houses on a hapless little town in Lonersville, Nevada—economic theories can often do as much harm as good, especially if you take them to be absolute answers in a conditional world. The best way to proceed when it comes to wedding economic theory to real world facts is to understand some of the basic themes in the overall market that most theorists use in order to establish their predictive prowess.

The truth is that when it comes to economics, you're already an expert. Chances are you have firsthand knowledge of how a growing or faltering economy has affected you. A growing economy makes it easier to, among other things, find a job that pays well. It also makes it easier to feel good about spending what you have earned. But be careful. Everything that rises must mimic Icarus and plummet featherless and bloody back to earth. Don't fall prey to sunny days without preparing for rainy ones. During tough economic times, jobs are as easily lost as they were to find in better times, unemployment climbs, and as unemployment climbs employers can reduce wages. This means they can expect to get the same level of work for less money. If that's not bad enough, while you are earning less money, it will also be harder to stretch a dollar to buy what it used to buy.

You don't have to have a Ph.D. in economics to become a savvy investor. Instead, you can familiarize yourself with some of the most common terms and frames of reference used by analysts, journalists, and investors alike in a matter of minutes. I call it "economics in a nutshell." And it's based on the most basic and commonsense principle of all: supply and demand. Supply and demand and scarcity and production, that is. The greater the demand, the less the supply and the greater the incentive to increase production (supply) to satisfy demand. If the resources needed to produce the item are themselves scarce, then the limited supply will self-regulate the demand by pushing the cost of the item above the means of the majority of those who want it. In this situation, profit is made by targeting high-end consumers. Likewise, if the resources needed to produce the item are plentiful and commonplace and the costs of production aren't high, then production can easily meet the demand to the point where the price of the item will be reduced in order to entice the majority of consumers who can afford it and not just those who need it. In such an instance, profit is made by volume sales.

Supply and demand is easy enough to understand. But there are a host of other terms which you will need to know in order to grasp what this economy of ours is all about.

THE PRIME RATE: The prime rate is the rate at which banks borrow money. Consequently, the prime rate plus one or more percentage points sets the floor for your lowest available lending rate at a bank. The lower the lending rate is, the greater the temptation and the ability are to borrow. Moreover, greater borrowing usually translates into greater spending, which is good for the economy even if it's not so good for you.

UNEMPLOYMENT/EMPLOYMENT RATE: This is one of the most watched statistics on Wall Street and, no doubt, your street. The higher unemployment is, the worse off the economy is likely to be or soon become. Why? In economic downturns, fewer people have money with which to invest and to purchase new big-ticket items like a car, a home, a stereo, etc. They're too busy trying to pay the rent or mortgage. The flip side isn't 100 percent rosy either. The higher employment is, the more nervous the bond market gets. The greater the number of people at work, the greater the demand for consumer goods. This increased demand usually drives up prices, creating what economists call an inflationary environment. However, during the past decade or so, stock investors have generally been as afraid of inflation as their colleagues on the bond side.

THE CONSUMER-DRIVEN ECONOMY

The following three indicators also will help reveal the state of the consumer-driven economy. These numbers tend to be robust in times of economic prosperity, down in a slowing economy, and out in a recession.

RETAIL SALES: Selling consumer items is good for the economy. This figure relates just how good things seem to be. Look at it from your own perspective: the more you buy, the more optimistic you seem to be about the economy, your job prospects, and your continued employment.

AUTO SALES: You can check this out for yourself based on the number of "sales" events that you see listed in the car-buying section of your paper every day, and the amount of the rebates being offered. Chances are, when "sales" are at their loudest and largest, actual sales of cars are at their slowest. Now, it's true that the auto industry is not simply cyclical, it's also seasonal—with more sales coming at peak times during a given year. But, during a slowing economy, and especially during a time of high unemployment, new car sales tend to tank.

HOUSING STARTS: New housing starts signal the strength of

the economy and bode well for related industries like banking, building-product manufacturing, and mortgage lending. These industries tend to be knocked down like a house of straw, however, when housing starts slow.

FUNDAMENTAL FACTORS

Fundamental factors are the comprehensive indices which employ mega-calculations (crunching sales and earnings numbers from hundreds or thousands of, for example, real estate agents or car dealerships) to produce a very small—but meaningful—indicator of economic health.

CONSUMER PRICE INDEX (CPI): This index is comprised of the prices of over 100,000 goods and services that we buy, including food, energy, cars, clothing, and new homes. As such, this index can be seen to present a picture of the overall cost of living. The Federal Reserve Board keeps a very close eye on this index, and uses it to help determine whether short-term interest rates should be raised (to slow borrowing and so reduce the chance of inflation) or lowered (to increase borrowing and so help spur spending, which, in turn, is a boon to the economy). It's an important index since your salary and the amount of your potential raise are likely to be directly affected by this figure.

PRODUCER PRICE INDEX (PPI): This figure reflects the direction of product prices. When this index rises it signals that businesses are raising the prices of the products they sell. While rising prices might seem like an obvious negative, this isn't necessarily so. In fact, often while businesses are raising their products' prices, the markets in which those products are found are offering rebates, coupons, or discounts to offset the potentially negative affect.

MANUFACTURERS' NEW ORDERS: New orders (of inventory) are how manufacturers gauge the relative strength and weakness of their business in the near future. Since new orders represent a demand for products (or lack thereof), this number can also be used to gauge the short-term future strength and weakness of a particular industry. Can the manufacturer meet the demand or will it have to spend in order to remain competitive? Overproduction is the real negative here, however, since overproducing (cars, cereal, or software) can lead to inventory that can't be sold for love or money.

INDUSTRIAL PRODUCTION: Industrial activity—the efficient production of basic materials required by manufacturers to produce their products—can serve as an advance warning of a market peak or valley. If industrial production is running at capacity, and materials are being purchased by manufacturers as fast as they can be provided, then the economy is ticking along nicely. If, on the other hand, the capacity that's being produced isn't being purchased at the rate of production, then inventory piles up and layoffs occur.

Purchasing Managers' Index: This index shows how much and to what extent industrial materials are being bought by manufacturers. When these manufacturers are buying, it's good news for the industrials.

Leading Economic Indicators: The U.S. Department of Commerce compiles a monthly report based on what it considers to be twelve leading indicators of the economy's strength. Taken as a whole, these indicators are used to help forecast the future climate for businesses in general. A monthly change is rarely significant (although it can reflect an anomalous event, such as bad weather that unexpectedly devastates crops). However, when the composite shows consistent gains (good for the economy) or consistent losses (bad for the economy), some investors feel inclined to raise their spinnakers (to capture the fair wind) or batten down the hatches (to helps secure them against a downturn).

As with the Dow Jones Industrial Average (defined and detailed in the next chapter), few people know what the 12 components are:

1. Average workweek of production workers.
2. Layoff rate in manufacturing jobs (see "unemployment," page 58).
3. Value of manufacturers' new orders for consumer goods and materials (detailed page 59).
4. Index of business information.
5. Standard & Poor's 500 Index (see next chapter or glossary for definition and details).
6. Contracts and orders for plants and equipment.
7. Index of private housing units authorized by local building permits.
8. Vendor performance (percentage of companies reporting slower deliveries).
9. Net change in inventories in hand or on order.
10. Change in prices of raw materials.

11. Change in total liquid assets.
12. Money supply.

Hold on. What is money supply, and how does it affect the economy and you? Good question. And one that brings up an important distinction—between fiscal and monetary policy. Fiscal policy is shaped by the raising or lowering of taxes which negatively or positively affects our demand (and ability to pay for) goods and services. Monetary policy, on the other hand, is governed by the Federal Reserve Board, and is used to control the direction of the overall economy by managing the supply of money in circulation —including what you have in your pocket and what's in your checking account. The supply of money in relation to the production of goods and services affects the pricing of products and services, as well as inflation. Too much money and too few goods can dampen interest rates but increase prices and inflation—and vice versa.

MARKET PSYCHOLOGY

Who said the market is driven by facts and figures? Well, of course it is—in part. But, as with all things human, psychology plays a significant role as well. The following indices help track this aspect as it relates to the market's relative strength or weakness.

CONSUMER CONFIDENCE: When times are good, consumers spend (typically beyond their means) with the confidence that they'll still be employed long enough, and still earn enough, to pay off the new car, boat, porch, and 64-seat home surround-sound theater they just charged on their Sears card. When times are tough, consumers cease to spend on fun in order to concentrate their earnings on the staples of life—food and shelter.

INVESTOR SENTIMENT: When the majority of investors (or investment advisors, depending on which sentiment index you're looking at) are bullish, it's time to get bearish. When the majority of investors are bearish, it's time to reconsider your cash position and look to getting fully invested. This index helps gauge the herd instinct, which is typically a more lemminglike (i.e., suicidal) path to follow than your own hard-nosed, analysis-driven stock buying. Still, momentum investors (those who look to where the herd is heading and try to get there slightly ahead of the masses) would argue that this index can be used to help gauge the directional flow of money into various sectors within the market.

BUSINESS CONFIDENCE INDEX: In 1996, *Fortune* magazine moved from an annual to a monthly survey of business confidence as reported by corporate America's Fortune 1,000 chief financial officers and treasurers (the people who need to be on target when it comes to how well their business is actually doing). Review this index regularly because those surveyed have their finger on the pulse of the economy as it relates to their particular business as well as to how it relates to the consumers who enable their business to thrive, survive, or be tested by tough times.

TOO MUCH OF A BAD THING, TOO LITTLE OF THE GOOD

The ebb and flow of our disposable income dictates, to a certain extent, our ability (and simply our desire) to invest. The following indices are closely watched by those who look for trends that can affect our ability as a culture to invest, and that affect where we do invest.

INSTALLMENT CREDIT (DEBT): OK. This may be hard for you to believe, but people use credit cards to purchase what they can't otherwise afford to buy outright. And the very same people use home equity loans and other sources of installment debt to buy a lifestyle that, without the debt, would be beyond their reach. You know from your own personal experience just how problematic this type of living can be. Sleepless nights, peanut butter for breakfast, lunch, and dinner (for one week out of every month after the paycheck runs out). This index shows just how overextended consumers have become—and it's not a pretty sight. For nearly two years after the 500-point stock market crash in October 1987, consumers reduced this figure quite dramatically. Now, we're way over the highest level attained back then. Taken together with the percentage of savings (under 4 percent), this number can spell tough times ahead for the two-thirds of our economy that depends on our ability to buy more and more and more stuff. Add to that the perilous job market and things look kind of shaky.

PERSONAL INCOME: If your income (in terms of annual raises) is rising ahead of inflation, it bodes well for industries that rely on your purchasing power—like retailers and car companies. If, however, your income doesn't keep pace with inflation, then your purchasing power is declining—bad news for the same industries.

MARKET MOMENTUM

Often, momentum creates opportunity or potential pitfalls for the unwitting investor. Momentum is basically the willed direction of a volume of money into or out of one stock or industry, one country or one region in the world. The movement of money, for whatever reason, makes the investment suddenly either very attractive or very undesirable. Momentum of money into one country's market, for example, can propel prices upward across the board. Many international funds attempt to use momentum to their advantage. But investors are better off not trying to time such events on their own. Better to spend the time carefully choosing successful companies or funds that use momentum as one investment criteria.

FUND FLOW: The flow of money into (and out of) mutual funds serves as an indicator of investors' interest in the various markets (stock, bond, foreign) as well as which industries they're interested in. Momentum investors often use this figure to gauge their own flow of funds in or out of the market. However, since so much of the money coming into mutual funds (over 75 percent of new money in 1995, for example) is retirement related—in the form of 401(k) or IRA money, for example—flow of funds may no longer be as telling as it was once believed to be. After all, retirement money is long term in nature—so the real story of the recent flow of money into mutual funds is that investors have awoken to the fact that they need to invest in their own future. Of course, this begs the question of what will happen to the stock market when these investors begin to withdraw their money to meet their retirement income needs. The answer may not be as devastating as you might think, since, after all, these investors will need to continue to grow the lion's share of their capital in order to fend off the inflation tiger. And what better way to do so than to stay invested in stocks? Still, you should mark on your calendar the year 2020— the year in which most of the demographic "baby boom" is likely to be in retirement. After that date, all bets in the markets are off (with the exception of stocks in funeral homes, that is).

Signs of the Times

Economics isn't a theoretical kingdom; it's the realm of the real world. If you know where to look for the signs, you might be able to track down some interesting investment leads. If nothing else, it will transform the next trip to the supermarket, mall, or Gap outlet from a dull trip to an informed shop. After all, you can readily gauge the retail side of the economy by looking for early and drastic sales on clothing you bought just last week for full price. What else? When you swing into your local gas station for a refill before you get to the mall, check out the pump prices. Have they risen or fallen since your last visit or from a month or so ago? Don't know? Take a note and track what you pay for a gallon of gas for the months ahead—there may be an energy investment idea there. As always, keep yourself attuned to the world around you. It's not just a Zen way of being; it's a way to tap into some of the more obvious investment ideas in town.

There are other, more standard real-world measures of the overall economy. The following few suffice to show you how to increase your own index of real-world economic activity.

Stock exchange seat: In order for a broker to be able to buy or sell shares on an exchange, he or she must have a "seat." There are a limited number of these seats, so the price of the sale of one seat can be seen to be an indicator of investment professionals' bullishness or bearishness—which, in turn, can be read as a contra-indicator. In 1987, for example, the sale of a seat on the New York Stock Exchange (NYSE) was recorded at $1,150,000 one month before the October crash. Little wonder, then, in early 1996, when the market had set record territory on top of record territory for over twelve months, that the sale of a seat for $1,250,000—a new record—was met with mixed emotions. Some saw it as a bullish sign, that a firm would be willing to spend so much for the seat seemed to say that the firm was convinced the market would support the price through increased business. Others were far more cautious, remembering the history of the last record-breaking sale.

Cab medallions: The limited number of available New York City (or your city's) taxicab licenses drives the demand for them—sometimes up (when business is expected to remain robust) and sometimes down (when the economy tightens, consumers walk). For a price history of medallions, City Hall would be the best starting place, although they may direct you elsewhere. Once you have that price history in hand, you can match its pattern to the market's and see what you see.

READ BETWEEN THE LINES! Investors must always be on the alert for potential economic benefits from far afield—as far afield as China, for example. In early 1996 the Chinese government issued a demand that every Chinese have not one but two eggs for breakfast. Before you go thinking about one billion people in need of a cholesterol drug, think about what it takes to get a fixed number of chickens to double their production. If you said more chickens, you're half right. In fact, it turns out that grain is a key ingredient. But China had already ramped up its grain imports—signaling their inability to manufacture the necessary grain to meet the new edict. The result was that U.S. grain manufacturers looked like the golden goose.

This chapter could go on to be a book in itself. But the truth is that you now have enough tools to begin to build your own frame of reference for potential investment opportunities that come about through the changes in our economy and in the global economy in which our markets participate. Of course, you'll want to know more about the markets which corral the securities that you might want to invest in—and that's what chapter 7 is all about.

READY RESOURCES

- *Forecasting Interest Rates*, by J. Schwartzman, McGraw-Hill.
- *Using Economic Indicators to Invest*, by E. Tainer, John Wiley.

CHAPTER SEVEN

Market Watch

When it comes to understanding the markets—stocks, bonds, mutual funds, real estate, commodities, precious metals, and more—it's easy to see why many people shy away. After all, so many markets, so little time—not to mention the risks of making a wrong decision—don't exactly add up to a welcoming invitation to learn how to succeed in the market. But, like learning some of the basics of economics which affect the markets you can invest in, coming to terms with the various markets and staying up-to-date on these ever-changing and potentially profit-making areas is pretty easy to do.

The marketplace has gone global; so, too, have the stock and bond markets. In fact, the average U.S. stock fund holds around 10 percent in foreign stocks. The upshot is that you need to keep tabs on markets both at home and abroad. For example, take a look at the chart on page 67. It illustrates how well the U.S. market did in comparison to the foreign markets in 1995. Historically, however, foreign markets have played a significantly positive role in building a successful investment portfolio (as detailed in chapter 14). The role of this chapter is to help you get to know the several markets and their wares, as well as the best ways to gauge their value.

When it comes to mastering the world and its markets, it's no

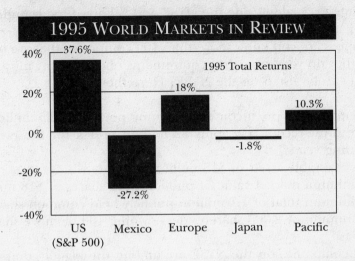

1995 WORLD MARKETS IN REVIEW

1995 Total Returns

- US (S&P 500): 37.6%
- Mexico: -27.2%
- Europe: 18%
- Japan: -1.8%
- Pacific: 10.3%

wonder you feel overwhelmed. As with the raw economic data that we found in abundance in the previous chapter, information on the various markets is plentiful—as are the pundits who extol the virtues of some markets over others. But we'll avoid the hype in favor of getting up to speed on the basics. Knowing where each market stands in terms of potential investment opportunities that suit your needs is the best way to determine where you want to invest.

THE STOCK MARKET

The following brief history of our major stock exchanges will help you wow an uninitiated guest or two at your next pub brew tasting. But, more important, it will help you get a sense of the differences between the three exchanges and their U.S. and global counterparts, as well as of the types of companies you'll find listed on them.

NEW YORK STOCK EXCHANGE (NYSE): Wall Street. 11 Wall Street, to be exact, is where you'll find our oldest, most venerable, and largest exchange. Launched in 1817 under a buttonwood tree (OK, look, this is the lore) on Wall Street—so called because of its wall erected to defend New Yorkers from northerly attacks—the New York Stock Exchange grew to its current size and shape virtually unrivaled by smaller, more regional exchanges, with one exception—the New York Curb Exchange (begun in 1842). That exchange grew along side the NYSE and is known today under the name it took in 1953, the American Stock Exchange.

Chances are you know more than 100 companies that are on the NYSE, but do you know the requirements one company must meet in order to be listed on the NYSE? Here they are:

- Demonstrate pre-income-tax earning power of $2.5 million for the most recent year, plus $2 million pretax for the two preceding years
- Net tangible assets of $18 million
- Minimum market value of publicly held shares of $18 million
- Minimum total of 1.1 million publicly held common shares
- Minimum of 2,000 shareholders owning 100 or more shares

The companies on the NYSE are among the bigger companies. In fact, the lingo is "large-caps," or companies with large capitalization—typically in excess of $3 billion. But big doesn't necessarily mean better. You know the expression "the bigger they are, the harder they fall"? There are plenty of Goliaths on the Street.

OK, biblical metaphors aside, what goes on at the NYSE on a daily basis? The buying and selling of stocks, of course. But what does a typical day on the NYSE look like? Outside of the image of pandemonium and paper chits flying everywhere, business as usual takes the following course: The gavel comes down and trading begins at 9:30 A.M. (EST) and the gavel comes down again signaling the end of trading at 4:00 P.M. (EST). Rarely does the market miss a scheduled beat. Between the gavels, a blizzard of millions of transactions take place. Typically, one transaction will take the following path: An order to buy or sell comes into the broker, and he or she either manually or electronically writes the order and places it with the brokerage firm whom he or she represents. The order is then sent to the floor clerk, who, in turn, passes the order to the brokerage firm's floor trader. This floor trader tracks down another floor trader with an opposite interest (to buy or sell, since for every buyer there must be a seller, and vice versa). The two traders meet and agree on a price. The order is agreed upon, written down, and returned to the floor clerk, who files the order and price of the transaction with the order department. This department issues an execution ticket to the brokerage firm's representative, who, in turn, lets the original broker know the transaction has transpired —and for what price. The broker then calls the client with the deal, and the client then receives a trade confirmation which, like a receipt, details the transaction.

If all the above sounds like a lot of leg- and paperwork, you're right. But, for orders of 1,200 shares or less, trades are handled on the Designated Order Turnaround (DOT) system, which is a computerized way to trade efficiently. Currently the DOT system accounts for more than 50 percent of NYSE trades. To learn the best ways to place an order, turn to chapter 16.

AMERICAN STOCK EXCHANGE (AMEX): Known as the market for "mid-cap" companies, the AMEX is based on Trinity—rather than Wall—Street, and is often referred to as the NYSE's little brother. AMEX-listed companies also must meet certain requirements:

- Pretax income of $750,000 or more in either its last year or in two out of three prior years
- Stockholders' equity of $4 million
- 500,000 shares of common stock available to the investing public
- A minimum public distribution of $1 million shares together with a minimum of 400 shareholders who each have 100 or more shares, or 800 public shareholders (i.e., not officers or directors of the company)
- Share price of $3 minimum (to start) with $3 million in public market capitalization

NATIONAL ASSOCIATION OF SECURITIES DEALERS AUTOMATED QUOTATION SYSTEM (NASDAQ): The Nasdaq celebrated its twenty-fifth anniversary in 1996, having grown from a tiny (100 listings) over-the-counter stock service in 1971 to its current 5,500-plus universe of stocks ranging from mega-Microsoft to micro-companies struggling to stay aloft. As a result, the Nasdaq is known as the market for "small-caps." In fact, many investors think that the Nasdaq is all small company stocks, but the truth is that as the Nasdaq has itself grown from puny to gigantic, so have many of the companies which list there, including Amgen (one of the few biotech companies to actually post earnings), Cisco Systems, Intel, MCI, and Oracle.

If some of its early comers have grown up, the Nasdaq is still a market for smaller companies which can't (yet) list on the NYSE big board or AMEX. Trading is done on a bid/ask basis, and is conducted thorough dealers who are members of the National Association of Securities Dealers (NASD)—electronically. Conceptually, the Nasdaq exists in virtual reality as opposed to on one street, but the NASD's headquarters is on Whitehall Street in New York City.

The following chart illustrates the performance of these three dominant markets over the last decade. (The NYSE is represented by the S&P 500 and the DJIA.) And, while past performance is no guarantee of future results, the bottom line is that all three markets, despite some notable retreats, delivered solidly positive returns in excess of inflation.

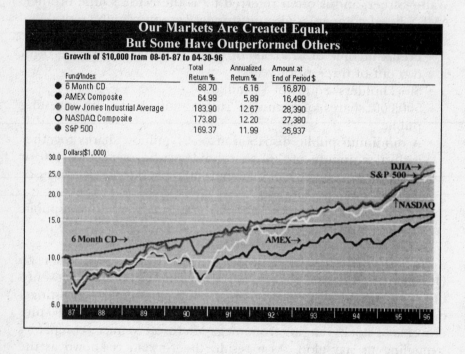

COMMODITY EXCHANGES

Some exchanges provide a place to buy and sell contracts on everything from stocks to pork bellies. Commodities are typically agricultural products: coffee, sugar, and corn are all commodities. Investors in commodities are placing bets on their future value. For example, if there has been an ice storm in Florida, orange juice contracts become very expensive since there will be fewer oranges to satisfy consumer demand for orange juice. The following commodity exchanges dominate the field. They are defined by the types of instruments their contracts are based on.

CHICAGO BOARD OF OPTIONS EXCHANGE (CBOE): This market serves as the most prominent source for auctioning puts and calls on NYSE stocks, Standard & Poor's (S&P) 100 and S&P 500 futures, and Treasury bonds. (For more on puts and calls, turn to chapter 15.)

AMEX OPTIONS EXCHANGE (ACC): This area of the AMEX is specifically designated for trading puts and calls on NYSE and OTC (over-the-counter) stocks.

CHICAGO BOARD OF TRADE (CBT): A major market for futures contracts on commodities (from coffee to pork bellies to soybeans), interest rate securities, and more.

NEW YORK COTTON EXCHANGE (NYCE): This exchange is dedicated to trading futures in cotton and orange juice.

REGIONAL MARKETS

In addition to the more famous stock and commodity exchanges, there are several regional exchanges which typically list smaller, more localized companies. The exchanges names, for the most part, are based on their location. So, for example, you have the Boston Stock Exchange, as well as exchanges in Cincinnati, Chicago, Philadelphia, and San Francisco (known as the Pacific Stock Exchange). If you live nearby, stop in for a quick look at how a trading floor works. You might have to call in advance (or, if you have a broker, ask him or her for an entree).

INTERNATIONAL MARKETS

Foreign markets offer investors a chance at some thrills—and spills. Not all foreign markets are created alike, however. Some, like the London Stock Exchange, are as solid as the White Cliffs of Dover, while others, like the Italian Market, resemble the frangible dunes of Cape Cod. The following table provides a list of established markets and their performances. You can see a wide divergence based on this table alone, as well as how many markets there are. (For more on the benefits of investing in foreign stocks, and there are some, see chapter 11.)

GLOBAL STOCK MARKETS

Index	% Chg.	In Local Currencies 2/01	52-wk Range		% Chg.	In U.S. Dollars[1] 2/01	52-wk Range	
The World	2.6	558.5	558.5–	440.8	2.3	748.5	748.5–	609.7
E.A.F.E.[2]	2.0	634.9	634.9–	506.1	1.4	1141.1	1156.2–	980.2
Australia	1.5	469.8	471.8–	388.1	2.9	313.7	314.7–	258.1
Austria	1.9	378.5	390.8–	331.0	0.8	937.1	1038.2–	852.3
Belgium	2.3	561.7	561.7–	433.2	1.2	915.0	921.0–	725.1
Canada	3.0	543.6	543.6–	436.6	3.1	427.5	427.5–	335.9
Denmark	–0.0	889.2	890.2–	705.9	–1.1	1155.0	1168.4–	957.3
Finland	2.7	146.2	211.8–	127.0	2.1	126.4	189.0–	115.3
France	3.8	644.5	644.5–	537.1	2.8	697.6	708.4	589.6
Germany	1.1	346.5	346.7–	273.3	–0.0	848.9	825.5–	707.5
Hong Kong	2.5	7565.4	7565.4–	4994.6	2.5	5434.2	5434.2–	3587.1
Ireland	0.3	233.5	234.3–	189.1	–0.0	219.6	22.6–	179.4
Italy	2.9	562.3	589.8–	486.7	3.7	222.5	230.2–	181.9
Japan	2.6	984.6	995.4–	715.3	2.0	3314.6	3524.6–	2914.2
Malaysia	–0.7	369.3	384.4–	307.8	–0.7	359.8	390.3–	300.2
Netherlands	0.4	550.5	550.7–	435.9	–0.7	1192.6	1228.4–	967.2
New Zealand	2.3	112.2	119.0–	101.7	3.4	115.1	120.8–	100.1
Norway	0.7	919.9	960.1–	781.0	–0.1	1008.3	1108.0–	896.5
Singapore	1.3	1336.3	1336.3–	1126.4	1.1	2894.7	2894.7–	2398.9
Spain	0.3	293.7	293.7–	223.9	–0.3	163.6	166.6–	121.3
Sweden	3.2	2366.2	2535.9–	1878.6	1.9	1757.7	1861.2–	1348.8
Switzerland	2.2	419.8	431.9–	315.2	–0.2	1480.8	1591.2–	1095.4
U.K.	0.7	1131.0	1133.1–	902.5	0.6	713.1	720.8–	601.7
U.S.A.	3.5	603.0	603.0–	444.7	3.5	603.0	603.0–	444.7

Base: Jan. 1, 1970 = 100
[1] Adjusted for foreign exchange fluctuations relative to the U.S. $.
[2] Europe, Australasia, Far East Index

Source: Morgan Stanley Capital International Perspective, Geneva.

EMERGING MARKETS

If foreign markets can sometimes throw investors for a loop, emerging markets are like a roller-coaster ride on a Mobius strip—unending volatility. While there are ways to minimize the risk of investing in emerging markets (for example, investing in a well-diversified emerging markets fund—or, better yet, in a well-diversified international fund which itself invests a small portion of its assets in emerging market securities), there is no way to bring the volatility of these markets in line with our own. Are the rewards worth the risks? Well, as the table opposite illustrates, not only are there several emerging markets to choose from, but, as is always the case, one

EMERGING MARKETS

In U.S. Dollars[1]

Index	% Chg.	2/01	1995–96 Range		Index	% Chg.	2/01	1995–96 Range	
Argentina	1.1	1372.5	1386.4–	1238.7	Peru[2]	4.9	238.8	238.8–	221.2
Brazil	6.2	694.9	694.9–	578.1	Philippines	–0.1	494.6	494.9–	441.5
Chile	–0.4	880.6	920.5–	862.3	Poland[2]	5.0	468.7	481.5–	362.7
China Free[2]	0.3	62.9	64.7–	54.4	Portugal	0.2	74.5	74.5–	68.4
Colombia[2]	9.1	109.7	113.5–	100.5	So. Africa	–1.3	279.3	283.5–	254.9
Greece	0.5	253.2	256.0–	233.8	Sri Lanka[2]	1.5	109.3	110.9–	103.9
India[2]	3.9	90.9	98.8–	87.5	Taiwan	–3.4	211.9	228.8–	208.2
Indonesia	2.5	581.7	581.7–	506.0	Thailand	0.7	566.9	571.3–	523.2
Israel[2]	–0.5	92.6	95.2–	90.9	Turkey	5.7	125.3	125.3–	100.2
Jordan	1.5	93.3	96.1–	91.5	Venezuela[2]	–5.6	66.7	75.6–	63.3
Korea	2.1	171.3	174.7–	162.1					
Mexico	0.2	837.7	850.6–	744.5					
Pakistan[2]	0.4	96.7	97.0–	88.8					

Base: Jan. 1, 1968 = 100
[1] Adjusted for foreign exchange fluctuations relative to the U.S. $.
[2] Base: Jan. 1, 1993 = 100

Source: Morgan Stanley Capital International Perspective, Geneva

or more of them delivers eye-popping returns in any given period.

Emerging markets are currently considered to be: Argentina, Bolivia, Botswana, Brazil, Chile, Columbia, Czechoslovakia, Ecuador, Egypt, Greece, Hong Kong, Hungary, India, Indonesia, Jamaica, Jordan, Kenya, Malaysia, Mexico, Morocco, Nigeria, Paraguay, Pakistan, Peru, the Philippines, Poland, Portugal, Singapore, South Korea, Sri Lanka, Taiwan, Thailand, Turkey, Uruguay, Venezuela, and Zimbabwe. Some markets in these countries are more established (in terms of longevity) than others. More new markets, especially from the former Soviet Union and China, are likely to emerge in short order. The commonality? Volatility in terms of the market, economy, and political maturity of each country.

Because these markets are emerging, rarely will you be able to time their periods of stability well. And failing to do so can leave you on the slippery slopes of a disastrous downside. (My recommendation is to avoid them, or keep your total exposure in them to under 10 percent.) Not surprisingly, when it comes to investing, most of us would be better off listening to Dorothy. She was basically right: there is no place like home.

However, some funds hedge their foreign stakes, for example, and by doing so neutralize the effect of fluctuations between the value of the U.S. dollar and the value of foreign currency. But before you rush out and invest only in those funds that fully hedge their currency (and there aren't many that are fully hedged), you should know that doing so can make the fund vulnerable to a strong U.S. dollar.

When investing in a foreign market, you need to be aware of how well the investments are doing relative to the market and country in which they're located, as well as to the currency in which they're denominated. The question is, what are your (or a fund's) investments worth in U.S. dollars—since, after all, it would be hard to buy this week's groceries with a bag of Thai bhats or Indian rupees. While the performance of various world markets is listed in easily accessible sources—from print to the Web—the performance of individual stocks, and the performance of those foreign stocks held by a domestic fund, are less easy to track down, and to track. However, there's a shorthand way in which you can keep tabs on the potential negative or positive effects of currency markets worldwide. Since the value of the dollar relative to most major international currencies is listed in many accessible places (such as the newspaper's business section), all you need to know is whether a stronger dollar is good or bad news for the foreign stocks you or your fund owns. A rising dollar relative to other currencies will translate into bad news for those investments that are denominated in those foreign currencies which are weaker by comparison; they will be worth less, but not worthless. If, on the other hand, the dollar is weakening relative to other currencies, then the value of the investments denominated in those foreign currencies will be worth more in dollar terms. If two funds, for example, were invested in the same stocks in the same foreign markets, and one fund was fully hedged and the other was unhedged, then the following would happen:

- If the value of the U.S. dollar is falling, the unhedged fund will outperform the hedged one.
- If the value of the U.S. dollar is strengthening, the hedged fund will suffer less than the unhedged fund, and so fare better by comparison.

Keeping tabs on the strength of the dollar versus other currencies is easy to do, and, as the above shows, a smart thing to do. But, just because the dollar spikes up or trips down, don't sell on short news. Instead, consider the prospect of the dollar's value over a longer time frame before making any moves.

Our Regulators

The Securities and Exchange Commission (SEC) was begun in 1934 to counteract the numerous stock-trading schemes which were plaguing the market and threatening its integrity. Then, as now, the SEC was the market's watchdog—and it got federal teeth to back up its regulatory bark. The SEC is headed by a group of five presidential appointees who oversee a host of attorneys and investigators. Their job is to ensure that the integrity of the market is maintained—as well as to prosecute those who violate the rules and regulations which govern fair and honest market practices. Additionally, the SEC works within the industry to ensure that investors are fully and accurately informed about the securities on the market. But, be forewarned: the SEC doesn't guarantee that you are informed—only that those who create the marketing materials provide accurate information. You'll need to do your own homework as to how the hype relates to the numbers.

The Industries

There are several ways to divide the overall market into the constituent parts that participate in it. The following main industries, or "sectors," are commonly agreed on, while the 90-plus subsectors (partially listed in the table on page 79) may be viewed more subjectively and creatively. "Industry" is a broad-based frame for several related businesses, while sectors are more business-specific. In the technology industry, there are several sectors including semiconductors and software.

To begin with, you'll need to get to know each major industry. From there, you can begin to unpack the constituent sectors and the companies that comprise each sector. Most companies concentrate in one or a few related industries, so their stocks can be similarly categorized by industry or sector. While you can break down industry into over a hundred narrow categories, the following ten broad sectors allow a more useful overview of the market's action.

Basic materials: These are the raw materials that manufacturers use to produce their goods. Aluminum, chemicals, paper and forest products, and steel (commonly referred to as "deep cyclicals") are prime examples. Companies which harvest and produce such raw materials tend to have their peak earnings in the later stages of an economic recovery, when increased demand for manufactured goods (from cars to homes) begins to outstrip the supply of raw materials (e.g., aluminum and lumber), resulting in price increases that go straight to the basic materials company's bottom line.

ENERGY: This is a big enough sector that it is usually considered separately from the other commodities making up Basic Materials. Energy companies are involved in oil, natural gas, coal, and/or energy services (oil exploration and pipeline equipment and service suppliers). As this is a commodity industry, supply and demand fundamentals heavily impact profits. Since oil producers can't count on OPEC to drastically cut production a third time (remember the 1970s?), the more typical good news for this industry comes from economic recoveries in established markets and strong growth in emerging markets. Emerging markets are providing an increasingly positive picture for this industry through their rapidly growing demand for cars and plants, and their need to fuel them.

CYCLICALS: Housing and auto manufacturers top this industry list. Sensitive to economic cycles, this group tends to rise quickly in economic upturns and slide back just as quickly during downturns. The success of this sector relies on the consumer's willingness and ability to purchase durable goods—which, naturally, slows during tough times and increases during better times.

NON-CYCLICALS: Also referred to as consumer staples, this sector includes food, tobacco, and sometimes drugs. (While drugs are often included in this category, most listings put them with other health-related companies.) Name-brand products have recently come on far stronger than generic products (although this wasn't the case in the early 1990s), and are likely to remain constants in the universe as more sales go overseas and more consumers want to associate their purchases with the best products. But, loyalty aside, the companies in this sector tend to produce basics we all need and would find it hard to do without.

HEALTH CARE: This industry includes those companies that make or sell products or services used in health care, with products primarily consisting of pharmaceuticals (prescription and over-the-counter) and medical devices, and services ranging from hospital and nursing home chains to HMOs and other medical insurers. The health care industry is susceptible to politics (in the form of federally mandated price controls), as well as rising pressures from HMOs and other large purchasers.

TECHNOLOGY: From semiconductor and computer manufacturers to software producers and telecommunications, this industry is likely to be a long-term success. All the major technology sectors should prove to be excellent long-term performers, benefiting primarily from the constantly improving performance of these products. Multimedia is the way this world is heading—but expect volatility in this high-growth sector.

FINANCIAL: Banks and savings and loans, brokerages, mutual fund firms, and insurance companies (life and property/casualty) make up this industry. While Mother Nature can wreak havoc on property/casualty insurers, she can also benefit banks that are called upon to loan money to rebuild. As a whole, this industry is sensitive to interest rates. Rising rates are typically a negative, while falling rates tend to be positive. Higher rates can dry up loan demand, while lower rates tend to encourage greater borrowing, increasing demand for loans, and are good for the securities markets. Economic growth also tends to bode well for banks and brokerages via increased loan and investment demand.

UTILITIES: These companies move electricity, natural gas, or data (e.g., phone messages) into homes and businesses. Because they tend to be stodgier, low-growth, high-dividend-paying stocks, they are generally most suited for more conservative equity-income investors. Because of their high, stable dividends, they are often held as bond substitutes, and they move closely with the prices of long-term bonds, making them the most interest-rate-sensitive sector. However, some telecommunications companies do have higher growth potential, with some of the newer areas, such as cellular services, often categorized with technology stocks.

MEDIA AND LEISURE: This conglomeration includes everything from TV broadcasting, newspapers, and advertising to restaurants, casinos, hotels, and cruise lines. What do these two very different areas have in common? They primarily exist to help people spend their free time. And each is too small to have its own category. While people don't give up watching TV during a recession, ad revenues do decline, hurting media companies across the board. As an investment sector, leisure is very sensitive to changes in peoples' discretionary income.

RETAILERS AND WHOLESALERS: Another smallish category; these firms include major discount chains such as Wal-Mart, as well as department stores, specialty retailers, and "category killers" such as Toys "R" Us. For the last several years, many retailers have been hurt by a major slump in apparel purchases. (Apparently, everyone bought all the clothes he/she needed in the 1980s, and with companies going casual, there's even less need for expensive replacements.)

When examining any of these industries, don't forget to unpack it into its constituent sectors. For example, with finance, you can examine each sector—banks, brokerages, and insurance—and scrutinize the performance prospects of the industry, sector, and individual companies. From there you can ferret out those funds that are most committed to the particular companies and sectors within one industry. And you can then measure that company's or fund's past and potential performance against a pool of its peers, as well as against an adequate market benchmark.

The opposite chart reflects an accurate mosaic of the types of industries that most publicly traded companies participate in. Why is knowing this important? For one thing, it's interesting in itself to see just how complex our markets and our world are. For another, especially when it comes to mutual funds, sector concentration may be the closest you can come to current weightings in any given fund. Knowing where the fund is concentrated will help you judge its performance in light of what you know about the sectors. And it will also help you avoid owning two funds that are invested in the same way (for more on the significance of determining your fund's correlation, turn to chapter 13). Likewise, when scanning the globe for new investment opportunities, you'll be far better off knowing in advance what industries are out there to choose from—so that you can wed what you know about the economy (for example, its cyclical nature) with your buying and selling strategies. In a given year, even an unusually positive one, some industries fare better than others—and some stand head and shoulders above the rest.

While you will need to select your investments based on your objectives and the investment's fundamental promise, you will also need to heed the dominant industry themes of the day. Known as top-down investing, it's basically a bird's-eye view of the forest (as opposed to a forester's view of each individual tree). First, you'll need to familiarize yourself with the major industry categories as well as their related subsectors. From that vantage, you can look at how those sectors relate to the overall economic and market envi-

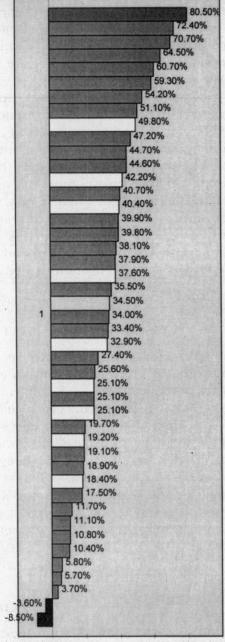

1996 MID-YEAR SECTOR PERFORMANCE

SECTORS

Sector	Performance
Biotechnology	80.50%
Oil, Drilling	72.40%
Aerospace & Defense	70.70%
Semiconductor	64.50%
Savings & Loans	60.70%
Pharmaceuticals	59.30%
Banks, Regional	54.20%
Airlines	51.10%
FINANCIAL	49.80%
Home Construction	47.20%
Beverage	44.70%
Computers (w/o IBM)	44.60%
CONSUMER NON-CYCLICAL	42.20%
Telephone Systems	40.70%
TECHNOLOGY	40.40%
Insurance	39.90%
Software	39.80%
Retailers (Drug-based)	38.10%
House Non-Durable	37.90%
S&P 500 INDEX	37.60%
Oilfield Equipment & Services	35.50%
Securities Brokers	34.50%
Gas	34.00%
Footwear	33.40%
UTILITIES	32.90%
Chemicals	27.40%
Food	25.60%
ENERGY	25.10%
Communications	25.10%
INDUSTRIAL	25.10%
Apparel	19.70%
CONSUMER CYCLICAL	19.20%
Mining (Diversified)	19.10%
Aluminum	18.90%
BASIC MATERIALS	18.40%
Real Estate Investment	17.50%
Paper Products	11.70%
Retailers (Apparel)	11.10%
Retailers (Broadline)	10.80%
Factory Equipment	10.40%
House Durable	5.80%
Clothing/Fabric	5.70%
Precious Metals	3.70%
Retailers - Specialty	-3.60%
Steel	-8.50%

BOLD = Major Industry Group
Source: Dow Jones Industry Groups

-20.00% 0.00% 20.00% 40.00% 60.00% 80.00% 100.00%

ronments. Doing so with respect to a particular company provides you with one way to gauge its prospects relative to the market and its industry peers. For example, General Motors is a car manufacturer that tends to do well in earnings in the later stages of an economic recovery when people are more willing to spend for big-ticket items.

With respect to mutual funds, sector weightings are perhaps even more critical, since a fund's investment character can be reflected in its sector weightings as much as in its stock selection. Not surprisingly, stocks and funds in the industry darling of the day (for example, technology stocks, and, within technology, software issues) tend to outperform those that are less focused in that industry and subsector. Sector analysis may sound difficult to wrap your mind around, but, thanks to the many user-friendly resources at your peck and call (peck, in terms of using on-line services), it's become much easier to note top- and bottom-performing industries and sectors as well as top- and bottom-performing stocks and funds.

MEASURING A MARKET'S PERFORMANCE

The science of measuring market performances is mathematically based, and so is less susceptible to error than analysis relating to each market, industry, and company. However, there's a lot of room for judgment in what gets included in an index and what gets left out. The following indices reflect the most commonly accepted ones in use today by experts and novices alike. You'll note that, not surprisingly, not all the indices are U.S.-focused. After all, since many of us invest abroad as well as at home—directly through buying Automatic Depository Receipts (ADRs) or indirectly through buying shares in an international or global fund—it's a good idea to get a grip on how all the markets we're investing in are performing.

MAJOR INDICES

DIVINING THE DOW: It's the most common, publicly accepted daily measure of the overall market. You've heard about it. You've seen it. You've talked about it. You've ignored it. But do you know what it is—the Dow Jones Industrial Average (DJIA), that is? Don't worry if you don't. Most people assume it's a good market indicator, and leave it at that. But it might surprise you to know that many market experts feel the Dow doesn't accurately reflect today's overall market. Such critics point to the fact that, for example, the 30 stocks which comprise the Dow are a slim reed on which to hang a daily picture of the more than 11,000 publicly traded companies. Moreover, the Dow's narrow band doesn't include the ever-widening playing field of new industries—most notably technology. While it's true that you will find IBM in the DJIA, you won't find market leaders like Microsoft and Intel. What will you find? Let's take a look at the 30 companies that make up the Dow Jones Industrial Average:

Alcoa	Goodyear
Allied Signal	IBM
American Express	International Paper
AT&T	McDonald's
Bethlehem Steel	Merck
Boeing	3M
Caterpillar	J. P. Morgan
Chevron	Phillip Morris
Coca-Cola	Procter & Gamble
Disney	Sears
E. I. DuPont	Texaco
Eastman Kodak	Union Carbide
Exxon	United Technologies
General Electric	Westinghouse Electric
General Motors	Woolworth

Aside from what the DJIA doesn't include, such critics find that what it does include biases it toward large-cap companies. The other argument against using the Dow as a standard with which to measure the market is that the way it calculates the average of the 30 companies is itself problematic, since it gives more weight to higher-priced stocks. So, should the Dow be replaced? NO!

Since 1896 (when Charles Dow introduced this index), the Dow has served to reflect accurately the movement and mood of the overall market. In fact, even when the Dow is compared to the broader indices that its critics propose as adequate replacements, the Dow withstands the test of time and accuracy. For example, when compared to the S&P 500 (a market-weighted capitalization which better reflects the market and, perhaps as important, serves as the benchmark against which many money managers and fund managers gauge their performance), the Dow shows little divergence—and the same can be said when the Dow is compared to other popular and significant indices like the Nasdaq Composite, the Russell 2000, and the Wilshire 5000 (all of which are defined and detailed below). The bottom line on the Dow, then, is that it continues to serve as an accurate and therefore adequate measure of the market. It's worth paying attention to, but not exclusively so. It's best used in conjunction with other indices that better reflect their particular markets.

S&P 500: Charles Dow created the first standard to measure the markets, and it was the only commonly accepted measure until 1928, when Standard & Poor's created a market-weighted index based on 90 stocks. Twenty-two years later, the S&P 90 had become what it is today—the S&P 500. Perhaps the most broadly used benchmark to gauge one's successes and failures versus the overall market, the S&P 500 is a tough performance standard to live up to. This index consists of 400 industrial companies, 40 utility companies, 40 financial companies, and 20 transportation companies.

NASDAQ COMPOSITE: The Nasdaq Composite Index is a market-value weighted average of 3,500 domestic over-the-counter (OTC) stocks. This index is becoming synonymous with the leading technology companies which comprise it (like Microsoft, Oracle, Cisco, and more). As such, you've no doubt seen this index gain wider acceptance as a market indicator in every media—from newsprint to TV. It's an excellent indicator of this sector of the market, although it can no longer be viewed as an exemplary small-company index since so many of its onetime small companies have become huge.

Indicative Indices

The following indices will help you cover the markets of the U.S. and the world in more detail. The more refined you become in benchmarking the performance of your individual investments (stocks, bonds, and mutual funds), the more interesting these indices become.

RUSSELL 2000: This index is used to measure small-company performance. The 2,000 companies in this index are also the smallest (in capitalization) companies in the Russell 3000 index (see below). Russell provides both a growth and value 2000 index which further refines your view of the stocks included in the small-cap universe (see pp. 126–27 for more detail).

RUSSELL 3000: An excellent overall stock market standard, it's comprised of the 3,000 largest U.S. companies (defined by market capitalization) and can be used to countermeasure the more narrow Dow and S&P 500 indices. The companies in this index represent over 95 percent of the total U.S. stock market.

WILSHIRE 5000: This is another excellent stock market index.

STANDARD & POOR'S MIDCAP 400 (S&P 400): If its large sibling is used to represent the overall market, this index is used to help investors gauge the performance of midsized companies (which are typically found on the AMEX).

WILSHIRE MIDCAP 750: This is another mid-cap index to watch.

WILSHIRE TOP 750: The 750 largest U.S. stocks comprise this index. If you're looking to get a take on the overall health of big-time corporate America as reflected by their stock performance, this is a superior index to scout out.

International and Global Indices

The most popular benchmark for international markets is commonly referred to as the "EAFE," which is shorthand for **Morgan Stanley Capital International Europe, Australasia, and Far East (MSCI EAFE).** EAFE has over 3,000 indices, but the following are the most relevant ones for most investors. Moreover, while Dow Jones provides equally useful international and global indices (found in the *Wall Street Journal* and on-line, among other places), the Morgan Stanley Capital International indices will help you know what to look for when you're looking at most market indices. Some are self-explanatory, such as **MSCI Europe, MSCI Pacific, MSCI Latin America,** and **MSCI Japan,** while others, like the **MSCI Free Indices** (which includes most markets in those countries that non-residents can invest in, including the U.S.), and **MSCI World** (which is comprised of 16 larger world markets, including the U.S.) are less so. Note that whether the U.S. is included in the index or not, when it comes to comparing international market returns, you need to ensure that the returns translate to U.S. dollars as well as local currency—typically, this is listed.

U.S. Bond Indices

Lehman Brothers cornered the bond index market—and remains the most popular litmus test for taxable and tax-free bond performance in the U.S. The **Lehman Brothers Corporate Bond** is a bond index that includes all publicly issued, fixed-rate, nonconvertible, dollar-denominated, SEC-registered, investment-grade corporate debt. **Lehman Brothers Government Bond** does for U.S. treasuries and agency bonds what the above index does for corporate debt. The **Lehman Brothers Government/Corporate Bond** combines the two. And the **Lehman Brothers Muni Bond** compares the performances of long-term, investment-grade, tax-exempt municipal bonds. And yes, Lehman provides indices for high-yield (junk) bonds and mortgage bond funds.

MARKET TRENDS

As with economic cycles, which can directly impact companies' performance (as well as funds which invest in those companies), so are there some interesting historical trends which have proven over time to affect markets or specific types of stocks within those markets. Two recurring and more prominent trends are the **January Effect,** named after the fact that January has historically been a very strong month for small-cap stocks—as have the early winter months; and the **Election Effect,** which is based on the historical trend (since World War II) that has shown the third year and the election year of a president's term tend to beat the market's (S&P 500) average return.

No matter what resources, cycles, trends, indices, or industries you turn to ferret out risks and potential rewards, you need to learn how to find and use this information. The next section will help you further distill your investment process by helping you tell one investment category from another, one investment from another, and one fund from another—in order to help you tailor your overall investment portfolio to your specific objectives.

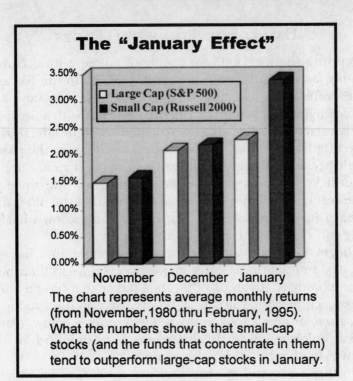

The "January Effect"

- □ Large Cap (S&P 500)
- ■ Small Cap (Russell 2000)

The chart represents average monthly returns (from November,1980 thru February, 1995). What the numbers show is that small-cap stocks (and the funds that concentrate in them) tend to outperform large-cap stocks in January.

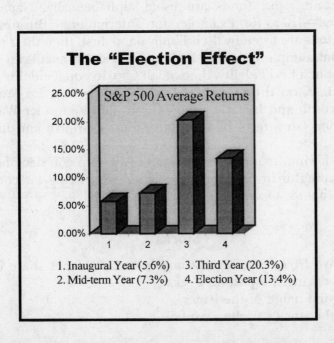

The "Election Effect"

S&P 500 Average Returns

1. Inaugural Year (5.6%)   3. Third Year (20.3%)
2. Mid-term Year (7.3%)   4. Election Year (13.4%)

USING THE FINANCIAL PAGES

You step into the local café for a mug of coffee, with a *Barron's* or *Wall Street Journal* under your arm. You walk up to the bar and ask for the coffee—black. Then you pull up your stool and lay the paper down, just like a miner from the Old West with a prospector's chart. The absence of a six-gun strapped to your side shows that prospecting for gold has become a lot tamer than in the past—but it hasn't become all that much easier to strike it rich. Sure, there are the lucky few who play the lottery and win. But, since you're like the rest of us, chances are you'll have to do it the old-fashioned way—earn it, save it, invest it. But if you don't know what you're looking for, chances are you won't find it.

To begin with, you will need to find a paper that lists stocks, bonds, and mutual funds. Most major papers do—in their business section, of course. If you can't locate a paper that has an adequate business section, visit your local library, or purchase today's *Wall Street Journal*, or take a look at the ready resources below. (And, yes, there's a quicker way to do this research on-line and/or on the Web; turn to chapter 20 for the scoop.)

From there, you will want to find the exchanges on which your stocks and funds are located. Note the following similarities: companies, bonds, and funds are listed alphabetically. Names are abbreviated—IBM, for example, for International Business Machines. Funds are listed by their family name first, then their proper name. For example, if you're looking for Fidelity small-cap funds, you would first find Fidelity, then Small Cap, to equal Fidelity Small-Cap Fund. If, on the other hand, you were looking for Warburg Pincus Growth and Income Fund, you would look under Warburg Pincus, then Growth, to find Warburg Pincus Growth and Income Fund.

The following financial pages primer will help you decipher the most meaningful investment information and help you compare the performance of various issues:

Stocks

- *52 Week Hi/Lo:* the highest and lowest price per share of the stock during the past 52 weeks.
- *Stock:* the name of the issuer.
- *Sym:* the stock's trading symbol.

- *Div:* the latest annual dividend paid by the stock.
- *Yld:* the stock's latest annual dividend expressed as a percentage of the stock's price on that day.
- *PE:* the price/earnings ratio (the price of a stock divided by the issuing company's past four quarters of earnings).
- *Hi/Lo/Close:* the stock's volatility expressed in terms of a single share's price movement. The close is what the price of the stock will open at on the next trading day.
- *s* or *x:* Symbols may appear in the left-hand column. A symbol here is further information that you should know about the company's stock. The paper will provide a key with the meaning of each symbol.

Bonds

- *Issue:* the issuer's name.
- *Coupon:* interest rate at which the bond was issued.
- *Mat:* maturity date (the year in which the bond matures).
- *Price:* the price the bond closed at. For example, a price of 98¾ means it closed at 98¾ percent per $1,000 of par value, or at $988.
- *Chg:* change reflects the amount the bond closed as compared with its previous day's closing.
- *Bid Yld:* the bond's yield to maturity.
- *CV:* the issue is a convertible bond, i.e., it can be exchanged for a fixed number of shares of common stock from the issuer.

Mutual Funds

- *NAV* (Net Asset Value): tells you what a share of the fund is worth today.
- *Offer price:* what you would pay (per share) were you to purchase shares in the fund that day.
- *p:* the fund charges a 12-bl fee.
- *t:* the fund charges both a 12-bl fee and a redemption fee.
- *NL:* no load, meaning there are no up-front sales charges.
- *r:* redemption charge. (Some are as high as 6 percent!)
- *x* (ex-dividend): new share buyers will not receive the fund's next dividend payout.
- *Note:* As with stocks and bonds, there may be a symbol listed

next to the fund you're interested in. Again, check the paper's key for the definition of the symbol.

More information on each of these characteristics of stocks, bonds, and funds can be found in Part III.

READY RESOURCES

As this whole section has amply demonstrated, when it comes to investing, information is never in short supply. The following resources barely scratch the surface (or airwaves, or virtual space), but they will help you unearth some of the best (i.e., useful and potentially profit-producing) information around. Moreover, purchasing some of these items could be tax deductible. That's right, you may be able to take a tax deduction for every investment-related book and magazine you purchase. What about CNBC and your cable TV? Don't count on it. On-line time? If you feel adventurous, you might explore this new territory for a possible partial deduction.

Caveat emptor (and caveat viewer and listener): Many of the sources listed here should be scrutinized by you much the way you would scrutinize a potential investment. Some provide more hype than true type. Others provide insight for a price that can be beat or can't be met—after all, if you're eking out $100 per month to invest, spending $100 for a source isn't exactly in your scope. (Hint: focus on your library.) Nevertheless, most of what you'll find below are acceptable sources for furthering your own research. Never become reliant on one, question all, and distill what's useful to you and your investment objectives.

PLUG-IN PUNDITS: Just as it's difficult to select the best stock or fund from the over-abundant crop, so it's difficult to know who among the many television and radio pundits is worth listening to (and who should be avoided). But, when time is short, there are several shows worth watching, and, of course, those which plainly are not.

The late-night hucksters with their no-money-down schemes are good for a laugh, but little else. To begin with, anyone who is trying to sell you something that sounds too good, or easy, to be true is probably telling a lie. Next, there are those who try to sell you something you simply don't understand. Avoid investing in any-thing—and anyone—you don't completely understand.

The more meaningful question is, who *can* you listen to?—and here, you're in luck. Of course, there's CNBC throughout the day for market updates and the occasional economic news. In addition, two of the best daily financial shows occur every night on TV: *Nightly Business Report* (PBS), after which you can turn to *Moneyline* (CNBC and CNN). You don't want to miss *Wall Street Week* (PBS)—tape it if you have to, since this show is the best overall summary of the market's recent activity and potential opportunities and pitfalls. CNN's *Moneyweek* is a good Wall Street week-in-review, too. For a more philosophical look at the way money is used in the world, tune in to *Adam Smith's Money World* (PBS). In radio land, tune into *Market Place* (National Public Radio, nightly at 7:30 PM, EST) and profit from news that any investor can use.

MAGAZINES: Subscribe to one of the following personal finance magazines: *Kiplinger's Personal Finance Magazine, Money, Smart Money, Worth, Your Money.* They're listed in order of my preference, but I recommend that you go to your library to compare them be-fore subscribing to the one that seems best for you. Not only are these publications an excellent resource for a broad range of in-vesting information, they're also a great source of new money-management, investing, and overall personal finance ideas.

NEWSPAPERS: The best daily source of investment news you can use is the *Wall Street Journal.* The *Journal* provides the best reporting on business in the business. Economic and market analysis, stellar and bombing bonds, the funds to watch and the funds to invest in—all are scrutinized. *Investor's Daily* is another investment news-paper that is widely read. And, of course, there's the eminent fi-nancial weekly, *Barron's.* These papers cost a bundle. As a result, you may want to subscribe to a monthly magazine and make a bi-weekly visit to your library for one or more of these excellent papers.

NEWSLETTERS: They aren't exactly a dime a dozen—or even $10 for one—but a handful of the many investment newsletters that are out there are worth considering. *Value Line* and *Morningstar* are obvious stock and fund investor choices—and deservedly so. *FundsNet Insight* also shouldn't be overlooked.

ANNUAL REPORTS: Every company publishes a year-end review of their financial health. You can get one—typically, free for the asking—by calling the company and requesting it. Of course, there will be a lot of hype, but there also will be some interesting narration and numbers, such as changes in management, marketing plans for the future, profit and liability statements—all of which will help you gauge your potential investment in that company.

ANALYSTS' RECOMMENDATIONS: Brokerage firms pump more pulp than most paper companies. Literally thousands of recommendations are produced by a handful of companies in a year or less. Nevertheless, analysts' reports are usually easy to understand and fact-based in spite of healthy doses of salesmanship inscribed in the rhetoric. As with an annual report, an analyst's recommendations should be taken with a grain of consumer-savvy salt. To get your hands on a report about a particular company, call a brokerage house and request it. Even if you have no intention of opening an account with the brokerage, they may be happy to serve you— so that they may be able to serve you again.

STANDARD & POOR'S STOCK REPORTS: These provide detailed performance analyses on thousands of stocks. Standard & Poor's also publishes a monthly Stock Guide which tracks the performance of more than 5,000 stocks. Both the reports and the guide are available in larger libraries and are useful sources for a company's history of stock performance and potential future value.

VALUE LINE INVESTMENT SURVEY: This survey covers 1,700 stocks and provides what some consider to be the best analysis in the investment industry. Your library should have it; if not, ask your library to get it. It's too expensive to buy on your own. (You can access much of the info on-line—see chapter 20 for details.)

ON-LINE INFORMATION: Participate in the information revolution—it just may enhance your investing skills and profit potential. America Online, CompuServe, and Prodigy provide easy-to-access and understandable on-line economic, investment, and business information. You also can buy and sell stocks, bonds, and mutual funds on-line. Chapter 20 deals with on-line investing in each of these principal players, and helps you navigate the Net to your advantage (rather than to your server's).

INTERNET: The Internet offers the widest range of raw data and wild opinion on all facets of the economy, markets, and investing. A lawless global village, it can be as easy to wind up with less than zero (especially after you calculate the cost of searching) as it is to hit a fountain of information that can change the way you think about an industry, fund, or company. Chapter 20 details some of the best methods for finding information in the World Wide Web.

Turn there before you turn your modem on. But before you go, take note of the following sources for focusing your watchful eye on the markets here and abroad:

- *Barron's*, (800) 544-0422.
- *Investor's Business Daily*, (800) 831-2525.
- *The Wall Street Journal*, (800) 221-1940.
- *Moody's Investors Service*, (800) 342-5647.
- *Learning to Invest*, Second Edition, by B. Wallace, Globe Press.
- *How to Read and Understand Financial News*, Second Edition, by G. Warfield, HarperCollins.
- *Fundamentals of Investments*, Second Edition, by G. Alexander, Prentice Hall.
- *Security Analysis*, by Graham and Dodd, McGraw-Hill.
- *Individual Investor's Guide Comp*, Thirteenth Edition, Login Publishers.
- *Investments*, Third Edition, by Z. Bodie, Irwin Press.
- *Hulbert Guide to Financial Newsletters*, Fifth Edition, by M. Hulbert, Dearborn.
- *Irwin Guide to Using the Wall Street Journal*, Fifth Edition, by M. Lehmann, Irwin Press.
- *How to Profit from Reading Annual Reports*, by R. Loth, Dearborn.

CHAPTER EIGHT

Beating the Benchmarks

You think you're about to settle into a single-malt when the man with the smell of stale cigars and too much Polo saunters up to you and begins to tell you all about his latest winning investment: the one that knocked the socks off the average return; the one anybody could have picked if they had just paid enough attention to what the world was telling the Street. The killing this guy made could have made you a fortune. But there you are—no back door to the wall you're propped against. You have to respond. You have to say something clever and competitive. You're scanning for the right investment—the one that delivered unbelievably good results. You can't think of one. In fact, you can't think of how to begin to measure what a truly good result is. What, after all, does beating the market really mean? Is it a good thing? Is it a necessary thing?

There's a lot of talk about beating the market. There are a few good books about it, including *Beating the Street*, by Peter Lynch. And while this chapter may be short, its lesson is critical to your overall investing success. Its lesson, in short, is that you must set mileposts to measure your portfolio's progress—or the lack of it. Failure to do so will mean that, like living without a budget or a financial plan, you're the investor equivalent of Casey Jones.

BEATING BENCHMARKS: When it comes to beating the market, you have to know which market you're referring to—and to what extent that market is an adequate benchmark of your investment's success. The truth is that, while it's important to judge a particular investment by the index to which it is most closely related, there are two solid milestones that you want to keep in mind at all times: a market index (the S&P 500) and an economic index, which relates to your wallet (the rate of inflation).

BEATING THE MARKET: For the most part, when people talk about beating the market, they mean beating a specific market index that they use as a benchmark against which they measure the success or failure of a particular investment and of their overall portfolio. Typically, this benchmark is the S&P 500—not exactly the father of all benchmarks (which, once upon a time, was gold, and now is the Dow Jones Industrial Average), but which is more correctly viewed as the mother lode of all indices. If your investment portfolio has been keeping pace with this index, let alone staying ahead of it, then you have been ahead of the majority of investors and their portfolios.

BEATING INFLATION: Inflation is a nemesis—no matter how "controlled" it seems to be today. That's why it's essential that you understand how inflation, in conjunction with all the more fancy benchmarks out there, affects your money at the core of its value, namely, its purchasing power. What is purchasing power? Think of it this way. You know how your uncle, who has told you countless tales of the value of a nickel in his day, could, with nothing but one dollar in his pocket, wine and dine a girl, take in a movie, and fly to Brazil for a wild, one-night gambling spree, and still have enough left to buy himself a breakfast special at the Blue Diner come Monday morning. Not seriously. But the value of that dollar in your uncle's day was far greater than it is today. George Washington looks the same on the bill, but his purchasing power has been eaten away. And it's inflation that reduced the value of the dollar's purchasing power. The purchasing power of $1 is reduced by 50 percent every fifteen years or so. This means that $1 today will be worth almost nothing in thirty years' time, thanks to inflation's slow but persistent nibbling. In fact, if you look at the value of $1,000 put in a conservative CD (among the least impressive investments in terms of performance) versus putting the cash in a drawer for the time period from March 1984 through February 1996, the results tell the tale: your $1,000 would be worth over $3,000 in the CD—but worth less than $300 in that drawer.

BEATING THE BENCHMARK OF INFLATION: Investing—in stocks and stock mutual funds in particular—has proven historically to be the only consistent way to beat the toll inflation takes on your pay. Failure to invest your money in instruments which beat inflation will result in your money becoming less valuable. If this happens, you'll be forced to live a lifestyle of diminishing returns. The only way to beat inflation is by increasing the value of your dollar ahead of the rate of inflation.

As long as your investments outpace the rate of inflation, you will be fine. It's when they fail to do so that you know you're heading for trouble. Determining how far ahead or behind the rate of inflation your interest-earning or investing accounts are is easy. Watch the nightly news. Listen for the rate of inflation. Look at what your investments are earning. For example, if you are earning 8 percent on your average stock funds and the rate of inflation is 3 percent, then you're doing all right. If, however, your bank CD is earning 4 percent and inflation is at 6 percent, you are fighting a losing battle.

It gets a little more complicated. You need to ensure that your overall investment portfolio is beating inflation as well as being in step with (or, preferably, ahead of) a meaningful market benchmark. For example, if you are earning 8 percent on your average stock funds and the rate of inflation is 3 percent, then you're doing all right so long as the S&P 500 isn't delivering a 10 percent return. You will also want to keep an eye on each individual investment in terms of its inflation-beating, market-beating, and industry- (or peer-) beating results. If it is falling behind on one point, it still may receive a passing grade. But if it's falling behind on two or more, you better get to the heart of the matter before your portfolio suffers the consequences.

NOT DEFEATING YOURSELF: Ultimately, if you invest in good stocks for the long haul, don't panic sell at market bottoms, or impulse-buy at market highs (or any time, for that matter), you will likely keep ahead of inflation and, if you've done your homework, be within reasonable proximity of meaningful market benchmarks. While this may seem like a facile way to comfort oneself, the truth is that those investors who brag most about their "timely" successes are also those who are most prone to the negative effects of market timing—buying and selling at the wrong time, as well as buying the wrong types of investments. There are those who say the market is a game, and others who call it a horse race. And for some it may be. But there's more than enough room for knowledge to play a key role in successful investment decision-making to encourage those who are thoughtful investors.

CHAPTER NINE

Uncertainty, Risk, and Reward

You're at lunch with a colleague. She asks what you did last weekend. You say, "Nothing much," while trying to repress the image of you, last weekend, sitting at home watching *Mortal Kombat*, followed by a Jackie Chan binge that left you craving some Szechwan. But that's as spicy as things got. It was raining out. The roads looked kind of slippery. And the Joy Luck wasn't delivering. You turned up the heat. Walked to the fridge. Pulled out a beer. Made some popcorn. Watched *Saturday Night Live*. "Nothing, really," you repeat. "How about you?" Her eyes light up. She plunges into a weekend you thought only Hollywood could manufacture. She was up before dawn, throwing instant coffee, two raw eggs, orange juice, and a papaya into a blender. She wanted a jolt. She needed to be fully alert. She had a plane to catch—But her ticket would leave her 10,000 feet in midair howling at the rising sun as she plummeted to the good ship Earth under her parachute. The rush of it. The lift and plunge of it. Your heart was pounding, and all you could say was, "No way."

Taking risks is something all of us do—to a greater or lesser extent. And therein lies the rub. Some of us are more risk-averse than others; we look both ways twice before crossing. Of course, taking risks for the sake of taking risks is a neurosis, not a challenge. The truth is that, when it comes to taking risks, even the most adventurous risk-taker looks before he leaps—and believes there's a better than even chance that he'll make it to the other side.

When it comes to investing, a critical point to remember is that risk, in and of itself, is not necessarily bad. In fact, some risks go hand in hand with potential rewards, meaning that, for some investors, the risks inherent in some investments may be worth taking. On the other hand, some investment risks are simply not worth taking. Each type of investment has its own specific risks, and there are also risks shared by each major category of investments; those risks are examined in detail in Part III. Before learning about these specific risks, it's essential to identify your own risk tolerance and learn how to deal with it.

If you are going to remain in control of your investments, you will have to learn to manage the risks involved. While this may sound trite, the truth is that too many savers are either swayed by their risk aversion to avoid investing altogether (which leaves their money prone to the damage inflation can do), or, perhaps more commonly, too many investors are enticed by sky-high returns on a current fund, or limitless heights promised by the arrival of a brand-new stock on the market. Sure, there's the middle ground of investors who have made the transition from saving to investing, who have not overcommitted themselves to extremely risky types of investments. Chances are, that's where you find yourself. But—and this is important to note—the majority of investors who are new to the market haven't experienced a full market cycle—from good, to bad, to good again. More than any other factor, an investor's risk tolerance is put to the test by a protracted down market since, as my uncle Ralph says, when the tide goes out, all the ships drop. In a down market, most securities are affected, although some are certainly affected more than others. That's why investors who want to build in a risk-averse portion to their overall investment portfolio select defensive stocks or funds that invest in them. For you, however, the best defense is a solid offense of growth-oriented stocks. Why? Time is on your side—time enough, that is, to weather a market downturn and ride the upsurge.

Simply defined, risk is a measure of how consistent and predictable a stock's or fund's returns are. Has a stock price risen steadily month to month, or has it swung in wide arcs? Does a fund deliver similar returns from month to month, or do returns look like they are attached to the pendulum of an overwound clock? Of course, as long as the up periods last longer and/or are substantially stronger than the down ticks, even a risky investment like small-company stock funds can prove to be more rewarding than a less volatile large-cap growth fund. (The reverse can be true, too.)

So why doesn't everyone invest in them? For one thing, small-company stocks are most appropriate (in large doses) for younger investors precisely because of their volatility; the older you get, the more defensive of your principal you'll become. But, for now, you want to focus on investments that build your principal. For another thing, the intemperate nature of small company stocks increases the risk that an investor will sell them in a down market (the worst time to get out—unless something has fundamentally changed with the fund itself). If you've done your research, then chances are the reasons you bought the stock or fund remain reasonable enough to hold on to it. Don't panic. Don't sell during a steep downdraft. Learn to tolerate risk—by testing your risk tolerance and matching investments to your level of understanding of the risks involved.

RISK TOLERANCE TEST

OK. This isn't exactly a scientific experiment here. But the following risk quiz is designed to help you gauge your risk tolerance as well as your ability to take the right kinds of risks—in life and when it comes to investing. What does one have to do with the other? Chances are you're already somewhat familiar with your risk-taking skills and desires; just take a look at such things as how you drive a car: whether you speed or not, change lanes or not, drive on fumes or never let the gauge drop below half a tank. And those attitudes, no doubt, impact on your feelings about your money. Take a shot at these questions and then take a close look at the explanation of your score on page 102.

1. Would you ever consider trying a sport like bungee jumping or parachuting?
       (a) yes   (b) no   (c) maybe
2. Have you ever decided to do something without knowing the potential consequences?
       (a) yes   (b) no   (c) almost

3. Have you traveled abroad?
      (a) yes   (b) no
4. Do you go to the ATM at night?
      (a) regularly   (b) sometimes   (c) never
5. Without looking at the top ten companies one of your funds invests in, can you name
      (a) all ten
      (b) more than five
      (c) more than one
      (d) less than zero
6. How often do you check the air pressure in your tires?
      (a) regularly   (b) sometimes   (c) never
7. If the pilot light in a gas stove isn't working, do you
      (a) light it
      (b) stand by while someone lights it for you
      (c) leave the house
8. If you had to rank your current investments from most to least risky, you would score
      (a) appropriate risk in relation to return
      (b) some risk, some return
      (c) no risk, low return
      (d) all risk, unlikely return
9. Does the probability of losing 10 percent or more of your total invested savings make you
      (a) not want to invest
      (b) want to invest a modest amount
      (c) ignore short-term dips
10. If you inherited a lump sum of money, say $25,000, would you
      (a) invest it all at once
      (b) gradually invest it
      (c) put it in a CD
11. Do you feel more comfortable when
      (a) you're in total control
      (b) sharing decisions
      (c) you're being told what to do
12. Would you risk everything for a potentially huge return?
      (a) yes   (b) no   (c) maybe
13. Which strategy suits you best?
      (a) taking your time to get to trust someone
      (b) trusting someone before you know them
      (c) trusting no one

14. Rank the following professionals in order of how much you trust them.
    - (a) car mechanic
    - (b) real estate agent
    - (c) banker
    - (d) broker
    - (e) airline pilot

15. The last time you pretended to know something when you didn't was
    - (a) just yesterday
    - (b) about one year ago
    - (c) never

16. You would rather
    - (a) impress your friends
    - (b) impress yourself
    - (c) impress your best friend or spouse

17. When you were applying for your latest job did you
    - (a) tell everyone you thought you would get it
    - (b) tell only a handful of people
    - (c) keep it to yourself until you actually got it

18. If you had to rate the riskiest thing you have ever done on a scale from 10 (being the most risky) and 1 (being the least risky), how would you rate yourself?
    - (a) 10   (b) 7   (c) 5   (d) 3   (e) 1

19. If you weren't guaranteed that you would get all your money out of the bank account it's now in, what would you be inclined to do?
    - (a) keep it in
    - (b) take it out
    - (c) keep in only the amount you were guaranteed to get back

20. In general you think that, compared to the stock market, banks are
    - (a) safer places to keep your money
    - (b) smarter places to keep your money
    - (c) safer and smarter
    - (d) safer, but not necessarily smarter

21. When you hear about the stock market, you think it's
    - (a) too risky to invest in
    - (b) too expensive to invest in

        (c) too risky and expensive

        (d) not too risky, but too expensive

        (e) worth the risks

22. When standing in line at the airport, you check to ensure you have your ticket

        (a) once

        (b) twice

        (c) at least twice

        (d) more than three times

23. When it comes to long-term commitments, you would say that you are

        (a) unshakable

        (b) mostly committed

        (c) susceptible to change

24. Are you easily influenced by others when it comes to making decisions about your well-being?

        (a) yes

        (b) no

        (c) sometimes

SCORECARD

Remember when your teacher told you that you could grade your own exam? Well, that's not in the cards. Instead, you'll need to score yourself based on the following key:

	A	B	C	D			A	B	C	D	E
1.	1	.5	0			13.	1	0	0		
2.	0	1	.5			14.	0	0	0	.5	0
3.	1	0				15.	0	0	0		
4.	.5	1	0			16.	.5	1	.5		
5.	4	2	1	0		17.	0	.5	1		
6.	.5	1	0			18.	1	1	.5	0	
7.	1	.5	0			19.	.5	0	1		
8.	.5	1	.5	0		20.	1	0	0	1	
9.	0	.5	0			21.	0	0	0	0	1
10.	1	.5	0			22.	1	1	.5	0	
11.	.5	1	0			23.	.5	1	.5		
12.	0	0	1			24.	0	1	.5		

Add up your score and check below for an explanation of your results.

20-plus. You are a well-rehearsed risk-taker who knows how to set reasonable limits in accordance with realizable goals. Not unwilling to take on a new challenge, you are also against leaps of faith for faith's sake. Chances are you could be a successful entrepreneur, which, by the way, is the same profile it would take to be a successful investor. You're willing to take charge of a new situation in an informed, objective way while, at the same time, you are able to recognize the potential pitfalls and calculate the consequences. You're also able to spot trouble before you're in it. To be a successful investor, you need to be able to tolerate and accomplish all the above without being overwhelmed by doubts. You're on your way.

10 to 20 points. Depending on where your score falls, you are either more or less likely to take risks with a greater or lesser degree of probability that there will be a reward waiting for you on the other side. You have tended to take either too much risk with too little advance thinking about the possible consequences, or too little risk without understanding the potential downside in terms of gain. As an investor, you will need to learn more about the potential risks and rewards in order to ensure that you flourish rather than founder when it comes to new investments which are better suited to your age and objectives. You will need to learn more in order to take on more risks, which, in turn, will help you increase your long-term chances of successfully achieving your investment objectives. In the chapters ahead, pay particular attention to the sections on each investment category's particular risks and potential rewards.

10 or less. You are, in varying degrees, either too willing to take risks without knowing and understanding the consequences, or too unwilling to take on necessary risks in order to achieve reasonable objectives. As a younger investor, you'll need to come to terms with the fact that some risks aren't worth taking while others decidedly are. Familiarizing yourself with appropriate risks and rewards for each type of investment vehicle within each investment category will help you overcome your timidity and/or tame your overconfidence when it comes to taking risks.

OVERCOMING UNCERTAINTY

Being uncertain is a natural condition, but so is growing beyond uncertainty. If it weren't, no child would crawl, no adolescent would survive into adulthood, and no adult would commit to self-determination when it comes to career and family. In investing, as in life, accepting uncertainty as a starting point—not as an end in itself—is a condition you'll need to evolve from. And, as with psychological growth, when it comes to investing, you'll need to come to terms with (and so take control of) your own past and present investment experience (or lack thereof) in order to reasonably ensure a more fulfilling future for yourself.

Knowing that investing in certain types of securities has proven effective in the past is one way to overcome any sense of foreboding you might have in the present. The best way to do this is to look at what would happen if you had made the wrong moves. Taking the worst-case scenario of investing in common stocks at market highs rather than lows might help. After all, conventional wisdom has it that this is the worst way to invest. And, while most investors won't ever repeat the poor performance results of investing new money at exactly the wrong time, if *you* did, you could take some comfort in the fact that you still would have fared very well. Take a look at the top chart on page 105, which shows the results of investing $1 rather than keeping it as cash.

What is immediately apparent from this chart is that, had you invested at the wrong time, you would have come out well ahead of where you would have been had you not invested at all (i.e., stuffed your money in a mattress). Making a classic mistake still turns out to be rewarding enough to make the move from saving to investing. But the types of stocks you would have had to have invested in—the more liquid, large-company stocks, right? Well, yes. But you would have fared better in small-company stocks over the same time period.

The bottom chart on page 105 is meant to help those who are reluctant to enter the market overcome their aversion. However, the truth of the performance lies in a hidden fact—that the money wasn't pulled out of the market on its downside. Your ability to commit to the market long term is of paramount importance when it comes to reaping the potential rewards investing has to offer. Every category of investment tends to diminish in volatility (swings from positive to negative returns) over time. In fact, as the volatility charts illustrate, time may be the single most important ingredient you can add to the recipe of what makes a successful investment.

What exactly is volatility? It's a relative term. In fact, the more accurate term is *"relative volatility"* or, more commonly, *"beta,"* and refers to the history of a security's or fund's range of rise and fall over specified time periods. To calculate the beta for a stock mutual fund, for example, divide the fund's standard deviation by the standard deviation of the S&P 500 index for the same period. What is a stock's "standard deviation?" It is the difference, or deviation, between its performance during a given period—say the last quater—and a benchmark like its average lifetime performance. You can use a market benchmark like the S&P 500 to measure a stock's standard deviation as well as its own performance history. Suppose you wanted to measure the standard deviation of a stock fund's beta against the S&P 500. If the S&P 500's beta is 1, and the stock fund's is 1.45, then the fund's standard deviation is 0.45. This means that the stock fund in question is 45% more volatile than the S&P 500 as a whole. If you want to buy shares in this fund, be prepared for a bumpy ride.

From beta to alpha. While this may be sounding like Greek 101, it's really Risk 101. Whereas a beta refers to a security's performance in terms of its volatility, an alpha mathematically measures a security's fundamental potential to deliver an expected return. A stock, for example, with an alpha of 1.45 would be expected to rise 45 percent in price. Low price relative to high alpha signals a potential buying opportunity.

Calculating a security's or fund's standard deviation or beta requires some doing, but there are several sources which do this for you for stocks and stock funds, such as *Morningstar, Value Line,* and several investment newsletters. Yours free at a local library.

MANAGING RISK

If you lift weights, or haven't repressed the memory of high school gym class, chances are you have heard the expression "no pain, no gain." Something similar applies to investing, although it's trans-

Power of Compounding

Even with the worst market timing, $1 invested in stocks each year
from 1946 to 1993 at the annual stock market high would have grown
to $1700 versus $245 invested in cash.

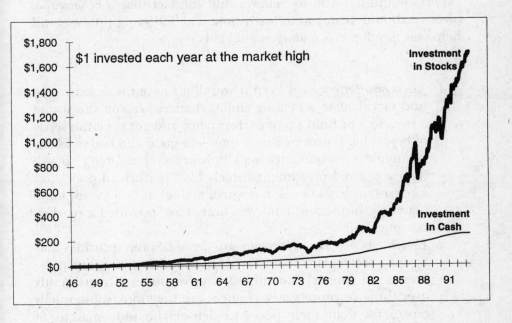

These three charts illustrate one point: Over time, stock and bond markets, as well as a standard
asset allocation for a conservative portfolio (of 60% stocks and 40% bonds) exhibit less volatility
over longer periods of time — and more volatility over shorter periods of time. The moral: Long-
term investing is more beneficial than short-term investing.

lated as "no risk, no return." And since risk is a constant in the investment universe, you'll need to learn how to adapt to it—and use it to your best advantage. You've already assessed your risk-taking tolerance; now you need the know-how to gauge whether a risky investment has real potential for reward.

Managing risk is only partially possible—no matter what some experts would like you to believe. But, the fact that it is *somewhat* possible should drive you to learn how. The following tip sheet will help you develop risk-management skills:

1. *Know past performance.* Even if you don't have the resources to find or calculate a beta or alpha, chances are you can locate a security's or fund's past performance and get a relative sense of how it has performed over time—in good and bad markets, economic environments, and industry cycles. Doing so will help you avoid investments which have performed poorly on a consistent basis (a risk not worth taking) as well as cull some better performers which, over time, have provided a market-beating return.

2. *Understand how the performance was derived.* Some securities may have a spectacular record for a few months, a year, or maybe even a bit longer. But, unless they've done so consistently over three or more years, chances are they took substantially more risk than their peers to deliver the wide margin of performance-related difference.

3. *Identify any significant changes in the economy, market, industry, and the company.* (If it's a fund, such a change could be a new manager.) While subsequent chapters will help you discern these qualities, it's worth keeping in mind that changes in any of the above categories will necessitate a review of the individual risks that may be increased (or decreased) as a result.

4. *Review your objectives.* If your objectives change, and your time frame for achieving them changes, then you have injected a degree of risk into your overall investment plan that did not exist when you put your portfolio together. Chances are you will need to review and revise your portfolio in light of these changes and the risks they bring.

5. *Review your portfolio's risk.* Each security or fund in your port-folio has a degree of risk which, when combined with the other securities or funds in the portfolio, creates an average

risk of your overall mix. You want to be sure that this risk remains in line with your tolerance and ability to manage it.

In 1987, a year which saw one of the worst days on Wall Street, even bearish investors—those who think the market will fall on their heads at any moment—made money, so long as they remained invested and didn't panic sell. You can't avoid risk. But you can understand it and look for ways to manage it to your advantage. That's what you'll need to do to be able to comfortably take appropriate risks and increase your potential to achieve your objectives. Sometimes it will be more difficult to stay the course—especially during intemperate markets. But the markets have never been dead calm, and will likely never be. The result is that you need to assess investment risks in relation to their specific rewards and particular potential for your overall portfolio. That's the best way to avoid the losses that uncertainty can yield and to maintain your prime directive: to invest in a better future for yourself.

PART III

Know the Basics Before You Invest

CHAPTER TEN

Bond Investing

What is a bond? Think of a bond as an IOU. When you purchase a bond, you're basically acting like a bank which lends money in return for (a) some interest and (b) ultimately, the return of the total principal amount that was lent. When you buy a bond, you are "loaning" the corporation or government the price of the bond; this is called the face or "par" value. In return, you are hoping to receive either one or a combination of: a high rate of interest, tax advantages, and/or safety of principal.

The distinction between long-, intermediate-, and short-term bonds is a key factor in a savvy bond investor's selection process. What do these words mean? The term of a bond, also referred to as its maturity, is the time the IOU becomes due and payable. The longer out that pay date is, the greater the risk of price fluctuation tends to be. The shorter the term, the less the bond's volatility. While long-term bonds perform better over time, shorter-term bonds can offer you a greater degree of certainty that your money will be returned to you when you need it.

As with stocks, there are numerous different types of bonds to chose from, and it's in your interest to familiarize yourself with them. Since many mutual funds hold some percentage of their assets in bonds, familiarizing yourself with the various types of bonds that are available to the investing public will help you better understand the risks and rewards each type lends to mutual fund portfolios. Even stock funds often have some bonds in their mix, and growth and income funds often have upwards of 30 percent of their assets in bonds or other types of fixed-income instruments.

Finally, bonds are barometers of Wall Street's take on the overall economy and specific parts of it. Learning to "read" bonds will help you grasp more than their own worth; it will help you see some underlying signals that the economy is sending to bond traders.

BOND RISKS

If stocks are often viewed as a walk on the wild side of investing, bonds are often viewed as a walk on the safe side, supposedly offering moderate but inflation-beating rates of return with lower risk compared to stocks or stock mutual funds. As a result, conventional wisdom suggests that bonds can and should play an important, counterbalancing role in most investors' portfolios. However, before you buy some bonds for your portfolio, be aware that there are two problems with the rosy rendition for bond investing mentioned above. First, bonds are not generally "safe" investments; there are risks inherent to each type of bond you can purchase. Second, and contrary to conventional wisdom—most of which is written from the perspective of those over age 45—bonds shouldn't necessarily be a part of your portfolio. In fact, if you're under age 35, they should rarely play a role in your portfolio. You've got the need and the time to risk short-term losses in your search for capital appreciation of your long-term investments. For shorter-term objectives, on the other hand, you can make a case for some types of bonds for objectives that fall within a two- to three-year time frame.

While no bond is risk-free, some are far safer than others. There are three main risks associated with bond investing; they should all be taken into consideration before you purchase any type of bond. It's important to keep in mind that, as in life, taking risks can be very rewarding—or downright punitive. Investing in some types of bonds is like taking new back roads to a familiar destination, while investing in others can be like trying to jump fourteen flaming buses with your mountain bike. Keeping the following risks in mind should help you avoid getting burned.

1. *Interest rate risk:* If there's one thing about bonds that you need to know, it's this: when interest rates rise, your bond's value declines—and vice versa. Thus, interest rate risk is the risk that your bond's market value will fluctuate with changes in interest rates. To be attuned to the overall interest rate scene, all you need to do is to tap into one of the on-line services for a bond market update or interest rate forecast. Failing that, read the business section of your paper—there you'll likely find current short-term interest rates as well as their earlier levels. If they're significantly lower than the previous year, you should probably stay away from bond investments.

2. *Call risk:* While rising interest rates hurt bonds, falling rates are good for bonds, sending prices above face value. However, in many cases a bond's issuer may "call" the bond prior to maturity, at par value or at only a slight premium to par value. This, of course, limits the upside potential of the bond in the face of falling interest rates. When a bond is called, you will have to reinvest in a new bond paying you less interest. Most bonds are callable, with the exception of Treasury securities, most of which are noncallable. The bond's fine print should spell out whether the issuer can call the bond, including any premiums required and any time/date limitations to the call. If you decide to invest in individual bonds, be sure to inquire about this often overlooked feature of bond investing.

3. *Credit risk:* This is also known as default risk and is the risk bond investors fear most—and most often hear about in the press thanks to the likes of junk bond king Michael Milken and, more recently, the Orange County, California, bankruptcy. Credit risk is the risk of losing your investment due to default by the bond issuer. Issuers default for several reasons, most typically because their business fails. And it is new or high-risk businesses (such as retailers) that are most likely to go bust or declare bankruptcy than, for example, the federal government, which can always raise taxes (or print money) to help pay you back. But, during the federal budget impasse of 1996, the federal government came under scrutiny from bond rating agencies, suggesting that even the U.S. government may no longer be a safe bet. The best way to safeguard yourself against default is to invest in highly rated bonds. While this is no

guarantee, it has proven to be the most successful way to hedge your bets.

Moody's and Standard & Poor's are the most highly respected agencies in the bond-rating business. Each firm provides a rating scheme designed to underline the degree of credit risk a potential bond investor is getting into. Among the ratings categories used by Moody's and Standard & Poor's are:

MOODY's	STANDARD & POOR'S	MEANING
Aaa	AAA	Best quality
Aa	AA	High quality
Baa	BBB	Medium quality
B	B	Minimal quality

Anything rated less than BBB/Baa is a junk bond.

Typically, lower-rated bonds offer a higher yield, but they also pose greater risk of defaulting. On the other hand, higher-rated bonds provide lower yields but greater chances of seeing full payment of interest and principal.

BOND TYPES

Like the various portrayals of James Bond, bonds have differing characteristics and don't act in the same way. The following types of bonds will help you sort through an investment category that many people invest in but few know much about. Even if you never invest in a bond, you will be able to impress your friends with some hip market talk and save yourself from investing in something that is often touted as safe but is, in fact, potentially rife with risks.

U.S. TREASURIES: The U.S. government regularly borrows money to fund its projects. Treasury bills—more commonly referred to as "T-bills"—are issued in amounts of $10,000, mature in three months to one year, and are sold at a discount. That means that you buy the bill at less than its face amount, and receive its face amount at maturity. Treasury notes and bonds have longer

terms and pay interest semiannually at a fixed rate. All are as free
from credit risk as a bond can get. (More on that below.) While
yields are lower than on other bonds (other than municipals),
Treasury yields are free from state and local income taxes (but not
federal taxes), so you may not be giving up much in yield to get a
Treasury's ultimate safety.

U.S. SAVINGS BONDS: Safe. Secure. Stable. Solid. Although they
don't offer the highest rate of return—4 percent—savings bonds
are a sound introduction to bond investing. With a required minimum investment of only $25, it's easy to start.

MORTGAGE-BACKED BONDS: Backed by pools of mortgage loans,
these bonds have names that sound like a long-lost relative—Ginnie
Mae, Fannie Mae, and Freddie Mac. These bonds offer high rates
of interest but require high investment minimums to get in. Moreover, in times of lower interest rates, when people refinance their
mortgages (billions of dollars of refinanced mortgages swept the
market in 1993 and 1994), mortgage-backed bonds are paid off
sooner than many investors expect or desire, and investors' principal has to be reinvested at the new, lower rates.

ADJUSTABLE RATE MORTGAGE (ARM) BONDS: If you're looking
for a bond investment to help you hedge your portfolio against
rising rates, this is a better bet than most. As rates rise, so too do
the payments of ARM mortgages. These increased payments allow
ARM funds to hold up relatively well compared to other fixed-
income securities. ARMs can offer the safety of a short-term bond,
but they typically pay a fairly low yield—like a short-term bond.

CORPORATE BONDS: Corporations in search of capital issue
bonds. In return for your investment the company pledges to repay
you the value of your investment at some specified future date, in
addition to making specified interest payments. However, corporate bonds vary in quality from AAA-rated bonds (almost as safe as
Treasuries) to the lowly junk bonds (euphemistically referred to as
"high-yield" bonds).

HIGH-YIELD (OR JUNK) BONDS: Junk bonds offer higher yields to
compensate for lower credit ratings based on the uncertainty of the
company's ability to repay the debt. One real advantage of junk
bonds is that they are less affected than most other types of bonds
by rising interest rates, although they still are hurt by them. Their
prices are more closely tied to the issuer's and the economy's well-
being rather than to interest rate levels. However, credit risks

generally outweigh the slim benefits of interest rate risks here—if you can spell junk, you can spell default. Historically, these types of bonds have promised higher yields for their higher risk, but sometimes the promise hasn't been kept, leaving investors holding thin air.

PREFERRED STOCKS: A preferred stock is like a bond in that it pays a fixed dividend. It is called "preferred" because its dividends must be paid before any dividends will be paid to common stock holders. But unlike bonds, the issuing company has no absolute obligation to pay the dividends. Preferred holders, unlike bond-holders, cannot force the company into bankruptcy. For that reason, many preferred stocks have a fair amount of credit risk, like junk bonds.

CONVERTIBLE BONDS: Convertible bonds offer you the option of converting your bond into common stock at a predetermined price. If you think the company is growing and the price of its stock will rise, then a convertible will enable you to capitalize on the company's growth rather than be locked in at a lower rate of return. The price you pay for the conversion privilege is, however, the fact that convertible bond yields are lower than those for other "straight" bonds. The yield is, however, generally greater than on the same company's common stock. (Mutual funds known as "equity-income" funds often invest in convertible bonds.)

MUNICIPAL BONDS: "Munis" are sold by states, counties, cities and towns, and other governmental and quasi-public authorities to finance everything from road construction to sewer systems. But before you flush this option down the toilet, consider the following fact: income from munis is federally tax-free, and in-state bonds are generally free of state and often local income taxes. Munis offer lower rates of interest, but their tax-free aspect increases their value. Like corporates, munis range in quality from AAA to junk.

BOND VALUES

Since a bond's value fluctuates and is not necessarily close to its par or "face" value, you must take both principal and yield into account to determine the return on your investment. Look at the following examples:

A $1,000 bond bought at par, with a term of 5 years at an interest

rate of 5 percent and that was held to maturity and sold, would
realize a return of $250;

$1,000 (par)
+250 (interest × 5)
$1,250
−1,000 (original cost)
$250 (return)

Taking a more complicated case, where the bond was bought at
$950 and sold five years later for $1,050:

$1,050
+250 (interest × 5)
$1,300
−950 (original cost)
$350 (return)

Current yield is easily derived by dividing the annual interest of
the bond by its price. When the bond is at par:

$$\text{yield} = \frac{\text{annual interest}}{\text{price}} \qquad \frac{\$50}{\$1,000} = 5\%$$

When the bond is selling for $950:

$$\text{yield} = \frac{\text{annual interest}}{\text{price}} \qquad \frac{\$50}{\$950} = 5.26\%$$

A bond's yield is what you actually earn on your investment only
so long as its price holds steady. Remember that as a bond's price
rises, its yield falls; and as a bond's price falls, its yield rises.

BOND INVESTING STRATEGIES

The following general strategies are designed to help you invest in
bonds. While bonds are often too expensive for the young investor
to get involved in via direct ownership, you might find yourself in
the position of being able to do so. Even if not, the strategies below
will stand you in good stead if you decide to take the more affordable and often as profitable option—investing in bonds through a
bond mutual fund (discussed in detail in chapter 13).

FOLLOW INTEREST RATES: Bonds may be attractive when they beat inflation, but they're plug-ugly when they don't. To get a handle on where inflation and interest rates are headed, stay informed about the markets and the economy.

If you think interest rates are going to head up, purchase the shortest maturity bonds (e.g., one year or less). If you think rates are going to fall, move into longer-term bonds (five years and up). But watch out. No one can predict the direction of interest rates with 100 percent accuracy, so you probably shouldn't try to jump back and forth between one-year and thirty-year bonds. When in doubt, keep the bulk of your income securities on the short end (three years or less). You've got plenty of time to practice on these before you lock into a long-term bond that even Houdini couldn't get out of.

LADDER MATURITIES: "Laddering" or "staggering" maturities means investing in a variety of maturities—some short-term (less than three years), some intermediate-term (three to ten years), and some long-term (ten to fifteen years) bonds. (Forget the thirty-year stranglehold for now.) This will help you hedge your bond market bets by reducing the risk of being mistaken about them. Another advantage to laddering is that it will give you a leg up in terms of being able to match your investments with your goals. For example, if you're planning on going to law school in a few years, you would do well to invest some or most of your assets in short-term bonds that will mature around the time you will enter.

BUY QUALITY: When it comes to investing directly in individual bonds, top-quality bonds (rated AAA or AA) are the best way to go. Individual investors rarely have the time or expertise to really investigate bond safety, or the assets to sufficiently diversify against default risk. The last thing you want to have to do is confess to your friends that you can't go out tonight because (a) you invested in bonds, and (b) those bonds turned out to be junk.

DIVERSIFY: As with stock investing, diversification is a bond investor's prime directive. Don't put all your eggs in one basket! This is very hard to do with direct bond investing because of the cost involved. For this reason, you will probably be better off focusing your early investment attention on mutual funds—stock mutual funds for sure, and perhaps a bond fund or two. And that's what the next chapter is all about. If you do want to own bonds directly, stick to a U.S. Treasury (if you're only holding one or a few bonds) or maybe AAA- or AA-rated munis or corporates (if you're holding several).

Short-Term Investing Strategies

The following specific strategies are designed to help you invest in bonds and their fixed-income equivalents. While bonds are often too expensive for the young investor to get involved in via direct ownership, many fixed-income investments (like bank CDs or money market accounts) are affordable and advisable as short-term places to park your cash (while being assured that the money you parked won't be towed away in the interim). In addition to these most conservative types of fixed-income investments, the strategies in the following section will help you understand the ways in which you can put your knowledge of bond risks and types to good use —i.e., making you some money. Regardless of the fact that you'd probably be best served by avoiding bonds altogether (for the time being), the following specific strategies will help you wed your bond investing ideas to real market scenarios. Also note that, in chapter 13, you'll come to learn about a more affordable option—indirect bond investing through a bond mutual fund.

Chances are that the closest thing you've come to in terms of investing money for a substantial short-term gain was either the office football pool or a Publisher's Clearing House Sweepstakes. When you need to safeguard a sizeable sum (like the amount needed for the down payment of a house), play it safe by putting your money in short-term investments.

If you need the money within two years, short-term CDs and money markets are the safest place, and super-short-term bond funds a possible alternative. Bank Certificates of Deposit (or CDs) and money market accounts offer you a reliable place for short-term cash and a better hedge against rising rates than more speculative short- and intermediate-term bonds. While it's true that a money market mutual fund delivers these as well, it fails to deliver one potentially important thing: a federal insurance guarantee.

A CD that is federally insured has several advantages over betting—for one thing, it's not against the law; and for another, it is usually insured (i.e., safe) up to $100,000. (Look for the FDIC logo on the door of your bank—or on the teller's window.) But while CDs are often a good temporary parking place for your cash, there are other equally or more attractive short-term investments that are worth considering.

U.S. Treasuries. There are some advantages to buying individual Treasury bonds. First, with Treasuries, you needn't worry about diversifying to minimize credit risk. Second, there is generally a yield advantage. This is mostly because you're not paying a mutual fund's annual expenses. Moreover, when rates are trending up, the money market you might buy is already holding lower-yielding securities, while you're free to buy Treasuries at the market rate.

Also, with individual Treasury bills you can generally go out a bit further than the sixty-day maturity typical of a money market without taking on any real interest rate risk (so long as you won't be needing the money before the Treasury bill matures). Similarly, but unlike a bond fund, any individual bond matures on a specified date. Regardless of where interest rates are at maturity, the par value of the bond will be paid (assuming there isn't a default). On the other hand, bond funds never mature. They are managed within a certain average maturity band and are redeemed at the prevailing market price of the bonds held in the fund. If you've designated your money for a specific purpose, it may be useful to know exactly how much money will be available on a specified date; an individual bond can give you this security.

In most cases, you'll want to buy a maturity matching your need for the money. If you expect to be buying a house in six months, buy a six-month CD or Treasury bill. When it comes to long-term performance, most varieties of bonds outperform the more staid CD. But remember, CDs are much less volatile than bonds: a CD investment is more appropriate if you're looking for a short-term parking place for your capital.

Let's look more closely at volatility. The often overlooked fact is that investing for the short-term (less than three years) in longer-term bonds (and bond funds) can be a losing proposition—and that rising interest rates decrease the value of bonds and the funds that invest in them, just as declining rates increase the value of bonds and the funds that invest in them.

Look at what happened to bonds, for example, in 1994 and 1995. Such wild gyrations exhibit what's known as volatility—the quality of instability and change inherent in an investment. The years 1994 and 1995 are great examples of how interest rate risk affects bond prices. Rising interest rates, which are always bad news for bonds, took their toll in 1994 as the Fed continued to raise short-term rates. CDs or money markets would have been a better place to be. Super-short-term bond funds (with a duration of less than one year) also held up well, since these types of bonds are the least interest rate sensitive. In 1995, thanks to a succession of Fed interest rate cuts, longer-term bonds more than quadrupled the return on a CD or super-short bond as yields hit new lows and prices rose dramatically.

Some bonds (and bond funds) are less interest rate sensitive than others. Historically, the least interest rate sensitive fixed-income investments deliver lower returns in exchange for the benefit of reliability of income. But while CDs, money markets, and super-short-term bond funds may be the best way to defend your fixed-income investment against the toll from rising interest rates, they won't really help you guard against the toll inflation will take on the overall purchasing power of your invested savings.

SUPER-SHORT-TERM BOND FUNDS. You can also look for super-short-term bond funds—funds with average maturities of less than one year. The advantage to investing in super-short-term bond funds is twofold: First, in a rising rate environment they'll be able to guard against the low or negative returns of (comparatively longer-term) short-term bond funds. Second, because interest rates on securities with a maturity of six to twelve months are significantly higher than a money market's securities, which have about a one month maturity, super-short-term bond funds will outperform money markets under most conditions—that is, when rates fall, remain steady, or rise slowly.

The bottom line on bonds is that it they are best left out of your overall investment portfolio for now. For one thing, the expense of investing in bonds is often prohibitive. For another, they're hard to track, analyze, and purchase. And, you have two better fixed-income alternatives: CDs (for the short term) and bond mutual funds (for the long term). Finally, when it comes to investing your hard-earned savings, there's a better investment alternative: stocks and stock mutual funds.

READY RESOURCES

- Bureau of Public Debt/Treasury Securities Information, (202) 874-4000.
- *Income and Safety*, Institute for Econometric Research, (800) 327-6720.
- *Buying Treasury Securities*, Federal Reserve Bank of Richmond, (804) 697-8000.
- *Municipal Bonds: The Basics and Beyond*, by David L. Scott, Probus Publishing.

- *The Dow Jones–Irwin Guide to Bond and Money-Market Investments*, by Marcia Stigum and Frank J. Fabozzi, Dow Jones–Irwin.
- *Guide to Investing in Bonds*, by D. Scott, Globe Press.
- *The Bond Book*, by A. Thau, Irwin Press.
- *All About Bonds*, by E. Faerber, Irwin Press.
- *Basics of Bonds*, by G. Krefetz, Dearborn.
- *The Bond Market*, by C. Ray, Irwin Press.

CHAPTER ELEVEN

Stock Investing

Forget those trendy cybercafés where jazz and blues are the buzz—or better yet, when you get to a cybercafé, tap into Wall Street on-line via one of the several sources (see chapter 20 for details). While you're there, look around for some better investing ideas. In fact, from here on out, you should keep an eye open to making your money grow, no matter where you are or where you go.

How? Take a look around you. If you're in a café, for example, consider where the coffeemaker is manufactured. Who provides the raw materials (the metals and plastics) for its construction? Where do the beans come from? How is the price of a plain cup of Joe determined? Who owns the joint? (Chances are you should own a portion of it, given the amount of money you pour into it!) When you step outside, are there other retail stores that are more (or less) crowded? What's the average age group in each store you browse? Do they have money to spend? Are they spending it on full-price items—or waiting for a sale? Are there more stores on the street or in the mall today compared to a year or two ago? And what about all those cybercafés springing up—how will they all survive? If only a few do, which ones will they be and why? And who needs to get wired on java when you can keep yourself frantic just trying to look at the world through an investment perspective?

To begin with, every investor needs to ask two basic questions: What's really going on? and How can I profit by finding out? The first answer to these two questions is itself basic—namely, that the best way to profit (in terms of increasing the current value of your savings) is to invest regularly, wisely, and well. But chances are you know this. The question then becomes—where to invest? Getting into the stock markets—either directly through owning individual shares of a company's stock or indirectly through purchasing shares in a stock mutual fund—makes particular sense for you and for everyone else young enough to have an investment horizon measured in decades. But, before you leap, let's take a look at some of the real risks of stock investing.

THE RISKS

The risks of stock investing are straightforward: the two most significant are the potential for decline in the stock's price (you buy a stock at $10 and it drops to $3) and/or the elimination or reduction of dividend income. If you bought the stock at $10, loss occurs when you sell your stock for $9.99 or less. Selling may still make sense—and it may not. In fact, since most stocks fluctuate in price, it may be best to hold tight and ride out the downward curve if you have reason to believe that there will be an upside. Doing so may enable you to see the stock price jump back from $3 to $14— or, as in the case with IBM, sell at $117 and buy it back at $60 to see it rise back beyond $100.

Right. Now that you have a clear picture of the benefits and risks of investing in stocks or stock mutual funds, let's unpack the stock investing trunk from start to finish. Read this chapter in its entirety. The modest amount of time you spend here will be amply repaid, for stocks and stock mutual funds will top your investment list.

TYPES OF STOCKS

The following stock guide will help bring you up to speed on the types of stock investments that are out there waiting for your green thumb. Once you familiarize yourself with them, you can begin to practice the fine art of making your money grow (while accounting for the risks you need to know) by implementing one or more of the stock investing strategies detailed below.

A common stock represents ownership of a (small) share in a company. Think of a share as one vine in a vineyard—either a very large IBM vineyard, wherein your one plant amounts to a tiny portion of the harvest, or a small Netscape vineyard, wherein the one plant is a somewhat larger part of the whole. Depending on how well the vineyard grows its vines and prepares the harvest, and how many vines you own, you will either be able to live off the harvest or have to look elsewhere for sustenance. Note that you could do well in the large vineyard or in the small (at either place, one vine makes about the same amount of wine), but the large vineyard may better rebound from bad weather, while the small vineyard may have more room for expansion in good conditions.

You can own stocks directly and indirectly. Direct ownership means that you "hold" an actual stock certificate or serial number which designates the number of shares purchased. Nowadays, stock certificates are mostly a thing of the past—although you may have inherited a handful or more, which may be the sole proof of your ownership. Today, electronic ownership is the rule in the U.S. market.

Indirect ownership refers to owning shares in a stock mutual fund. The advantages of indirect ownership are examined in the following chapter on mutual funds, so for now suffice it to say that mutual funds offer individual investors several advantages over direct ownership. Mutual funds can be comprised of a pool of one or more of the following: stocks, bonds, cash, and/or options. This chapter will focus on mutual funds primarily comprised of stocks. With this in mind, the benefit of indirect ownership of stocks through a stock mutual fund is that, with a small amount of money, you can purchase shares in a well-diversified portfolio of stocks.

The following list of stock types is comprehensive but not all-inclusive. Consider these the most common types of stocks—and realize that in each type there are likely to be a few rotten individual stocks. The good news? Knowing what to look for and diversifying will help ensure that one rotten stock doesn't ruin your overall portfolio.

BLUE CHIPS: Blue chips are traditionally thought of as the highest quality of all common stocks. Blue chips are typically larger, solid performing, dividend-yielding companies. Examples of blue

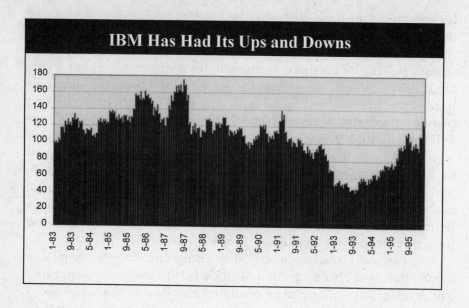

IBM Has Had Its Ups and Downs

chips are Coca-Cola, General Electric, and IBM. However, these giants can fall as mightily as the small. For example, let's take a look at IBM's performance during the decade between 1985 and 1995 as shown in the chart above. As you can clearly see, you could have easily lost money owning shares in IBM at the wrong time. Fortunately, it's just as evident that, had you sold at the high and bought at the low, you would have done very well for yourself.

Like other stocks, a blue chip can be characterized as a growth, a value, or a cyclical stock (or somewhere in between). The difference?

GROWTH STOCKS: Growth stocks present investors the opportunity to invest in companies that promise to increase their stock's market value through earnings growth. They tend to be smaller companies and/or in rapidly growing industries. (But they could, like Wal-Mart, be large players expanding market share in a mature industry.) Because investors expect their earnings to grow, growth stocks tend to be expensive relative to their current earnings. Growth stocks typically rise in value more than other stocks, but they are far more volatile and subject to greater declines in price, too. Growth stocks should be the choice of your generation: they're more exciting, can be more rewarding over the long term, and are less likely to get you caught in the web of trying to time a specific economic cycle—and you can afford the greater risk for the potentially greater reward.

VALUE STOCKS: Value stocks are stocks that are cheap relative to earnings or assets. Value stocks tend to be stodgier players in slower-growing, mature, defensive, or cyclical areas; they are basically the opposite of growth stocks. However, almost all fund managers claim to be seeking "undervalued" stocks, or say that even their highest-flying holdings are cheap relative to their (predicted) future earnings.

CYCLICAL STOCKS: Cyclical stocks are stocks in companies whose earnings fluctuate more than average with business cycles. Examples of cyclical industries are housing, automobiles, paper, and steel. Correct timing is the key to successful cyclical stock investing. Get the cycle wrong and you will know what it feels like to land on your head without a helmet. Crash! As with growth versus value, the cyclicality of stocks is a continuum. Some stocks are in the middle and might be considered cyclical by some investors and not by others.

There are other ways of categorizing stocks by distinct characteristics; it behooves the potential stock investor to know more about them.

INCOME STOCKS: Income stocks are those paying a substantial or above-average dividend income. Income stocks are most often value stocks—stocks in companies that are typically in more stable, mature industries. The stability enables these companies to provide the steady dividends that are a source of income for many retirees or, more relevant from your vantage point, a source of reinvestment capital. (See page 192 for more on the benefits and strategies of dividend reinvesting.) Examples of income stock industries would be utilities, telecommunications, and energy—but even many pharmaceutical companies (not exactly a stodgy industry) fall into this camp.

There's a revolution or two underfoot these days in both the telecommunications and utilities industries. On the one hand, telecommunications companies are developing new modes of communicating (cellular as opposed to cable, satellite as opposed to cellular), so look for some increased volatility in the decade ahead—as well as the potential for greater profit in this group. But watch out: the new technology is leading to significant downsizing and consolidation in the industry—a plus if you're on the right side of the investment; but, again, added volatility will have to be

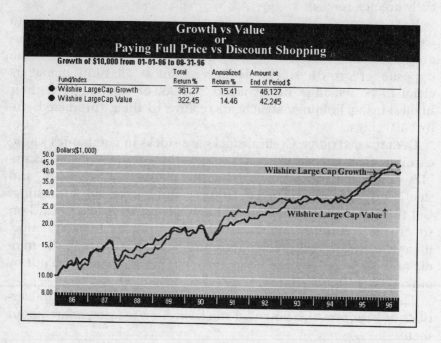

Growth vs Value
or
Paying Full Price vs Discount Shopping

Growth of $10,000 from 01-01-86 to 08-31-96

Fund/Index	Total Return %	Annualized Return %	Amount at End of Period $
● Wilshire LargeCap Growth	361.27	15.41	46,127
● Wilshire LargeCap Value	322.45	14.46	42,245

weathered. The revolution in utilities is a far more sleepy affair involving both regulatory changes on the federal and state levels as well as industry consolidation. While such a conservative type of stock is not necessarily recommended for you, with some diligence you can track down smaller companies which stand to benefit from this old-fashioned industry's change from coal burning to cleaner, more efficient fuels. (For example, who manufactures gas turbines, and who makes the necessary parts for those turbines?)

PREFERRED STOCKS: A preferred stock is really more like a bond performancewise (yawn!) in that it pays a fixed dividend. These "stocks" are generally more appropriate for income investors—i.e., the blue-haired, denture-driven, Ex-Lax cocktail crowd. Use the tooth index on this one—if you have 100 percent of your teeth, then you can avoid this group 100 percent.

PENNY STOCKS: Penny stocks, so called because you can often buy them for under $1 per share, are highly speculative. Danger is the name of this investment game. Investing in a speculative penny stock entails investing in a company with way above average share price fluctuations and a higher risk of loss for all or most of your investment compared to most other types of stocks. Many penny stocks are also the creation of less-than-scrupulous brokerage firms. While the lure of these stocks is that you can own a lot of them with relatively little money, this is one case where more is decidedly not better. Often, they are like holding a wheelbarrel of coal instead of a handful of diamonds. Invest only what you can afford to lose —or better yet, avoid these stocks altogether. If you want to be a high roller, concentrate on a very volatile but often more promising group of stocks known as IPOs.

INITIAL PUBLIC OFFERINGS (IPOs): IPOs are new issues of new companies' stocks. Such companies issue stock in order to generate capital to expand their business and/or to buy out company founders and venture capitalists. Bottom line: be forewarned. One of the reasons that IPOs come so highly recommended is that the investment bankers who back their launch, as well as the brokerages who have come in line, need to sell their inventory of shares in the IPO—just as much as the IPO needs to sell more of whatever it makes in order to sustain itself as a viable company. Flashy new stocks are also often flashes in the pan. Nevertheless, every stock was, at one time, an IPO. As a result, you needn't avoid IPOs on principle—the way you should avoid penny stocks. Instead, concentrate on the individual promise of the company and its long-range profit potential. It certainly helps if you are familiar with the company's products, or know someone who is. That's a great, grassroots approach to starting your investigation. It can also lead you to becoming overenthusiastic, since you might feel that the product is so good it can't help but do well.

FOREIGN STOCKS: Many foreign stock markets have outperformed the U.S. stock market long term—and many haven't. As the economy goes global, foreign stock investing will likely provide choice investment opportunities. The difficulty will be in selecting the right stocks in the right country at the right time—and how best to invest in them. Since the country and company may be foreign to our language and frames of usual stock-investigation reference, you'll be up against difficulties that you would not normally face when investing in the U.S. Nevertheless, taking advantage of stocks in a foreign country such as France, Great Britain, Japan, or Germany can make sense. After all, they have well-established stock markets, and information abounds on these countries and their companies. But when it comes to hot emerging markets such as

Hong Kong and Taiwan, you may experience information deprivation. In which case, be fearful.

There are four ways to invest in foreign markets: (1) directly through a foreign stock holding, though that's pretty hard to arrange; (2) directly through American Depository Receipts (ADRs; see below); (3) indirectly through shares in U.S.-based multinational companies (like Procter & Gamble, Bausch & Lomb, and Kellogg—since 40 percent of their total sales are derived from foreign markets); and (4) by buying international and global mutual funds (see page 158).

What exactly is an ADR? ADRs are receipts for shares in a foreign corporation that are traded in American securities markets such as the New York Stock Exchange. These tend to be larger foreign companies in established markets (blue chips). Examples include British Airways, Honda, and Toyota.

SPECIFIC STOCK ANALYSIS

You'll need to know what to look for in an individual stock that may have piqued your interest. The following questions will help you begin the process of determining the possible profit and risk potential of a given stock. Keep them in mind whenever you are thinking about a particular investment.

- Is the company in a growing industry?
- What are the industry's prospects for future growth?
- Does the company have, or have the potential to get, a significant share of its particular industry's market?
- How successful has the company been in its industry?
- Does the company have a history of profitability that is above average for its industry?
- If the company is relatively new, has it shown that it is likely to be successful in the industry?

There's more to reviewing a particular stock than a general feel for its potential. The following will help you get acquainted with some analytical fundamentals, as well as refresh your mind about those you visited in chapter 7.

- *Dividend:* a cash distribution a company makes to its shareholders. At many companies, dividends can be reinvested in more shares of stock (good), but even if you do so, they count as taxable income. A stock's dividend yield is its annual dividend divided by its share price.
- *Earnings per share (EPS):* a company's net income divided by the average number of shares outstanding. A company which reports income of $1 million with 1 million shares outstanding would have an EPS of $1.
- *Price/earnings ratio (P/E):* the price of a stock divided by its actual or estimated earnings. If a stock sells for $20, and it has $2 of earnings per share, it has a P/E of 10. The P/E ratio is used by most investors as one way of determining whether a company's stock is fairly valued. Not surprisingly, companies with little or no earnings tend to have sky-high P/Es—but, in the case of many newer, smaller companies, this may be acceptable if earnings seem likely to take off.
- *Debt to equity ratio:* an often overlooked source of risk, since a company with sizeable debt may be unable to compete—in research and development, or in ability to withstand a slowdown—against a rival that's debt-free. Sound like you and your best friend?

You can dig deeper! Look at the company from the bottom up. Doing so will require that you get your hands on their latest annual report as well as on any analyst reports you can find. Be careful to weigh your own analysis on a par with the "experts." Often, experts are best used to direct your questioning process rather than for answers to adhere to. Look for the following key markers when analyzing an individual company's annual report:

1. Long-term debt: How much long-term debt has the company taken on? If it's greater than 40 percent of capital, or high relative to its competitors, tread lightly. Heavy debt can prove to be a severe competitive handicap in a slow economy, since competitors who are cash-flush can continue to grow their business unhindered by debt payments.
2. How much working capital does the company have? The more it has, the better able it should be to stay competitive within its own industry (although that industry itself might still be one to avoid).

3. How old is the company's plant and equipment? If it's brand-new and paid for, so much the better. If, on the other hand, the factory was built in the Etruscan Age, then updating costly equipment has to be factored in to your estimate of the company's short-term growth capacity.

4. Review the following ingredients in the company's annual report in order to spot performance trends, strengths, and weaknesses within the company:

   • Sales—the backbone of any company, comprised of three basic elements: volume, product range, and selling prices. Are the company's sales volumes increasing? Are they increasing at an above- or below-average rate compared to its competitors? Is volume being moved because prices have been slashed (and how does this affect overall profitability)? Are comparable products competitive, and competitively priced? How does the company's price-to-sales ratio (share price divided by per-share sales) compare within the industry?

   • Profits—the *sine qua non* of business. Is the company making any money on its sales? Do profit margins compare favorably with the rest of the industry? What is the stock's P/E ratio? Is it reasonable compared to its competitors and/or its prospects for growth in profits?

   • Cash flow—generally defined as net income with depreciation and amortization charges added back (since these aren't real cash expenses). Cash flow is the amount of cash the business is generating for management to reinvest, service debt, and pay dividends. It's a useful indicator of a particular company's ability to provide its own capital while maintaining a desirable earnings or dividend record and without having to borrow money or sell additional stock.

   • Book value—the stated value of all of the company's assets. How many times book value (the price-to-book ratio) is the stock selling for, and how does that compare within the industry? Don't necessarily avoid paying several times book value; many assets may be grossly undervalued (for example, a company-owned building bought forty years ago which has risen substantially in value but is still listed as the original "value").

INVESTING STRATEGIES

Dissecting a company's profit potential can be a fascinating exercise in and of itself, but it won't guarantee that you will be able to select a winner. Combining all your research, from the broad questions of economic cycles and market competition to the particulars of patents and earnings reports, will at least help you avoid the pitfalls of an impulse investment. As in shopping, where impulse buying rarely gets you what you need or want, so in investing you need to be cool, calculating, and clear about what you are buying and why. The following approach to stock investing will help you and your investments keep on course—no matter how bumpy the ride.

THINK BEFORE YOU BUY: Too many first-time (and some experienced) investors leap before they look. Hot tips, a cover story, a fast-talking broker can all conspire to trick you into buying a stock you don't know much about. Be sure to tie your shoes before walking down the road to a new investment. Request and read the company's annual report and Form 10-K before investing. (You can obtain these documents directly from the company, from your broker, or through the World Wide Web.) Also, stay informed about the economy, markets, industries, and subsectors that could potentially affect the performance of the company and its stock.

KNOW WHY YOU'RE BUYING: Buy stocks that fit your investing plan—and not someone else's idea of what's a good thing. While you want to be convinced there's a "story," or a plausible scenario for an improved earnings outlook, beware of "sure things." Look for companies that have dominant positions in their fields, or are likely to become dominant in the future. Also, examine each stock's performance history to see whether its potential volatility is acceptable to you.

SCAN FOR PROMISING INDUSTRIES: Target industries that seem most likely to succeed, and don't be fooled into thinking that the industries that are on top today will be there tomorrow. If the industry of a company you're thinking of investing in seems likely to fail or become moribund, give it Das Boot. If, on the other hand, it seems like it's ahead of its time, like virtual reality, you may be able to ride the stock to the top. If the industry has long-run promise, it's that much easier to find stocks (and time periods) that will prove profitable.

DIVERSIFY: This is the prime directive of investing. You've heard me say it before: never put all your eggs in one basket, but beware of overdiversification, too. Overdiversification, especially with smaller amounts of money, can lead to nothing more than a record-keeping, fee-paying headache. It's easier to keep track of a dozen stocks than a hundred, and a dozen stocks, if they're sufficiently different, can provide sufficient diversification.

BUY LOW AND SELL HIGH: If you haven't heard this maxim yet, wait another minute and you will. Every expert will tell you this—and it's as obviously true as it is difficult to achieve. Remember, when the market is hot everyone wants to get in—but that's when prices are high. Try a contrary approach—researching companies you want to invest in and hoping for a temporary dip in their prices—then lock in.

KEEP YOUR EYE ON THE MARKET: As discussed in detail in the previous chapter, keeping tabs on the market's current and expected condition requires little effort and can provide maximum gains. But when it comes to investing in an individual stock, your vigilance can really pay off. For example, if your stock falls with the market, but you're convinced it's fundamentals are sound, you may want to buy more shares. If, on the other hand, the stock rises to above fair value on the strength of a bull market, you may want to sell.

INVEST FOR THE LONG TERM: Buying and holding onto your stock investments is an historically proven smart money move—but it's harder to do than most investors realize. The difficulty comes with market volatility and individual stock price volatility. It's hard to hold on to what you've got when its value is taking a nosedive. Still, if you have reason to believe in the fundamental strength and the future promise of the company, then stick to your guns. Generally, you'll come out ahead—as the market has so far continued to gain over time. Consider a holding period of ten years or longer as a time-proven way to earn inflation-beating returns. Concentrate on knowing what to buy, since buying well will reduce your need to sell. Also, remember that investing for the long term is in your best interest—so long as you have selected stocks in quality companies with quality management.

HOW TO CUT YOUR LOSSES

Everyone concentrates their energies on how to buy stocks, but there's an equally significant and often overlooked piece to this investing puzzle—knowing when to sell. As with buying, there are no guaranteed ways to *always* sell when the stock has hit its high or is threatening to become a fallen star, but there are warning signs. For example, if the company whose stock you are investing in cuts its dividend, stops dividends, or does not increase its dividends when others in its category are doing so, then it may be time to sell. Another sign to sell may be when the stock hits a high that is equal to or ahead of even the rosiest projections for it, or when its price gives it an absurdly high P/E ratio. Such peak performance can foretell a precipitous fall. However, it may be only a temporary one—so long as you have tied yourself and your investment dollars to a strong company. If not, you might be better off cutting the cord and hoping for a soft landing in another stock or mutual fund investment.

Although there are no foolproof methods for selling (or buying) stocks, the suggestions and guidelines in the previous section should be kept in mind. It's inadvisable to try and time the market by buying a stock today that you think you can make a killing on for a few tomorrow's. A good rule of thumb is to not invest in a stock with the intention of selling it in the next two or three years. Instead, concentrate on those stocks that potentially provide longer-term rewards.

Every investor gets bitten by the hand they thought would feed them. If one of your golden opportunities turns out to be worth less than a plug nickel, then you've missed the opportunity to sell at a livable loss. Some stocks will catch even savvy investors by surprise and plummet almost overnight. But most solid-seeming stocks don't vanish instantaneously. Instead, their demise tracks out over a long enough period of time that, with the proper diagnosis, the attentive investor will have enough advance warning to get out before they're left with truly painful losses.

How can you spot a "rotting" stock in your portfolio's barrel of good ones—before it turns rotten, that is? One way is to see how it performs relative to its benchmark. If, for example, you own a stock whose benchmark is the Russell 2000 (small-cap stock index), and it has not kept up with this index's average over three or more consecutive quarters, then start asking why. But don't jump to conclusions—selling too soon is often the way investors wind up missing out on a big gain and losing money. Instead, go back to the drawing board that led you to select the company in the first place. Are the fundamentals still as believable now as they were when you first bought the stock? What has changed in the company or industry that could account for the glitch in performance? Is the change temporary or a trend toward worse times ahead?

There's another important aspect to selling a stock that is easy to overlook—especially if you have determined that you want to sell. That aspect is the individual stock's position in your overall portfolio. If the stock plays a particular role—for example, it's your only exposure to an industry that you continue to believe will do well—then by all means hunt for another company within the industry to purchase with the proceeds of the sale of the fallen-from-favor stock.

Finally, always evaluate the selling of a stock in light of your capital gains and the taxes you'll have to pay on them. Often, there are more (and less) beneficial times to transact the sale of a stock —and you could wind up saving (or losing) yourself some money if you take (or fail to take) the tax factor into consideration. (For more on tax strategies, see chapter 24.)

READY RESOURCES

There's no shortage of stock investing books on the shelves of your bookstore and library. There are also dozens of stock investing newsletters—some great, some useless. The following list includes both books and newsletters. I recommend requesting newsletter samples and borrowing books from your local public library before making any purchases.

- *S&P Reports On Demand*, (800) 292-0808, (800) 221-5277.
- *Value Line Investment Survey*, (800) 833-0046.
- *The 1996 Nasdaq Company Directory and Fact Book*, NASD, (202) 728-8000.
- *This Is Not Your Father's Stockpicking Book: Profiting from the Hidden Investment Clues in Everyday Life*, Derrick C. Niederman, Times Books.
- *Beating the Street*, by Peter Lynch, Simon & Schuster.
- *One Up on Wall Street*, by Peter Lynch, Simon & Schuster.
- *How to Buy Stocks*, by Louis Engel and Brendan Boyd, Little, Brown.
- *Fundamentals of Investing*, by Lawrence J. Gitman and Michael D. Joehnk, HarperCollins.

- *Classics: An Investor's Anthology*, edited by Charles D. Ellis, Dow Jones–Irwin.
- *Buying Stocks Without a Broker*, Second Edition, by Charles B. Carlson, McGraw-Hill.
- *How to Read a Financial Report*, by John Tracy, John Wiley.
- *Handbook of Key Economic Indicators*, by R. Rogers, Irwin Press.
- *Learn to Earn: An Introduction to the Basics of Investing*, by Peter Lynch and John Rothchild, Fireside.

CHAPTER TWELVE

Real Estate Investing

Whoever said a home was a castle didn't have to scrounge to pay rent for a one-bedroom apartment, let alone make the leap into actual home buying. But, despite the difficulty of saving up a sizeable enough down payment, many of us cross the threshold from apartment dwelling to home ownership before we turn thirty-five. True, fewer of us do so today than in the generation before us—and it's not because we're slacking. For the most part, it's because we're *lacking* (the money) to make the move. So why bother to buy a home? Why not stay put and let the landlord do all the snow shoveling, painting, plastering, and lawn mowing? Well, from the day we're old enough to differentiate between our playpen and the home we shared with our benefactors, we've been told what a great investment a house is—just about any house, but "location, location, location" should ring some bells.

Is a home a good investment? Well, not as good as your parents might want to have you believe. What about those no-money-down gurus who huck their sun-splashed success on late night TV? Nope. They've got it wrong, too. The truth is that the value of buying a home and the potential value of investing in real estate are not the same, and rarely do the twain meet when it comes to buying a home and making a good investment.

BUYING YOUR HOME

A home may not be the good investment it once was, but home ownership is still likely to top the list of the single biggest investments you ever make. The best way to avoid the money pitfalls that many others have encountered is to anticipate the costs that you will incur when it comes to buying your new home. That will also avoid your having to sell some of your longer-term investments to meet a short-term need. Coming up with a down payment, which typically runs from 5 to 20 percent of the cost of the home, is a first hurdle many would-be home buyers fail to get over. For example, a $150,000 house will likely require a down payment of anywhere from $7,500 to $30,000. In addition, you can count on paying from 1 to 3 percent of the mortgage amount in closing costs, including "points," the charge for preparing the mortgage.

Of course, you'll also need to estimate how much home you can afford to buy. After all, if you can't afford the mortgage payments on a $150,000 home, there's no need to build up a savings amount of $30,000 before you start looking. That's why, before you start looking, you should come to terms with how much house your income can legitimately support.

There are several ways to estimate how much mortgage you're likely to qualify for. These days, most banks and mortgage lenders (and personal finance software) will be happy to do this for you. Typically, your monthly mortgage payment shouldn't exceed 28 percent of your net or post-tax monthly income, or 32 percent of your gross or pretax monthly income. Including the mortgage payment, lenders look at your total monthly debt obligations—from credit cards to car and student loans. The line in the lending sand: your total monthly obligations shouldn't exceed 36 percent of your gross monthly income. Obviously, the less debt you owe, the larger the mortgage and/or the better the rate you'll be able to qualify for.

You can estimate what your monthly mortgage payment will be by using the following table. For example, if you're thinking of qualifying for a $150,000 30-year mortgage at 8.25 percent, multiply 150 × $7.52 per $1,000 = approximately $1,128, your monthly principal and interest payment.

Payment per $1,000 of Loan

Interest Rate (%)	15 Years	30 Years	$100,000 Loan Monthly Amount	
			15 Year	30 Year
7	$ 8.99	$6.66	$ 899	$666
7.25	9.13	6.83	913	683
7.50	9.28	7.00	928	700
7.75	9.42	7.17	942	717
8	9.56	7.34	956	734
8.25	9.71	7.52	971	752
8.50	9.85	7.69	985	769
8.75	10.00	7.87	1,000	787
9	10.15	8.05	1,015	805

Not only will buying a home be the biggest deal you're likely to make in this lifetime, but once you've purchased one, you'll need to view the potential benefits of refinancing your existing mortgage if rates dip 1 percent or more below your current rate. Your home mortgage is very much like a fixed-income (bond) investment which can and should be actively managed from the standpoint of interest rate sensitivity. As you can see from the chart above, even a 1 percent change in your mortgage rate can mean a significant savings to your pocketbook.

Investing in Real Estate

There are two ways of thinking about real estate investments: owner-occupied (your own home) and non–owner occupied. There is one way to do the former, and several ways to participate in the latter. If you do not own your own home free and clear—that is to say, you no longer have mortgage payments—then you should not consider investing in real estate. Instead, concentrate your investment dollars in historically more rewarding investments: common stocks and the funds that hold them.

Traditionally, real estate has been one of the more common foundations on which people have built wealth. But, as many veteran homeowners will tell you, it is also possible to lose a great deal of money in the real estate market. Like all good investments, real estate opens the door to risks as well as potential rewards. If you own your own home, you may be troubled by deteriorating real estate markets or delighted by stable or rising prices; and if you own your home for long enough (ten or more years), chances are you'll run the gamut of those emotions, since real estate values tend to move in long-term, demographically and job-based cycles.

Location is one way to hedge your bets. A solid locale, one with a well-diversified mix of ages, incomes (tending toward the higher end), with good schools, and near a source of good jobs, is hard to beat—and harder to find. But, if you're flexible, and are able to move beyond either U.S. coast (inwards, and/or to the South), you might be able to find a way to make money by investing in other properties. If you are a potential real estate investor—tempted by the "bargains" flooding the market in some locales—educate yourself thoroughly before buying. There's one golden rule of real estate investing (which I just made up): if you can't afford to buy your own home or condo, forget about investing in one!

Many investors think that they know enough to invest in a piece of property simply because they know the area. And while that's a great start, it will hardly lead you toward the most successful real estate investments. When it comes to investing in real estate—either in the form of your own home or in potentially income-producing properties—there is one critical drawback compared to stocks and bonds (and mutual funds): you are putting money into an illiquid investment—namely, one that you can't simply sell overnight if you need the money or want to get out. In fact, unlike, say, a mutual fund, where you can sell if you don't like the new fund manager or the fund's increased concentration in a particular industry, you can be hamstrung by bad news if you buy or invest in real estate—all the way to ground zero if it so happens that the building burns to the ground and you let your insurance lapse, or the land turns out to be a former hazardous dump site, or the local factory or military base shuts down, sending property prices plummeting. In such worst-case scenarios you'll find it hard to recoup your down payment, and may even have trouble paying back the bank.

Fortunately, most of us won't run into worst-case scenarios. Instead, when it comes to our homes, we're more likely to see the value inch along with the rate of inflation. Not a great investment, but at least you'll build a part of your retirement savings successfully so long as the home's value does at least keep pace with inflation.

Real estate investors may also find more bargains on the lot than in previous years. In the 1970s, as inflation took off, housing prices jumped and many homeowners with low fixed-rate 1960s mortgages saw windfalls. But the late 1980s and early 1990s saw many property values plummet back to earth from those lofty levels. Markets have come back a bit, but the hardest-hit segments of the real estate investment market, like condominiums, might still provide some hidden gems which can actually produce income for the smart investor.

When it comes to real estate investing, let *caveat emptor* be your guide. Or, better yet, come to terms with the ways to evaluate a potential real estate investment (see the checklist below), then consider if there are any viable options in your neck of the woods. But before you open the door to potential real estate investment opportunities, be sure to slam the door closed on the following:

- Most limited real estate partnerships (i.e., those not publicly traded)
- Time-shares
- No-money-down real estate seminars
- Unimproved land
- Uninspected property
- Foreign property

Younger investors (who don't have enough money to buy a whole apartment building) invest in residential rental property in order to produce more income for themselves. A typical investment might be purchasing a single condo or a two-family house. Both can potentially provide a steady secondary source of income while at the same time increasing in value. The location and condition of such properties will affect the price of them—as well as your ability to obtain a viable rent from them. But there are several other factors you need to consider before making such a significant investment, including the zoning laws and renter population. Chances are, buying near a large university will net you a steady flow of willing renters, but the wide pool of potential renters may prove to be a shallow one in terms of their ability to pay the rent you need for the investment to succeed. Also, with students comes the increased potential for hassles and transience.

Be sure you get to know the place before you invest in it and have the answers to the following questions:

1. Is the property in a location which has a solid history of appreciating values?
   [ ] yes   [ ] no
2. Have you researched the socio-economic factors (employment, roads, taxes, zoning laws, demographics, transience) that can affect the property's value as well as the property's ability to generate a consistent cash flow?
   [ ] yes   [ ] no
3. Is the property conveniently located for prospective renters? Which of the following are nearby?
   [ ] Public transportation
   [ ] Grocery store
   [ ] Retail shopping
   [ ] Recreation
   [ ] Schools
4. When was the last time the roof was done?
   [ ] 15 or more years ago
   [ ] 12 to 7 years ago
   [ ] Less than 5 years ago
5. Have you received the following?
   [ ] Complete rental history
   [ ] Complete history of utility costs
   [ ] Complete history of water billing
   [ ] Complete history of maintenance
   [ ] Complete history of tenant complaints and legal actions
   [ ] Complete history of the electrical or heating systems
   [ ] Complete history of reported crime
   [ ] Complete history of property damage and repair costs

Remember that the real estate agent showing you property is representing the seller—not you. Therefore, you'll need to be reasonably assured that your agent isn't "bumping the market," quoting not actual rent but what it "ought to be" according to his or her sense of the overall market level. Note that it's also important to see if the potential property's rental history shares common ground with apartments in the same location (same size and condition), as well as any significant demographic or economic changes in the area. Each, or all, could affect the ability of the history to repeat itself.

The main problem with investing in real estate for income is that it is difficult to locate properties that are priced low enough so that the rental income is sufficient to cover the cost of your investment. In order to investigate a property's potential merits or lack thereof, use the "rent multiplier" method, which enables you to evaluate a property by comparing the total price you'd have to pay for it with its current gross annual rental (not just last year's but over its rental history). Of course, there's no guarantee that a property that passes the rent multiplier test will deliver the goods, but the traditional rule of thumb is that any property selling for more than seven or eight times its gross annual rental will be unlikely to deliver sufficient rental income to cover your costs (mortgages and operating expenses), let alone make you a profit. Here's how it works:

1. Selling price: $210,000
2. Gross annual rental: $18,000
3. Rent multiplier = the selling price divided by the gross annual rental

A two-family property selling for $210,000 generates $18,000 in annual rent:

$$\text{Rent multiplier} = \frac{\$210,000 \text{ (selling price)}}{\$18,000 \text{ (gross annual rental)}} = 11.66$$

In other words, the property is selling for 11.66 times annual rental, and is probably not going to be a good investment. Of course, you can ensure a positive cash flow by sinking a large down payment into the property—but you'll only be scuttling yourself. First, you're already having to compensate for the property's lack of inherent value. Second, and perhaps more important, you're tying up your cash in a negative investment—as opposed to investing it in a positive one, like a stock mutual fund.

There are tax benefits to direct ownership, however, that need to be included: from maintenance and depreciation deductions to real estate taxes and mortgage interest allocable to rental use, which can be subtracted from rental income and all claimed as deductions. This can be a significant sum, but it still may not make the property a better-than-average investment.

Despite the fact that there are better investments out there, many younger investors are drawn to real estate as a potential source of secondary income. Some achieve this goal truly and well. In fact, I have a friend who spent ten years buying a small kingdom of multifamily rental properties which he, in turn, used to help finance graduate school costs for himself while still supporting his family of three. His costs were substantial (he went to Harvard's business school), but unlike many of his fellow students, he didn't have to overburden himself with loans. But for every successful real estate investment story there is at least one story of losing some, most, or all of the initial investment—or more. But, if you think the risk is worth taking, then by all means familiarize yourself with the following real estate investment options that are out there waiting for you.

1. Single home, condominium, or cooperative apartment: Investing in a single-family home is among the most costly and least flexible forms of real estate investment. On the other hand, investing in a condo, co-op, or single apartment could reap rewards—especially if you buy during a down market. Generally cheaper than equivalent single-family homes, condos and co-ops provide you with the benefits of direct ownership. However, there is a lack of overall control with this type of investment which should give you some cause for concern. For example, despite the fact that each unit is individually financed, if one owner defaults on his or her condo and co-op, the other owners may have to assume the defaulting owner's share of operating expenses.

As with a house, when it comes to owning a condo or co-op, there are more expenses involved than the mortgage. There are condo fees and there are meetings to attend. The condo association (typically comprised of the owners) oversees the common areas like entranceways, yards, and parking lots, which typically are jointly owned by the owners. They, or the majority of the owners, and not just you, will decide what money to spend on maintenance and improvements. There are also potential problems when it comes to wanting to change the outward look of your condominium.

Despite the drawbacks, condos and co-ops can make solid sense for rental purposes. To test a potential condo's worth, make sure the renter pool is there and that the rental income is sufficient to support your ownership costs by employing the rent multiplier method shown above (or a more detailed analysis of all expenses).

2. Multifamily: Two-, three-, and more family homes that are often owner-occupied can provide you with positive cash flow, increased tax advantages, and a roof over your own head. You might even be able to live "rent free," although you'll have to ensure that the mortgage payments are made in full. Multifamily dwellings require a greater initial investment (it's a bigger building), but the cost per unit can be lower than with a single condo, and your ability to qualify for a mortgage is based on rental income as well as your ability to pay. Down payments can be a problem, but lenders have become more flexible in recent times. All the other potential pitfalls are multiplied by two, three or more times (from tenants to the costs of insurance)—but so are the potential benefits. One generic drawback might be location, since multifamilies abound in lower-income and more transient neighborhoods. But this can work in your favor since there are typically a greater number of renters and lower property values in such neighborhoods.

3. Second home: The demand for second homes (particularly those near the water) is likely to increase as the boomers age and look for places to retire to. One of the more interesting ways to invest in this phenomenon is to consider buying a second home which can serve as an investment rental property in season, and a place for you to get away to during the off season, with long-term potential for increased resale value. Note that if a vacation home is rented for fewer than fifteen days a year, the resulting income need not be reported to the IRS. If, however, the residence is used solely as a rental property, all income must be reported.

Don't invest in a second home for the short term. Most likely, the rental income you'll receive will be insufficient to cover your total expenses. Instead, consider it as a long-term investment—so long as the location and demographics are likely to materialize buyers down the road.

4. Land: You know those ads that promise forty acres of hunting, fishing, fields, and forest? Typically, the ads don't tell about the lack of water, electricity, sewage, and roads. Consider too that land doesn't generate any income, your cash that could be invested elsewhere is staked to it, financing is costly as well as difficult to arrange for unimproved land, and the land's value is likely to remain the same (i.e., a bad investment) unless there's a potential for development (in which case there would likely have been a long line of developers ahead of you). Zoning and environmental issues can wipe you out overnight. Avoid the forty acres, or you may wind up looking like a mule's relative.

5. *Commercial property:* Chances are commercial properties—office buildings, malls, industrial plants—are beyond your direct financial reach, but you could invest in them via either a limited real estate partnership, a real estate investment trust (REIT), or a REIT mutual fund.

REAL ESTATE INVESTING STRATEGIES

Becoming a landlord isn't all it's cracked up to be, but when it comes to the potential for the best returns—and the most risks—owning an investment property yourself is the way to go. If this is for you, make sure you are ready for the monetary, legal, and psychological demands that even a single investment condo can rain down upon you.

1. Limited real estate partnerships: Limited real estate partnerships pool money from a group of investors in order to purchase larger properties like a mall or apartment building. There are some advantages to limited real estate partnerships, from simplified purchasing (you get a prospectus and send a check to the general partner), to smaller initial investments, to no management responsibility. It's the general partner's responsibility to find tenants, fix the sink, unplug the toilet, collect and bank the rent, file the tax reports, and all other management duties. Moreover, unlike owning a property outright, your legal liability is limited to the total amount you have invested in the partnership, so your other assets are not at risk.

You can estimate the worth of a potential limited partnership investment by doing the numbers in advance of your actual investment using a method called a capitalization rate, or "cap rate." To determine the cap rate of a potential investment property, try the following formula:

$$\text{Capitalization rate} = \frac{\text{Net operating income}}{\text{Total amount invested}}$$

For example, a limited partnership investment in a mall requires a total investment of $1,500,000 and has an estimated net operating income of $125,000. The cap rate is $125,000/$1,500,000, or 8.3 percent. A cap rate of 8 percent or greater is considered desirable. So is this investment worth it?

Well, there are several disadvantages—beyond a forecasted soft commercial real estate market for years to come—including the fact that you are basically giving up control of your investment to the general partner. For this reason alone, investing in limited real estate partnerships makes less sense than direct ownership. And for those just starting out, this type of real estate investment will not generate the kind of cash flow you could generate from direct ownership. That's because the general partner takes a cut for commissions paid to set up the partnership, to operate the property, and —upon liquidation of the partnership—the sale of the property. Remember that the people who sell you these partnerships are the ones who stand to make the most money from the deal—not you.

2. Real estate investment trusts (REITs): REITs are companies which invest in a pool of real estate or mortgages. REIT shares trade on major stock exchanges like the New York Stock Exchange, which means that you can buy shares in a REIT (and so avoid the drawbacks of investing directly in real estate), avoid the pitfall of illiquidity that dogs direct real estate investments and limited partnerships, and—similar to a mutual fund—participate in a diversified portfolio of real estate (or mortgages) which you couldn't afford to do by yourself. Moreover, like investing in a mutual fund, REITs offer the prospect of professional management. Of course, there are drawbacks—like the unavoidable fact that REITs suffer from bad real estate markets just like the other types of real estate investments that are available to you. If only you could buy a mutual fund that invests in REITs, maybe you'd be able to enjoy the benefits of an even more diversified portfolio of real estate investments that just might stand a better chance in a down market—and still capitalize on any boom. You're in luck; the next chapter will show you how.

CHAPTER THIRTEEN

Mutual Funds Investing

Mutual funds are by far the most popular form of investing today. And that's not too surprising given their many benefits and low cost, especially relative to investing directly in stocks and bonds. In fact, they're the single best avenue for your investing plans—at least in the beginning. But, in addition to the many positive features that funds offer most investors, there are some pitfalls you'll need to avoid—not the least of which is the common mistake of thinking that mutual funds are guaranteed to deliver positive results. And for those of you who have been (or have just begun) investing in funds, take note: there are many ways you can enhance your control over your overall mutual fund investment portfolio.

YOUR VERY OWN MUTUAL FUND PRIMER

What exactly is a mutual fund? A mutual fund is a professionally managed, diversified portfolio of stocks, bonds, money market instruments, or other securities. Each fund is comprised of many investors' money, "pooled" by the fund manager or managers to purchase these securities. Pooling the money gives you the potential benefits of a larger and more diversified portfolio than your money alone could purchase.

However, you'll still need to know what is in the pool, since otherwise it's easy to get in over your head without realizing that that's what you've done. Mutual funds don't magically protect you from the market's eddies. The value of your fund shares still depends on the value of the stocks and/or bonds owned by the fund. And the value of the stocks and/or bonds the fund holds still depends on the market risks they are subject to (as discussed in the previous chapters).

It used to be that mutual funds represented an easy way for investors, large and small, to avoid the complication of picking a large portfolio of stocks and/or bonds. A decade ago there were under 500 mutual funds and well over 3,000 stocks trading on the NYSE. Today, there are still over 3,000 stocks trading on the NYSE; however, you must now choose the best mutual funds from a selection of over 7,000 funds—with 1,000 new funds in 1995 alone.

Mutual Fund Advantages

Selecting the best mutual funds to invest in has become quantitatively and qualitatively more difficult. And, while we'll sort this out together below, it's important to note that the advantages of investing in mutual funds remain the same today as when they were first introduced back in the early 1940s. For example:

- *Performance has been a principal strong point:* Beating inflation as well as a comparable market index is one objective every investor must come to terms with. The average stock mutual fund has delivered a solid inflation-beating return. But—and this may come as a surprise to you—the average stock fund hasn't outperformed the S&P 500 index. In fact, the average stock fund's 15-year annualized total return (through July 1996) was 12.6 percent, versus the S&P 500's 15.2 percent return for the same period. Some significant down years in the early 1970s set funds back a bit—but that's not the real story. The real story is that the majority of funds fail to beat the S&P 500 but some do—meaning that you need to learn how to select the best funds.
- *You can invest in a fund even if you have only a small amount of money:* Some funds have no or low (i.e., under $1,000) minimum investment requirements while others, it's true, have minimums that range from $1,000 to $1 million. Note that you

can usually open a tax-advantaged account (like an IRA or Keogh) for $500 or less. The majority of funds offer a low-cost way to start investing today—i.e., around $2,500 for taxable accounts and $500 for tax-advantaged accounts like your IRA.

- *Diversification is the mutual fund's principal benefit:* Mutual funds are a low-cost way to diversify a small amount of money in a broad range of stocks, bonds, or other securities in various industries, markets, and/or countries. The advantage of diversifying is twofold. First, it helps reduce the overall risk of your investments. Second, it can enhance your total return.

- *Convenience is another plus:* Mutual funds make it easy to invest regularly, through automatic investing, dollar-cost averaging, and their presence in your 401(k) plan. Taken together with 24-hour-a-day toll-free phone numbers, Internet Web sites, and the advent of mutual fund networks, in the past few years convenience has been further enhanced. (See below for more on mutual fund networks.)

- *Researching mutual funds is within your grasp:* Mutual funds are relatively easy to research. Current information abounds—so much so that it may take you a while to locate the funds you own in the business section of your paper. Fortunately, with the advent of on-line hosts like American Online, CompuServe, and Prodigy, you can re-create your portfolio in virtual reality and get a nightly update as to where you stand. (Nightly, since most mutual funds' values are determined at the close of market each day.) And, yes, you can also order an electronically personalized version of the *Wall Street Journal*—so long as you have an e-mail address—which can ferret out your funds from the reams of otherwise overwhelming data.

- *Information is as close as your phone, modem, and library:* Performance records, the year's top performers and dogs, fund manager interviews, and detailed analyses of potential risks and returns and past strengths and weaknesses which might affect your funds in the future—all are daily, weekly, and monthly topics for the dizzying number of sources available to you. In fact, as one quick glance at the Ready Resources section at the end of this chapter shows, the on-line services and the World Wide Web have netted some of the best information available.

- *Professional management:* Mutual funds are managed by experienced investment professionals whose business it is to perform well for their shareholders; failing could be harmful to their current job and career path, not to mention your hard-earned money. But keeping track of fund managers has become about as difficult as tracking professional baseball players. If they perform well, they themselves become a hot commodity. That's why it's important to know who is managing your fund (and what their past fund records have been)—and who *was* managing your fund prior to the current manager. Why? The fund's performance record might be attributable to someone else—which, depending on that record, could bode ill or well for you. One more ingredient in the manager's mix is his or her credentials. While performance, like action, tends to speak louder than words, some managers who are new to the scene may share some professional traits in common with veterans—namely, professional designations like Chartered Financial Analyst (CFA), which is the most highly regarded certification in mutual fund town. (Chapter 17 has the lowdown on this and other professional designations as well as a review of the range of financial advisors available to you.)

• *Wide range of investment choices:* As you will see in the section on pages 154–55, there are dozens of types of mutual funds to choose from. And while this range of choices makes it easier for you to select funds that match your objectives, it can also make it harder to determine these objectives in the first place. Fortunately, if you have access to a personal computer, there are a bevy of automated resources at your beck and call. (You can create a mutual fund screen to quickly sort through the abundance and locate the best funds for your objectives and your particular portfolio.)

• *Liquidity:* While actual trades are made once a day, you can place orders to buy and sell mutual fund shares over the phone 24 hours a day. Thus, this investment is, for the most part, as liquid as water, which is a good thing if you want to get in or out of the market. However, there are instances where selling your funds (or buying them) can prove to be a difficult proposition—and one in which you can lose big money by untimely delays. The section on buying and selling your funds on page 207 will help you avoid such pitfalls—or, in the worst case, forewarn you about them.

Mutual Fund Disadvantages

What? There are disadvantages to investing in mutual funds? Oh, come on. What are you, some holdover commie looking to destroy the very fabric of our God-given country? Sorry. But there is potentially bad news on mutual funds:

- *Fluctuating value:* OK, so this isn't really a disadvantage—it's just the nature of the game. But many investors mistakenly think that mutual funds are a safe house for their money. The reality is that some funds are built of brick and mortar—and others are made of straw soaked in gasoline. And while we'll talk about ways to discriminate between marketing huff and puff and down-to-earth facts for most types of funds, you'll need to keep in mind that mutual funds, like the securities they invest in, have risks. A fund's value can fluctuate with changing market and/or economic conditions, the same risk as if you buy individual stocks and bonds.
- *Fund fees:* If you buy $1 million worth of shares in a fund, you might be able to wrangle a free lunch out of the company—otherwise, get used to the fact that you'll pay some amount for investing in most funds. But just because you have to pay something doesn't mean you should pay the highest amount possible. There are no-load funds (which charge no up-front sales commission, but may include one on the back end—if you sell shares in the fund before a specified date), low-load funds, and load funds (which can charge a sales commission of up to 8.5 percent of the money you invest). There are also a host of other fees you need to watch out for which are explained in detail on pages 170–71.

Funds, Performancewise

Performance is attractive, but can be deceptive when it comes to determining whether one fund's performance is better or worse than others. There are two performance terms you need to know inside and out: Net Asset Value (NAV) and total return.

- *NAV:* A fund's net asset value is determined by adding up all the fund's holdings (its assets in securities and cash) and dividing by the number of shares outstanding. For a no-load fund, the NAV is the share price you see listed in the paper—and the price per share you would pay (to buy) or receive (if sold).

- *Total return:* Total return tells you how well your investment is doing. It measures the fund's total investment performance by adding the fund's yield (dividend or interest distributions) and capital gains distributions to any undistributed capital appreciation (change in NAV).

TYPES OF MUTUAL FUNDS

Mutual funds come in two distinct flavors: open- and closed-end. Open-end funds are by far the more popular. They're the funds you find in the mutual fund section of your paper, and number in the thousands. Closed-end funds are listed in the stock pages of your paper and trade like stocks while acting like bonds; they number under 200. There are many types of funds to invest in, but the funds themselves invest in one or more of the core investment categories listed below. Of course, each core category itself is made up of dozens of investment vehicles. The three major fund categories to invest in are stock-, bond-, and money market funds:

1. *Stock funds:* A stock fund, also referred to as an equity fund, invests in individual stocks of large, and/or medium, and/or small companies, here and/or abroad. Stock funds are characterized by the kind of companies they invest in, and by the fund's specific objective.
2. *Bond funds:* A bond fund invests in bonds of companies or governments as varied as those the stock funds invest in. Bond funds tend to be more conservative when it comes to risk and growth.
3. *Money market funds:* Money market funds are the investment world's equivalent to a bank's money market deposit account or savings account. Money market funds won't really make you money (after taxes and inflation), but are a good place to store your short-term cash because they offer liquidity (easy access to your cash) and stability of principal (least risky).
4. *Real Estate Investment Trust (REIT) funds:* REIT funds invest in REITs, which are corporations that invest in real estate or mortgages, and which trade on the NYSE. REIT funds aren't

numerous, and are more suitable for more conservative investors as a source of income.

5. *Closed-end funds:* As already mentioned, closed-end funds, unlike open-end funds, issue a fixed number of shares, and trade just like a stock on the New York Stock Exchange (NYSE), American Stock Exchange (AMEX), or the Nasdaq. Since they're traded like stock, you don't go through a mutual fund company to purchase or redeem shares in closed-end funds. Instead, you purchase them through your broker—and pay him or her commissions.

All of the above categories are detailed below.

Stock Funds

Stock funds are the most appropriate place for you to invest your money and for you to concentrate your investing dollars. As you get older, you'll want to shift more money to bond and money market funds because these typically show less short-term volatility than stocks. However, in your youth, it's best to focus on investments that present the opportunity for substantial growth. Stock funds are your answer. They should be the choice of the new generation—that's you. There are numerous types of stock funds you can invest in; for example:

- Aggressive growth funds invest in stocks of new companies, industries, and/or more speculative ventures in an attempt to achieve very high returns. Objective: maximizing capital gains.
- Growth funds invest in somewhat more established companies whose earnings are expected to steadily increase. The objective: achieve a rate of growth that beats inflation without taking the risks necessary to achieve occasional spectacular success.
- Small-company funds (commonly referred to as small-cap funds) invest in smaller companies whose earnings are expected to steadily increase. Objective: capitalize on small-company growth potential while focusing on earnings.
- Growth and income (G&I) funds tend to invest in more established companies whose stock tends to pay significant dividend income. They may also hold some assets in bonds. These funds vary in aggressiveness, but tend to have less growth potential

than the previous groups. Objective: significant price increases combined with current income.

G&I funds will no doubt come to serve a central, centering force in your overall investment portfolio. However, for now, these funds generally present a too-timid approach to the markets, investing in overly conservative securities, and should be used as a small, stabilizing percentage of your overall portfolio. For example, you could place 10 to 15 percent in an S&P 500 index fund. Often classified as growth and income funds, these funds try to match the S&P 500 index which, over time, have performed better than the average stock fund which tries to beat the market. An index fund could be the first and best G&I fund you ever own, but keep it under 15 percent for now—or better yet, give yourself a G&I fund down the road—for your fortieth birthday, perhaps.

• Income funds generally invest about half their portfolio in dividend-paying stocks and the rest in convertible securities and bonds. Objective: current income is the primary objective, and long-term price increase is a secondary one. This type of fund is not generally suitable for younger, more aggressive investors.

• Balanced funds invest in common stock, preferred stock, and bonds. Objective: current income, growth, and lower-than-pure-stock-investing risk. Like an income fund, this is not generally suitable for younger, more aggressive investors.

Bond Funds

Bond funds have limited potential for long-term gains, and are generally more suited to retirees than to investors who haven't yet moved to a golf community. My suggestion: Avoid bond funds altogether for the time being. Invest in bond funds down the road —when you reach middle age. And then, invest only a small portion (no more than 20 percent) of your money in bonds. You'll gradually increase this percentage as time goes on, but for now, you're young and stand to benefit most by investing in good stock funds. Unless you're within five years of funding a child's college tuition or within ten years of retiring, stick to stock funds. Nevertheless, as an informed investor you ought to know all your options—bond funds included.

Bond funds are often mistakenly thought of as safe, sure-thing, income-producing investments. Except for funds that invest solely in shorter-term government bonds, this simply isn't so. Bond funds have a significant degree of risk, particularly when rising interest rates reduce the value of the instruments they invest in.

Only by examining both interest rate and credit risk in relation to how they affect a fund's performance in different market environments can you be assured that the bond fund you've selected matches your overall investment objective.

A fund's *duration* reflects its sensitivity to interest rates—its interest-rate risk. This is an important factor to consider given that different bond funds hold bonds of widely varying durations. For example, if interest rates were to rise by 1 percent, a fund with a duration of ten years will (all other things being equal) fall 10 percent, while a fund with a duration of half of a year would fall only 0.5 percent. (When rates decline, bond prices rise, and a fund with a ten-year duration would appreciate 10 percent in response to a 1 percent decline in rates.)

A reliable way to evaluate the speculative and/or conservative bonds in a given fund's portfolio is to note the letter ratings from Moody's and Standard & Poor's in tandem with discerning the economic health of the companies in the fund's portfolio. The primary types of bond funds include the following:

- Short-term bond funds invest in a mix of government and corporate bonds with maturities of one to five years. Objective: income with limited exposure to interest rate risk.
- Intermediate-term bond funds invest in a mix of government and corporate bonds with maturities of five to ten years. Objective: higher immediate income.
- Long-term bonds invest in a mix of government and corporate bonds with maturities of 15 to 30 years. Objective: steady source of income.
- High-yield bond funds (a.k.a. "junk" bond funds) invest in below-investment-grade-quality bonds that offer potentially high profits at the expense of higher risk. Needless to say, these can be volatile. Objective: higher-than-average yield.
- Municipal bond funds (better known as "munis") invest in bonds of state and local governments. Note that while muni bond prices are hard to find, muni bond fund prices are not. Objective: tax-free income.
- Single-state funds invest in bonds only from one state. Since interest earned from these funds is free of state (and often

local) as well as federal income taxes, single-state funds often
provide the highest tax-equivalent yields. Objective: double tax-
free income.

International Funds

An essential subset of stock and bond funds is international and
global stock and/or bond funds:

- International stock funds invest only overseas in the stocks of
  several countries or regions. Objective: take advantage of foreign stock market opportunities.
- Global stock funds invest in a combination of foreign and U.S.
  stocks. Objective: take advantage of both foreign and domestic
  investment opportunities, often hedging against currency risk.
- International bond funds invest in foreign government or corporate bonds. Objective: income, diversification, and hedge
  against a depreciating dollar.

International stock funds, like growth and growth and income
funds, present a wide variety of investment opportunities and, yes,
risks. Some international funds concentrate their assets in established European markets, others in a combination of European and
Japanese securities. Still others participate in whole or in part in
the combustible emerging markets. Taken together with the economic, political, and currency risks that investing abroad visits upon
you, you'll need to keep your eye on the country and portfolio
diversification in order to rest assured that you've selected the best
international fund for your particular portfolio.

Why invest abroad at all? It's profitable, to a degree. A globally
diversified portfolio can help you guard against a potential U.S.
market correction, as well as benefit from a rebounding market
beyond the U.S. In fact, as the chart opposite shows, investing a
portion of your assets abroad long term can land you risk-adjusted
returns that prove to be better than with a pure U.S. portfolio. But
it can also place your portfolio in harm's way if you attempt to time
the markets or overconcentrate in one market.

The same benefits of diversification apply abroad as well as at
home. But with an international or global fund, you'll need to focus
on country as well as stock diversification. When it comes to diver-

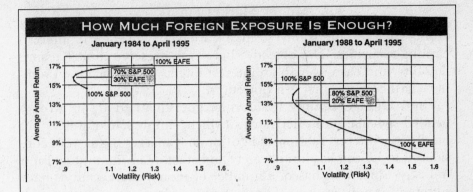

HOW MUCH FOREIGN EXPOSURE IS ENOUGH?

January 1984 to April 1995 — January 1988 to April 1995

After a spectacular '93 foreign stock funds suffered through 1994. This year, Europe has been stellar, while Japan has been a downer. For the past 10+ years the Morgan Stanley Europe, Australasia, Far East Index (EAFE) has beaten the domestic S&P 500 Index. The foreign index has shown greater volatility, but because foreign and domestic markets are not perfectly correlated, a portfolio combining these two indices can have a bit less risk than either index alone, while sporting a return greater than can be obtained from just domestic stocks. (For the past 11 years, a combination of about 70% domestic and 30% foreign stocks has shown the least volatility.)

Shorter time periods have proven less successful for foreign investments. For the past 7+ years, a portfolio of about 20% foreign stocks has shown a bit less volatility than an all-U.S. portfolio, even though the EAFE has had much greater volatility. However, the EAFE lagged the domestic market for this period, and you'd have obtained a better total return by investing exclusively in the U.S.

You should note that your "domestic" fund may already hold 20% to 30% in foreign stocks.

sification and international funds, investors often think of global funds. These funds tend to deliver less stellar returns *but with less risk* than a straight international fund. Geographical diversification is their main benefit. You can also add to your diversification by putting together two or more narrowly drawn international funds, but in that case you'll need to determine how closely the international funds correlate. Of course, funds with "Europe" in their name perform relatively similarly, and downright differently from, for example, Japanese or emerging market funds. However, while this is the case for the most part, it's not always as clear-cut—especially among funds with the generic "International" or "Worldwide" designations.

Money Market Funds

Money market funds invest in a variety of short-term interest-earning securities. The objective here is to preserve capital, assure liquidity, and earn as high an interest rate as can be achieved without sacrificing the first two objectives.

Until Orange County, California, got squashed by its wrong-headed speculation in derivatives (which, simply stated, were a bet on the way interest rates would go), money market funds were considered to be the bastion of safety and stability in the mutual fund industry. Since that fiasco, a number of money market funds have suffered from derivatives. (For the first time in sixteen years, a small institutional money market fund fell below $1 per share). All of which may lead you to ask how safe money market funds are today. The answer is that they are not as safe as an FDIC-insured bank money market account—but still, they're pretty close. The key is to ensure that your money market fund isn't propping itself up on a house of derivative cards. You can find out by finding the answers to the following:

1. Does your money provide an unusually high yield? If it does, or if it has high expenses (as revealed in the prospectus), then it could be using derivatives. Call and find out.

2. If your fund does use derivatives, what types does it use? Steer clear of funds that are peppered with them.

3. Regardless of what your money market invests in, the best thing you can do is stick with a fund that is part of a large fund company. A large firm is more likely to have the financial strength to compensate a fund for any losses. But more important, a large fund group would have a bigger incentive to help out a troubled fund, if only to pacify their existing clients in other funds.

Closed-End Funds

Mutual funds come in two distinct flavors: open- and closed-end. Unlike open-end funds, closed-end funds issue a fixed number of shares. While closed-ends tend to perform like whatever type of stocks or bonds they invest in, moving up or down with the net asset value (NAV) of their investments, there is no guarantee that you will be able to buy or sell a closed-end fund at this price.

Closed-end prices are set by supply and demand in the market.

Often, closed-end funds trade at significant discounts or premiums to the actual value of their portfolio—i.e., with a closed-end you can often pay "too much" or, just as often, get a bargain. With an open-end fund, new shares are created whenever a new investor steps up to the plate—and you buy shares in an open-end fund directly from the fund company (or through a fund network, bank, or brokerage) at the NAV price (although often with some load or other fee charged). With a closed-end fund, the number of shares is limited, and, unless you get in on the initial offering (more on that below) you don't really buy closed-end shares from the fund company, you buy them from another investor who is selling.

The only time you're likely to be solicited to buy shares in a closed-end fund is during its initial offering. Why? That's when the brokers can make a big commission. Typically, for every $100 you invest, commissions eat up around $7, and only the other $93 goes to work for you. It rarely, if ever, makes sense to buy a new closed-end fund at this time. Unless you want to reward your broker for exemplary service and advice, wait until after the fund has been available for a while and buy it on the open market. Then the commissions will be more like 1 percent, not 7 percent or more.

How should you judge a closed-end fund? First, if the fund doesn't meet your investment objectives (e.g., for growth, or for stable income), you must avoid it. Second, if the fund's management has shown a poor record and/or management expenses are out of line with the norms for open-end funds, you should probably stay away. Stock funds' expenses shouldn't exceed about 1.5 percent, with some leeway for aggressive small-cap growth funds and international funds, while bond fund expenses should be well under 1 percent, again with some leeway for funds investing in junk bonds and convertibles. Finally, even if the underlying fund looks good and appropriate, if it's selling at a significant premium to the value of its holdings (its NAV), you should stay away, at least for the time being. Remember, there's probably a no- or low-load open-end fund that's just as good.

When is a good time to buy a closed-end fund? Closed-end funds are generally attractive when they are selling at a significant discount to their NAV. (This information can be found in *Barron's* magazine each week.) You can often buy $100 worth of assets for $95 or less. Optimally, you can buy discounted shares in a closed-end fund when its investment niche is out of style, then when the area recovers you'll make money from both a higher NAV and from the elimination of the discount. (You may even sell your hot fund for a considerable premium!)

There's some truth to the cynical interpretation that closed-end funds exist largely because there are brokers willing to sell a new closed-end fund for a fat commission. But closed-ends do have another, more legitimate reason for existing. The managers of many open-end funds, especially specialized funds that invest in illiquid securities like stock in foreign companies or small domestic companies, have to spend a lot of time waiting for the right securities to come on the market at a good price. If they have to dump these securities to meet shareholder redemptions one day, they may have trouble finding similar replacement securities when their shareholders are buying a week later. To avoid such problems, many open-end funds levy redemption fees on short-term traders, but that is only a partial solution to the problem of shareholder redemptions. If half a fund's shareholders sell out in the same month, it will be little consolation to fund management (or the other shareholders) that they had owned their shares for more than a year! The manager of a closed-end fund, on the other hand, has complete confidence that he won't have to be dumping illiquid securities and raising cash to meet shareholder redemptions—because there aren't any redemptions. This gives him the freedom to concentrate assets in promising, but illiquid, securities.

Closed-end investors who dump their shares at the same time will suffer exaggerated market losses because (unlike open-end fund investors) they lack the power to force the fund's management to buy the shares back at their NAV. But, paradoxically, shareholders in general benefit from their lack of power, because it allows the closed-end fund's managers to invest in these promising but illiquid securities in the first place, and to avoid dumping the securities at sensitive times.

For this reason, closed-end funds make the most sense as a vehicle for investing in narrowly defined portfolios of illiquid securities, and many of the most notable (and worthy) closed-end funds are single-country funds. In fact, if you look up the name of just about any European, Pacific Rim, or fast-growing emerging-market country in your newspaper's stock tables, you're likely to find a closed-end fund or two (e.g., the Japan Equity and Japan OTC funds on the NYSE).

More Fund Types

The following funds can offer you the possibility of investing in a single country, industry, market, or new fund. While this may sound like an advantage, the truth is that these funds often present the highest degree of risk, since they focus their investing on a single area, industry, or market. Nevertheless, these funds also present potentially higher returns than most other funds.

- Sector funds invest in the stocks of a single industry, such as biotechnology, electronics, health care, utilities, and so on. If, for example, you think an industry is about to take off or rebound, then a sector fund may prove to be the best way to invest your money, as opposed to buying stocks in companies in the industry directly. Because of their focus on a single area or industry, sector funds behave more like individual stocks. Also as a result of this focus, sector funds often top the list of the highest-performing mutual funds for the year. Unfortunately, the same funds that top one year's list are often found at the bottom of the next year's.
- Index funds invest in an index, like the Standard & Poor's 500 or the Wilshire 4500, for example. Objective: duplicating a broad section of the market in order to safeguard investors against below-market returns (but also eliminating the possibility of above-market returns).
- Socially responsible funds limit their investments to companies considered to be socially responsible. (For more on creating a criterion checklist that will help you screen funds with a conscience that matches your own, see chapter 19. However, be sure that your conscience isn't your only guide, so that you research and screen out poor-performing funds, too.) Objective: achieve an adequate return without sacrificing the moral imperative.

    There is no common definition for social responsibility. As a result, each fund's holdings will differ. Some, for example, will base their investments on companies to avoid (e.g., tobacco, alcohol, defense) while others will base their investments on companies to include (e.g., those that tend to promote women's issues, or that provide health insurance for the domestic partners of employees). But perhaps the biggest concern ought to be the performance of such funds historically versus "conscienceless" funds—after all, your money is used in a more focused manner when you actively support the charities you believe in through tax-deductible donations, as opposed to purchasing an investment product which supposedly does the work for you.

• New funds are not exactly a "proper" category, but they are a phenomenon within the overall industry that you can't avoid —and so need to know about. Like IPOs (initial public offerings) in the stock world, new funds present investors with a dilemma: whether to invest or not to invest, that is the question. New funds can provide investors a substantially rewarding investment opportunity. But with over a thousand new funds starting up in 1995 alone, it's hard to know where to look for the most promising new funds to invest in.

All funds were new funds at one point in time. But investing in new funds can be a risky business. Unless, that is, you can afford the time to research and cull those funds that offer real promise. Many investors view new funds from the largest fund families as their only source of new funds. Here, logic dictates that if a company has produced some of today's top-performing funds, their new progeny will prove to do likewise come tomorrow. But the fact is that new funds from even the most successful families can wind up losing your money. In short, fund-family name recognition isn't the best way to scan the fund horizon for the best possible new investment opportunities.

• Single-country funds focus on one particular country's stocks and bonds, while most international and global funds invest in several countries on one or more continents. By far the most volatile of the bunch, single-country funds are generally best avoided unless, as in the case of Japan, the country is the largest market outside the U.S., with well-established markets, industries, and accounting practices.

You'll still have to do your research on such funds, however, since funds concentrating in the same single country can invest in different types of markets—as well as hedging or not hedging their bets against currency fluctuations.

• Emerging-market funds concentrate in developing markets, countries, and economies, unlike the majority of international funds, which invest in countries with well-established markets and economies. The results can be spectacularly good— or bad.

How to Tell One Fund from Another

Every fund publishes a prospectus. The prospectus designates the type of fund (aggressive growth, balanced, etc.), details the specific objective of the fund and its past performance, states how the fund will be managed, and much more. To get your hands on a fund's prospectus, simply call the fund company and ask for it to be sent to you. (Or you can download the prospectus from Galt Technology's Web site—check out chapter 20.) Once it arrives—and it will arrive quickly since you're their business—you may be a bit shell-shocked by the bombardment of information contained within each prospectus. (For a thorough understanding of how to read a mutual fund prospectus, request a copy of *An Investor's Guide to Reading the Mutual Fund Prospectus*, cost 40¢, published by the Investment Company Institute, P.O. Box 66140, Washington, DC 20035-6140.)

In 1995, as part of a pilot project, the SEC began producing "Profile Prospectuses," two-page fund profiles which serve as crib notes for prospectus readers and which include: the fund's objective, investment strategies, the types of securities in which the fund will invest, any special investment practices, risk factors, expenses, and past performance. While the pilot program remains restricted to only a handful of funds and only a handful of fund families, they may catch on—which will prove to be a boon for you. When asking for a fund's prospectus—which you must do for every fund you invest in—ask for the profile prospectus, too. Who knows, you might get lucky.

Why is a fund's objective so important? Although it's only a paragraph or two long, a fund's objective tells you most of what you need to know. The objective indicates what types of investments the fund invests in, what the fund manager's goals are, as well as what the manager's investment strategies will be. Risk, reward, and your personal objectives and goals can be measured against this objective.

Selecting a Fund That's Right for You

Selecting the mutual funds that suit your investment means, objectives, and goals is not a simple task. Neither was learning to ride a bike, but I'm sure you mastered that pretty quickly. The trick is partly in choosing the right vehicle and partly in getting the balance of the thing. Once you have these two in check, you will be able to select a suitable group of funds that will help you stay in the investment seat no matter how bumpy the market ride gets. First, you will need to make sure that your investment vehicle is in working order. Then you will be able to map out a course that puts your investing know-how to the real-world test.

The following questions will help you keep focused on the answers you most need:

- What is the fund's objective?
- What is the minimum investment?
- What loads and other fees are charged?
- How well has the fund performed relative to its peers and index?
- How long has the fund been in existence?
- How is the fund managed?
- Who is the fund manager and how long has he/she been at the helm?
    Did he/she manage a different fund prior to this one and how did it do?
- How can you purchase and redeem shares?

Mutual fund investors all share one basic goal: to make more money. Yet making more money won't help you achieve financial independence if the money isn't slated for specific goals and objectives. It is your goals and objectives which should dictate not only how much money you're investing in mutual funds, but also which types of funds you're investing your money in.

Fund Analysis

Stock funds can be parsed by their investment style (value versus growth), their capitalization (the size of the company the fund invests in—large-cap (over about $3 billion), mid-cap (between $1 and $3 billion), small-cap (under $1 billion), or micro-cap (under $500 million), as well as their industry concentrations. Knowing each of these parts helps you picture the fund as a whole as well as how one fund is likely to correlate with another. Remember, you don't get added diversification when you buy two funds that invest in the same things! As you analyze the funds you might invest in, consider the following:

INVESTMENT STYLE: Value-style managers focus on stocks that are currently selling at low prices relative to their book value and/or earnings (price-to-book and price/earnings ratio). Value funds typically invest in mature, slower-growing stocks, like industrial equipment manufacturers and financial service companies. Growth-style managers, on the other hand, seek out rapidly growing businesses—even if the company's stock price is higher than the general market. That's why you'll find technology, health care, telecommunications, and other rapidly growing industries in growth funds.

Value funds typically tend to outperform growth funds in periods when the economy is recovering from a low point. (Economically sensitive stocks, like capital goods manufacturers, benefit as other companies expand capacity.) In a maturing economic recovery, growth funds tend to gain ground. Companies in these funds aren't hurt as much by an economic slowdown as are companies found in value funds.

INDUSTRY CONCENTRATION: Investment style determines the types of stocks a manager is most likely to own, as well as the fund's industry concentrations.

CAPITALIZATION: Capitalization refers to the size of companies. Companies with large capitalization are, for example, name-brand companies such as Coca Cola, Proctor & Gamble, Ford, IBM, and Intel. Companies with small capitalization are often start-ups you may not have heard of, such as Zoll Medical. A fund's median market capitalization can clue you in to its inherent volatility as well as its stock selection. For example, many investors mistakenly think that value-style funds are inherently less risky than growth-style funds. You'll have to dig deeper to get at the real risk-related difference between these two investment focuses—since a fund's average market capitalization often reveals more about its inherent volatility than does its investment style. In fact, if you took two value funds with similar industry concentrations, you might be surprised to find a wide divergence in terms of their volatilities. One way to explain this is to look at each fund's holdings. Is one large-cap oriented (focused on steady, reliable, liquid performers), while the other focuses on more volatile, small-cap issues? Chances are the answer is yes. Similar investment style and industry weightings don't necessarily mean similar volatility.

CORRELATION: Your ability to put together a well-diversified portfolio depends on your ability to discern such similarities and differences. The "correlation matrix" (page 169) illustrates the performance similarities, or the *correlation*, among a representative group of funds. (The table compares monthly total returns over the past three years.) If you do hold two growth funds with a high correlation, chances are the growth portion of your overall portfolio isn't as diversified as it could or should be. On the other hand, if you own two growth funds with a very low correlation, you've achieved added diversification.

The table clearly shows how closely the growth funds' returns correlate with one another. Simply put, for any two funds, there is a number, called the "r^2," which shows what percentage of one fund's performance can be explained by the other fund. Thus, as you can see in the shaded columns, Invesco Growth Fund's r^2 when compared to Gabelli Asset Fund is 71 percent. (A fund's r^2 when compared to itself is 100 percent.) The top row of the table shows each fund's correlation with the S&P 500 Index—the best overall benchmark for U.S. stock investors (although it does have its limitations as a benchmark for small-cap funds).

Founders Growth and Invest Growth, which are both invested in larger-cap technology stocks, have a high r^2 (81 percent); thus, owning both offers little in the way of additional diversification. On the other hand, owning both Crabbe Huson Equity and Wasatch Mid-Cap, which have a low correlation (32 percent), would improve your overall growth group diversification—not surprising, given each fund's different industry emphasis. Crabbe Huson Equity owns virtually no technology, preferring instead financial services (8.9 percent), transportation (8.8 percent), energy (7.5 percent), and retail (7.4 percent), while Invesco Growth favors technology (26 percent) and consumer staples (16 percent). Note that you need to keep your eye on each fund's velocity as well as your portfolio's overall velocity.

Once you're clear on what you want your mutual fund investments to accomplish, take the following steps:

GROWTH FUND CORRELATION MATRIX

S&P 500	20th Century Ultra	Brandywine	Columbia Growth	Crabbe Huson Equity	Fidelity Growth Co	Fidelity Magellan	Fidelity Value	Founders Growth	Franklin Balance Sheet	Gabelli Asset	Heartland Value	Invesco Growth	Janus	Kaufmann	Managers Special Equity	Neuberger & Berman Guardian	Oakmark	Oberweis Emerging Growth	PBHG Growth	Permanent Portfolio Aggressive Growth	Robertson Stephens Value + Growth	SteinRoe Special	T. Rowe Price Small-Cap Value	Vanguard Explorer	Vanguard PRIMECAP	Wasatch Mid-Cap	Yacktman	
100	40	38	75	67	59	65	65	56	51	74	29	66	83	37	51	84	55	34	22	65	37	58	44	42	73	45	50	S&P 500
	100	88	66	45	85	66	43	89	33	55	35	70	49	77	74	51	35	72	73	70	44	61	48	71	63	53	15	20th Century Ultra
		100	68	41	84	66	40	82	33	53	37	66	53	80	76	51	38	78	68	68	48	59	51	74	65	45	11	Brandywine
			100	70	78	64	60	77	49	74	40	83	81	66	79	80	68	61	51	78	41	77	62	74	83	53	40	Columbia Growth
				100	59	57	69	55	47	70	38	74	60	44	62	71	60	42	32	63	30	61	55	46	63	32	37	Crabbe Huson Equity
					100	75	53	85	36	60	39	82	72	79	80	72	45	74	60	78	54	69	56	78	79	62	27	Fidelity Growth Co
						100	62	76	42	63	21	66	65	54	61	71	32	48	40	68	64	59	46	46	72	38	14	Fidelity Magellan
							100	53	51	69	37	66	57	46	59	70	56	33	31	44	31	72	45	41	58	29	20	Fidelity Value
								100	38	72	37	81	66	73	76	61	44	67	70	73	51	69	58	72	68	54	18	Founders Growth
									100	65	38	43	42	24	42	50	48	21	27	38	16	48	49	35	39	19	20	Franklin Balance Sheet
										100	48	71	68	50	66	67	67	44	44	63	29	75	65	55	61	38	25	Gabelli Asset
											100	47	35	46	54	34	47	41	32	32	17	37	53	46	26	27	18	Heartland Value
												100	72	66	74	74	59	64	46	70	45	77	67	74	71	55	28	Invesco Growth
													100	48	62	81	55	41	33	68	39	61	47	55	72	44	38	Janus
														100	86	53	47	85	74	59	53	67	45	86	59	56	24	Kaufmann
															100	65	66	74	68	70	44	79	62	84	66	52	28	Managers Special Equity
																100	59	42	35	66	42	70	51	53	72	44	37	Neuberger & Berman Guardian
																	100	41	39	46	18	66	57	57	51	31	37	Oakmark
																		100	62	61	53	54	41	79	60	56	25	Oberweis Emerging Growth
																			100	47	35	53	39	62	38	34	11	PBHG Growth
																				100	42	55	48	64	77	47	33	Permanent Portfolio Agrsv Grwth
																					100	32	34	41	50	51	19	Robertson Stephens Value + Growth
																						100	62	71	63	51	21	SteinRoe Special
																							100	52	45	37	15	T. Rowe Price Small-Cap Value
																								100	60	61	32	Vanguard Explorer
																									100	58	40	Vanguard PRIMECAP
																										100	42	Wasatch Mid-Cap
																											100	Yacktman

1. Determine how much you can invest. Once you've determined what your investment objectives are, you'll need to figure out how much of your hard-earned money you can and are willing to invest.
2. Figure the percentages. Once you know why you're investing and how much money you can invest, you'll need to figure out how to divvy up your money among different types of funds. Why different types of funds? Because doing so will enable you to fit your investments to your goals and take advantage of the benefits of diversification. Figuring out what percentages to place in which types of funds is asset allocation plain and simple.

3. Select the funds you think will be best based on the prospectus objective and performance record as well as your individual investment means, objectives, and goals.
4. Know what fees you have to pay. Fees really make a difference. Consider the following. If you invest $10,000 in a 4 percent load fund that turns in a 10 percent performance for the year, you earn the 10 percent, but not on $10,000. Instead, you earn 10 percent on $9,600. That's $400 short of a no-load fund investor. However, just because a fund says it's no-load doesn't mean that there are no fees associated with it. There may be a redemption fee, and every fund charges management fees in one form or another. The trick is to find the funds whose fees are (far) more reasonable than others and whose performance is still solid. To do this, you will need to do your homework—a task made easier by the resource room at the end of this chapter. For now, let's look at the range of mutual fund fees that can affect your investment dollars.

- *Load:* A load is an up-front sales commission charged and deducted from your initial investment amount. (Load charges range as high as 8.5 percent but are more commonly in the range of 3 to 4.5 percent.) There's little reason to purchase load funds when there are so many good no-load funds to choose from.
- *No-load:* No-load means no initial sales commission fee. No-load refers only to up-front sales commission charges. Many no-load funds have other fees (listed below). Nevertheless, no-load funds tend to be the best way to invest in mutual funds because more of your money is going to work for you.
- *Back-end loads:* Also known as "redemption fees," this is a fee charged to the net asset value of your shares when you sell them. Either your profit is cut or your loss is increased. No matter how you look at it, this load sucks.
- *Deferred loads (contingent deferred sales fees):* On the surface, a deferred load seems as lousy as a back-end load. A deferred load is charged by some funds if and only if you redeem your shares before a specified time—typically a few years. While this may not be to your advantage if you're investing for the short term, the principle of discouraging investors from jumping into and out of the market in short shrift is a good one.

- *Reinvestment loads:* Some fund companies dock your dividend, interest, and capital gains should you decide to reinvest them. Any fund which does this is discouraging a very wise investment choice—reinvesting dividends. Drop any of these funds from your list of possible investments.
- *12b-1 fees:* Some funds deduct the costs associated with advertising and marketing themselves from the fund's overall assets. The charge associated with such deductions is called a 12b-1 fee, and ranges as high as 1.25 percent. Some funds feed a portion of the fee to the broker who sold you the fund.

5. Consider a fund network: If you want the simplicity of one statement and one phone number, but don't want to limit yourself to one fund family, consider a fund network, such as those at Charles Schwab, Fidelity, or Jack White. Each has hundreds of funds available without any transaction fees, and many hundreds more with modest fees.
6. Open the account: You can do this either by investing directly or through the fund company or by opening a brokerage account. The following fund phone book should help you get started; note that this is only a partial listing, the business pages of your phone book will list others.

Fund Family	Phone	State
Artisan	800-344-1770	MN
Babson Fund Group	800-422-2766	MO
Benham Group*	800-472-3389	CA
Berger Group	800-551-5849	CO
Berwyn Group	800-992-6757	PA
Bramwell	800-272-6227	NY
Brandywine Funds	800-656-3017	DE
Cappiello-Rushmore	800-343-3355	MD
Cohen & Steers	800-437-9912	NY
Columbia Funds	800-547-1707	OR
Crabbe Huson Funds	800-541-9732	OR
Dodge & Cox Group	800-621-3979	CA
Dreyfus Group	800-645-6561	NY
Federated Funds	800-245-2423	PA

* Benham has merged with 20th Century.

Fidelity	800-544-8888	MA
Fidelity Funds Network	800-544-9697	MA
Founders Funds	800-525-2440	CO
Franklin Funds	800-342-5236	CA
Gabelli Funds	800-422-3554	NY
Harbor Funds	800-422-1050	OH
Heartland Funds	800-432-7856	WI
IAI Funds	800-945-3863	MN
Invesco Family of Funds	800-525-8085	CO
Jack White Network	800-323-3263	CA
Janus Group	800-525-3713	CO
Kaufmann Fund	800-261-0555	PA
Lexington Group	800-526-0056	NJ
Lindner	800-995-7777	MO
Loomis Sayles	800-633-3330	MA
MAS Funds	800-354-8185	PA
Meridian Fund	800-446-6662	CA
Merriman Funds	800-423-4893	WA
Montgomery Funds	800-572-3863	CA
Mutual Series Fund	800-448-3863	NJ
Neuberger & Berman Group	800-877-9700	NY
Oakmark Funds	800-625-6275	IL
Oberweis Funds	800-323-6166	IL
PBHG Growth Fund	800-932-7781	PA
Permanent Portfolio Funds	800-531-5142	CA
PIMCo Funds	800-800-0952	CA
Robertson Stephens	800-766-3863	CA
Royce Funds	800-221-4268	NY
Safeco Mutual Funds	800-835-4391	WA
Schafer Value Fund	212-403-2900	NY
Schwab Network	800-266-5623	NY
Scudder Funds	800-225-2470	MA
Seven Seas Series Fund	800-647-7327	MA
Sit Group	800-332-5580	MN
Southeastern Asset Management	800-445-9469	TN
SteinRoe Mutual Funds	800-338-2550	IL
Strong Funds	800-368-1030	WI
T. Rowe Price Funds	800-638-5660	MD
Tweedy Browne	800-873-8242	NY
20th Century Family	800-345-2021	MO
Vanguard Group	800-662-7447	PA

Warburg Pincus Funds	800-257-5614	NY
Wasatch	800-345-7460	UT
Yacktman Fund	800-525-8258	IL

7. Keep accurate records of how much you've invested, and where. It's been a while since we mentioned the term "active file." Remember to set up a file for your investments, and to keep it current with statements that you receive.

8. Keep tabs on your funds' performance. The quickest way to do so is to call your fund's 800 number and ask them. But remember, the market is a fickle provider. That's why keeping track of your funds' performance is a necessary, ongoing process. You may not buy this, but it's kind of fun looking at the financial pages in your newspaper and seeing how your funds are doing. Of course, if they aren't doing well, the fun goes out of the picture pretty damn fast. But don't let a bad day or two cloud your judgment. For that matter, don't let a few lousy months or even a year do so. If you've selected a good fund and still believe in its fundamental ability to succeed over the long term, then stick with it. Making a move based on short term market fluctuations will only increase the likelihood of an overall poor investing performance.

Further, make use of the many good financial-planning magazines available to you at your library, bookstore, and/or newsstand.

9. Regularly increase your investments. Plan on investing regularly. Plan too on increasing the amount you invest as you get older and have more disposable income. Chapter 14 details several ways to build an actual portfolio of mutual funds to suit your age, income, and objectives.

There's no guaranteed path to success. But when traveling in unfamiliar territory it is always advisable to get a map, rather than ask for directions from random strangers. Following the "map" provided in this chapter will help you start on your investment journey.

READY RESOURCES

As with stock investing, there's no shortage of fund information available to the avid reader. The following list of newsletters and books should be sufficient to get you going.

- *Morningstar Mutual Funds* (and other publications), (800) 876-5005.
- *Individual Investor's Guide to Low-Load Mutual Funds*, American Association of Individual Investors, 625 North Michigan Avenue, Chicago, IL 60611, (312)280-0170.
- *Straight Talk about Mutual Funds*, by D. Vujovich, McGraw-Hill.
- *Individual Investor's Guide to Low Load*, Fourteenth Edition, Aaii, Login Publishers
- *Bogle on Mutual Funds*, by J. Bogle, Dell Trade.
- *Building Your Mutual Fund Portfolio*, by A. Fredman, Dearborn.
- *Fundamentals of Fund Analysis*, by J. Ritchie, Irwin Press.
- *Getting Started in Mutual Funds*, by A. Lavine, John Wiley.

CHAPTER FOURTEEN

Creating Your Own Investment Portfolio

An investment portfolio is like a painter's palette. And, in a sense, being an investor is like being a painter. Your chances of creating a success of your overall work depends to a large degree on your range of skills and experience, as well as on the materials you can apply to the canvas to ultimately express your potential for failure or success. An investment portfolio is the palette from which you bring your investment objectives to life. And, as selecting the paints for the palette is potentially limiting or liberating for a painter and his or her work, so selecting the types of investments for your portfolio's palette will prove to be either restrictive or rewarding. Fortunately, your investment portfolio is a work in progress, and you can learn to quickly adapt and revise so as to secure a better total return picture for yourself.

Whether you have $100 or $1,000 to invest, you can plan a portfolio that will help you achieve your investment objectives. In fact, even if you have $0, zip, nada, zilch, you can profit today by planning your investment portfolio of tomorrow. Planning a portfolio requires prior knowledge of several investment-related steps—from knowing where you stand financially to coming to terms with how the economy and securities markets work to understanding and selecting the best types of investment vehicles to get you to where you want to go. That, of course, is what the first three sections of this book are all about. From the vantage point of knowing the many investment alternatives that are out there, you can begin to contemplate the process of applying what you know in order to create a better world for yourself.

You still feel overwhelmed? No wonder. With over 6,500 mutual funds and over 11,000 publicly traded stocks (plus hundreds of bonds and real estate opportunities) to chose from, the mind boggles. But you can always go back to any chapter to refresh yourself on a particular subject or investment vehicle. Moreover, when it comes to building a portfolio of investments for yourself and your objectives, there's more than one way to keep a clear head and focus on the best investment alternatives for you. To begin with, you'll need a plan.

PLANNING YOUR PORTFOLIO

Planning your portfolio requires reviewing, and potentially revising, your life. That's the only way to ensure that your investment objectives make sense for you, and that you can achieve them.

AGE: Your single biggest hidden asset is your age. Sure, you may feel that being older means you are somehow automatically richer —but just ask anyone who worked for AT&T back in 1995 and they'll tell you that ain't necessarily so. In fact, with the uncertain job market that exists today and is likely to persist throughout your lifetime, you need to be prepared for the loss of a job or, even more likely, for your desire to change careers or places of employment. Part of your portfolio planning will require you to view your investments in light of your overall financial planning, so that both are working in harmony to achieve your desired ends of a financially secure life from start to finish.

Because you are still young, you can afford to take on more risk in the types of investments you select for your portfolio—and, if you have selected the right type of investments, more risk has, over time, delivered more rewards. In short, you have more time and a greater ability to create a sizeable worksheet to retire on. (Perhaps even to retire *early* on.)

LIFESTYLE: If you're spending everything you make on fun, believe me, you're heading for some very depressing times in the not-so-distant future. If you don't start saving today, and you haven't started investing yet, the longer you wait the more sacrifices you'll have to make just to stay in the game. What do I mean? Let's take a look at two 25-year-olds. One invests $100 every month in a 401(k) plan starting at age 25, but he stops at age 35 and never invests another penny. The other doesn't start investing until age 35, but he keeps plugging $100 per month into his account until he retires at age 67. Who wins? The early bird of course!

CURRENT INCOME: Your current income obviously affects the amount of money you have to invest. But don't make the common mistake of thinking that postponing investing until you make more money is the best way to go.

At 27, earning thirty grand, you're barely making ends meet. After all, there's the rent, the car, the student loans, the bars. So you say to yourself that in a few years, around age 30 or so, you'll be earning thirty-five grand, maybe even forty. Since this is a reality check, let's not use the rosiest sum. Let's compromise and say you'll be earning $37,500. Will that amount guarantee more disposable income for you—you know, more money to invest? Not likely.

First, taxes. Taxes on your thirty grand run approximately 28 percent federal and 5 percent state. Let's say that remains constant—you go from $20,000 after taxes to around $23,500—a $3,500 lift, despite the $7,500 increase in income. But now you'll want to add to the equation the toll inflation will take. Let's say inflation remains under control at around 3 percent per year. Further, let's say that your income increases from $30,000 to $37,500 in $2,500 increments ($2,500 × 3 years = $7,500). By the end of year one, your $30,000 loses about $800 worth of purchasing power. By the end of year two, your $31,666 loses about $950 of its purchasing power. Year three, your $33,333 loses nearly $1,000. By year four, the year you were going to begin to invest, your $37,500 has lost $1,050 in purchasing power for the year. Your cumulative loss of purchasing power is now nearly 10 percent—your total supposed advance. And if graduate school is part of the scenario, you've been set back big-time. Add to this equation the likely changes in lifestyle that will occur, and the increased expenses to boot—you no longer buy wine by the screw-top jug, you want better skis and bindings, and, of course, your credit debt has skyrocketed.

Am I getting through to you? Don't panic. I've been there myself. The message, for those who have opted for real-life learning as opposed to real costly higher learning, and who haven't yet begun to invest, is to: just do it. Once you have a clear idea of your overall investment objectives, you can develop an investment plan designed to help you achieve those objectives. Your investment plan is based on your ability to determine:

1. What you can invest. Many of us feel as if we have little or nothing to invest. More of us, however, are beginning to invest in our future, through retirement plans like 401(k)s. The benefits of doing this are inarguable—so long as you view your 401(k) or other tax-advantaged, retirement-oriented investments as an active portfolio in its own right, as well as a part of your overall investment plan. (Part V has more information on retirement-oriented investment plans.) But you also need to focus on investing for your shorter-term objectives. What's an optimal percentage of your income to invest? A minimum of 5 percent of your take-home pay, for starters. But you'll need to ramp up your participation to 10 percent within one to two years—once you've got your overall financial house in order.

2. What you're investing for. If you're investing for your retirement, you can afford to be far more aggressive in terms of the investments you select for your portfolio. If, on the other hand, you're investing for a short-term goal like the down payment on a home in two years' time (or less), then you'll need to be far more conservative with the bulk of your money—or at least with the amount you'll need for your purchase. But don't think that you shouldn't also be investing for much longer term goals like your retirement. You should! The key is to proportionately allocate your savings to appropriate investments relative to your several objectives.

3. What rate of return you'll need to achieve your objectives. You'll need to invest in order to stay ahead of inflation and in step with the market. Using 3 percent as an inflation rate, and 8 percent as a conservative market standard, you need to find investments which will deliver an average annual return of at least 8 percent. Where does history tell you to turn? Stocks, and stocks alone, can generate returns of 8 percent or higher in the long run.

4. What asset allocation will optimize your chances of success. What percentage of your hard-earned savings should you place in, say, each mutual fund category, i.e., growth stock fund, small-company fund, and/or international fund? If history can be repeated, concentrating your assets in stocks, and, in particular, in large-cap growth and small-cap value stocks—and the funds that invest in them—is your best bet.

Asset Allocation

I like to think of asset allocation as the bones of the portfolio, and individual investments as the flesh. Asset allocation decisions are critical to the overall performance of your portfolio—not simply as it stands today, but, going forward, in how well it will are in tough and robust markets. When coming to terms with asset allocation, you'll need to factor in much of what you already know: economics, stock markets, interest rates, inflation, investment vehicles, taxes, and your career. This is part of what makes investing interesting, but it can also serve to frighten some individuals away from investing altogether—or in part. Either move is in the wrong direction, since, after all, you're in the driver's seat when it comes to ensuring that your investment decisions are in line with your personal objectives. Of course, you can work with a financial advisor to further your own interests. But even there, you'll want to know enough to make informed decisions—and to be certain that your advisor is at least as informed as you.

If you have just started investing, or have been investing for some time, you will need to review your portfolio to ensure that it's allocated appropriately. Chances are you'll need to make some adjustments. You will also, no doubt, find that one or more of the individual investments (a stock or fund, for example) could be replaced with one that is more in keeping with your allocation decisions, which, in turn, reflect your investment objectives. I'm not advocating changing your asset allocation often. In fact, if you've done your allocation job well, you will have to review it only on an annual basis—or when sudden and dramatic lifestyle changes (marriage, children, a new career) occur. On the other hand, you will want to be more attuned to the performance of the individual investments which comprise your portfolio. Again, making many changes isn't on my top-ten list of things to do with your portfolio. But keeping up-to-date on your investments, and their related industries, makes sense.

The following steps will take you through a core asset allocation plan from start to finish. Once you cross the asset allocation finish line, you begin the second leg of the investment biathlon—selecting investments for your portfolio.

To begin with, determine your objective. In this instance, let's say it's building a retirement war chest. Your objective (given your young age) determines the investment categories you want to place your assets in. Before you even begin to do this, however, you'll need to make a geographical decision: what percentage of domestic (U.S.) and foreign assets do you want in your overall allocation. Here, the younger you are, the more you may want to invest overseas. But this is only true to a point. In fact, foreign markets tend to be far more volatile than ours—which means some will rocket twice as much as the U.S. market in a given time period, while others will plummet twice as far—or further.

Step 1: At home or abroad, the younger you are, the more important it is to concentrate on categories that have the highest growth potential. There's one: stocks. With that in mind, consider the following allocation for your portfolio:

Stock	*Bonds*	*Real Estate*
100%	0%	0%

Step 2: Since you're not investing in bonds or real estate, you have leapt ahead of the need to determine the percentage of your assets you want to invest in each category and have landed on the need to decide how you want to invest in stocks. There are two options: direct ownership of individual securities and indirect ownership through stock mutual funds. Unless you have amassed over $25,000 (and possibly even if you have), investing in stock mutual funds makes the most sense. Why? You easily get the benefits of being fully invested in the stock market with the benefits of broad diversification. So your portfolio would look like this:

Stocks	*Stock Funds*
0%	100%

Note: To get the diversification you need through direct ownership of individual stocks, you'd need to own an absolute minimum of a dozen stocks. And these would have to be chosen very carefully, and primarily from the standpoint of diversification; thirty stocks is a more practical minimum to diversify most investors' portfolios. One fund, on the other hand, can offer you well over 100 stocks in one basket. But owning one fund generally isn't the way to go —since it would bias your portfolio toward a single investment style and manager's focus, which, in turn, would no doubt favor some industries over others. How many funds is enough? You don't need thirty—in fact, don't go overboard with the number of funds in your portfolio. Instead, concentrate on how and where each fund is invested. Five funds should be more than sufficient and you probably shouldn't invest all your money in a single family's funds. Again, doing so could bias your portfolio toward one way of participating in the markets the funds are invested in.

Step 3: Determine which major stock fund category you wish to invest in, as well as what percentage you want to invest in each category. As you learned in the previous chapter, mutual funds come in several different packages—and stock funds come in several different flavors. Selecting the ones that best meet your objectives is crucial to your overall investment success. The following is one possible allocation among major stock fund categories—together with percentages of assets allocated to them—that could potentially suit your longer-term objective:

Aggressive Growth	*Growth*	*International*
50%	30%	20%

Step 4: Now you need to decide how you want to allocate your investments in each stock fund subcategory (here defined by investment style and market capitalization, as well as country allocation). For example:

Small-Cap Value	*Mid-Cap Growth*	*Large-Cap Growth*	*International*	*Industry*
25%	20%	25%	20%	10%

Step 5: Selecting the specific funds to match your percentages is the next step, but not the final one. In fact, there is no final step to this process—it's ongoing until the day you die (and, if you plan

your estate well, you can control your investments from beyond the grave). To begin with, you'll need to build a fairly aggressive portfolio. Let's see how it's done.

CREATING YOUR MUTUAL FUND PORTFOLIO

Building your own portfolio is within your means. And since a solid underpinning of mutual funds, especially for younger investors, will likely be your design, keep the following architectonic in mind.

1. Know your objectives and risk tolerance. You will need to build a portfolio which offers you both the (somewhat conflicting) benefits of industry diversification and the potential rewards of asset concentration while not overstepping your own ability to tolerate the inherent risks.

2. Know your funds' objectives and risks. (To help determine a fund's objective and risk level, turn to chapter 13.)

3. Find out the fund managers' performance records and investment styles. While past performance is no guarantee of future results, average-annualized one-, three-, and five-year returns will help you get a sense of how a manager has done, and might continue to do. Be sure to compare these returns with those of other like-invested funds. What if the manager is new to the fund you're thinking of buying? Find out what his or her record was at a previous fund. Investment style tends to divide itself into two camps—value and growth. Each camp has a history of performance that is well reflected in the Wilshire Growth versus Value Index, as illustrated by the chart opposite.

   As discussed, investment style is a macro concern, while capitalization is a more focused one. You'll want to have a blend of small-cap value, mid- and large-cap growth funds—in addition to a well-diversified international fund (i.e., one which resembles the country weightings in the EAFE index; see chapter 7 for details).

4. Determine what types of industries and stocks every fund and each manager typically invests in. This may take a lot of research—but not a lot of time. In fact, you can call directly and ask the funds you're thinking of buying (or the ones you own) for this information. True, the information may be a bit

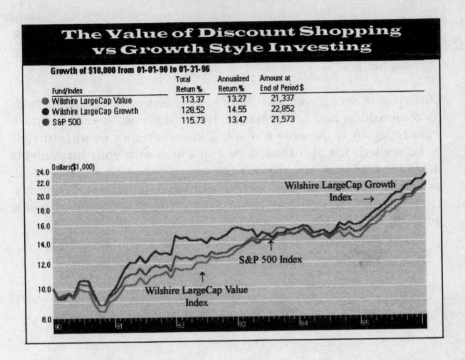

The Value of Discount Shopping vs Growth Style Investing

Growth of $10,000 from 01-01-90 to 01-31-96

Fund/Index	Total Return %	Annualized Return %	Amount at End of Period $
Wilshire LargeCap Value	113.37	13.27	21,337
Wilshire LargeCap Growth	128.52	14.55	22,852
S&P 500	115.73	13.47	21,573

stale—three months old or so—but it's still relevant. Another way to pursue the question is to research past issues of several personal finance magazines such as *Money, Kiplinger's,* or *Mutual Fund Magazine.* Your fund and its manager may have been profiled in one or another.

5. Establish how the funds in your current (or potential) portfolio correlate with each other. Thinking that owning many funds automatically guarantees diversification is perhaps the most common mistake fund investors make. How can you tell if the funds you currently (or potentially) own are likely to behave similarly when the market rises, flat-lines, or falls? The easiest way is to look at the factors mentioned earlier (i.e., if the funds' objectives and holdings are similar, the funds are likely to perform similarly). There's also a more technical way to derive correlation. This will require some doing, since you'll need to accumulate monthly returns for each fund over a thirty-six-month period. If you can plug these numbers into a Lotus or Excel spreadsheet, it's fairly simple to determine their correlation. Correlation can tell you how closely the funds' performances move together—as well as against an in-

dex which best reflects them, like the S&P 500 for growth funds, the Russell 2000 for small-cap funds, or the EAFE for international funds. (See chart on page 169 for an example.)

Once you've set up your portfolio, you'll need to keep track of both its composition and performance. Reviewing your investment portfolio regularly is the only way you'll know whether or not it needs to be revised. It's also fun. Staying in touch with your investments helps keep at least one of your fingers on the pulse of a very real, as opposed to ideal, world. Don't panic over sudden market moves. Don't get overconfident on upswings. Just trust that investing wisely and well will, in the end, help you meet your objectives.

PART IV

Smart Investing Moves You Can Make

CHAPTER FIFTEEN

Your Best Investing Moves

He was the one who was always coming up with new ways to strike it rich. Whether it was buying a load of oranges off a truck whose refrigerator had gone berserk and frozen the lot ("I'll make a killing in frozen orange juice") or throwing his whole month's paycheck into a sure-thing stock in a company that sold parcels of land on the moon, this guy was the one who had a "gift" for discovering unique markets and ways to invest in them. But every time you saw him coming, you turned and headed the other direction. In fact, when it came to his more down-to-earth investments, you actually found a good use for his "insights"—you simply did the opposite of whatever he said, and so far, you've come out ahead. The trouble is, he's doing so many things these days, it's hard to commit them to memory so that you can act accordingly.

There's a better way to school yourself in the best ways to invest. In fact, the following are among the best ways to get into the market and regularly add to and protect your investments. But don't try to commit them to memory. Act on them.

WAYS TO INVEST IN TODAY'S MARKET

1. Automatic investing: Automatic investing is a great way to begin and to stick with a regular investing program. You can have a set amount deducted from your bank savings or checking account and placed in an investment account with a mutual fund company or brokerage. The logistics of setting up an automatic investing account are easy. All you need do is to request an automatic investment account from your brokerage or mutual fund company. The rest is as easy as spelling out your name, address, and bank account.

2. Dollar-cost averaging: The prime directive of successful investing is to buy low and sell high. Dollar-cost averaging's aim is to do just that by investing a fixed sum of money at scheduled intervals. In this manner, you are automatically buying more shares when the prices are low, and fewer when the prices are high. But don't look to it to guarantee a dramatic increase in the performance of your investments. Instead, look at dollar-cost averaging as the tortoise's strategy for winning the race.

Here's how dollar-cost averaging works:

Period	Amount Invested	Price	Number of Shares Purchased
1st	$260	$ 9	28.88
2nd	260	8	32.50
3rd	260	6	43.33
4th	260	8	32.50
5th	260	10	26.00
	$1,300		163.21

Total amount invested over 5 periods: $1,300
Number of shares purchased: 163.21
Average market price: $8.20
Average cost: $7.96

Like automatic investing, dollar-cost averaging is also a great way to discipline yourself to invest on a regular, scheduled basis. And the effect of both is basically the same. However, dollar-cost averaging is an investment method, whereas automatic investing refers to a method of withdrawal and deposit. The discipline of dollar-cost averaging helps you keep your cash flowing into investments which, in turn, stand an excellent chance of providing you with a brighter financial future. There's no way to predict when to buy low, but dollar-cost averaging gives you your best overall shot at doing so. How? As the example above illustrates, investing on a regular basis can average out in your favor. Of course, if the stock is a dog that won't get up—or worse, one that keeps going down —then dollar-cost averaging won't help you.

3. Lump-sum investing: Is it better to invest your money in a lump sum or, given the market's recent heights, to gradually invest that sum in regular increments? The answer is that, historically, investing the lump sum right away is your best move—but the answer isn't always easy to swallow, because doing so naturally makes many investors nervous.

If you receive money in a substantial lump sum (e.g., an inheritance, or you were injured in an accident and your lawyer has made good on his ambulance-chasing TV promo), or you've been hoarding money in a savings account and are now ready to invest it, then you'll need an investing strategy which can help you cope with short-term market uncertainty.

The most aggressive form of investing your lump sum would be to invest it all at once, 100 percent in the stock market if your objective is growth. In fact, this is generally the best way to invest because it puts your money to work immediately—but it is also psychologically a difficult way for many investors to act.

Why? Let's say you inherited $10,000 from your grandmother and put it all in the stock market, only to watch the market immediately slip from the high point of your investment. Watching your inheritance diminish isn't exactly what you had in mind when you invested the money—and many investors, especially those who are relatively inexperienced with the markets, panic and sell after a few down months. But, historically, this has been the wrong move to make. Investing a lump sum even at a market high puts you ahead of those who invested at the high and then sold out lower. The key is to stay invested.

If you think your tolerance for risk might be less than meets the eye, don't worry. Investing your lump sum in scheduled increments will still deliver the goods (and may even let you sleep better at night). The following lump sum investing strategy is designed for the more cautious investor but nonetheless should help you remain steadfast to your goal of investing no matter what the short-term

market moves. It suits your age and ability to reap the rewards of
taking some additional risk rather than potentially retreating from
your entrance into the market.

This is, in essence, a form of dollar-cost averaging. The following
timetable should help you get into the market in a relatively pain-
less way. As the timetable indicates, you go from 100 percent cash
(invested in a money market mutual fund) to being fully (100 percent) invested in stocks within the first twelve months of this investment program.

% FULLY INVESTED WITHIN NEXT:

Investment Category	Now	3 Months	6 Months	9 Months	12 Months
Stocks	0	25	50	75	100
Cash	100	75	50	25	0
Total	100%	100%	100%	100%	100%

4. *Value-averaging:* This is another "automatic" investment
method. Value-averaging's principal idea is to keep the value of
your investment growing by a constant dollar amount. Rather than
a set amount each month, you put in just enough to keep your
investment on target. If the value of your shares goes up during the
month, you put in less (or even take some out). If it goes down,
you put in more.

However, even though your percentage return may be greater
with value-averaging than with dollar-cost averaging, total profits
may be lower, because you invest fewer dollars. In short, since you
put less money in as the share prices go up, you inhibit yourself
from taking full advantage of a bull market. To be able to keep
true to the method, you'll need cash in reserve for the months
when your portfolio goes down. Since you may need this reserve
money, it shouldn't be in the market, and since that money isn't
in the market, you'll need to account for the effect of its not being
invested in order to calculate a meaningful total return.

Value-averaging can outperform dollar-cost averaging in times of
great market volatility combined with the lack of a sustained upward
or downward direction.

5. *Stock purchase plans:* You may work for a company that offers a
stock purchase plan as part of its overall incentive package. A stock

purchase plan enables you to buy stock in the company at a discount. In this way, you automatically come out ahead. But how long you stay ahead depends on the company's performance over time. You will need to do the same fundamental research on your own company's strengths and weaknesses as you would for any company you're thinking of investing in. For now, consider this option a double-edged sword. It does provide a great way to cut the cost of investing, but it also can cut your investment legs out from under you, especially if you put all your investment dollars into the stock purchase plan. The solution is to make use of this option as only one part of your diversified portfolio program.

6. *Stop your losses:* Using stop-loss orders can help you limit your losses on stocks. They enable you to set a floor in a given stock's price below which you are unwilling to go. For example, you buy a stock at $8, and you place a stop-loss order at $6 to avoid too much damage from any sudden market downdraft. (On the other hand, if the stock fluctuates to $6, you'll sell out at that low price, and maybe miss the bounce back to $8 or higher.) But stop-loss orders can also help discipline you on the upside, to lock in a profit. For example, say the stock you bought at $8 more than doubled to $20 per share; you can put a stop-loss order in at $16 to lock in your double. (But, if the stock dips to $16 temporarily, then surges forward to $23, you won't be able to participate in the gain.) In times of increased market uncertainty, a stop-loss is a walk on the safer side and could wind up saving you from some deeper loss. On the other hand, if the stock's price falls quickly enough, you may not get out at your stop-loss price but rather may have to accept a lower bid. Typically, for every seller there's a buyer—but not every seller will get the price he or she wants.

7. *Buy and hold:* If you've done your research, and you're not trying to time the market with the stocks or stock funds that you've purchased, then you should be able to buy and hold for the long term, since high quality stocks (like the market in general) have tended to gain ground over time. What about small companies? Here you may find yourself buying and selling more frequently, but the same truths apply: if you have carefully selected your small-company holdings, then chances are you'll fare well over time—far better than a merely inflation-beating return.

Conversely, studies have shown time and again that trading in and out of the market on a regular basis not only racks up numerous brokerage fees and/or taxable gains, and increases your stress level remarkably, it also tends to deliver worse results over the long haul. This isn't to say that you shouldn't be actively managing your portfolio. Instead, it is meant to be a lesson in diligence (to begin with) and patience (to profit by).

8. *Revise the "7 and 7" strategy:* Many long-term investors swear by this old standby for purchasing stocks. It's based on the principle of buying low P/E (price/earnings ratio) stocks with relatively high dividend yields. It's called a "7 and 7" strategy since the original P/E target was a ratio of 7 or less with a dividend yield of greater than 7 percent. This discipline helped investors buy out-of-favor stocks in companies that they had determined were fundamentally promising (i.e., no major long-term problems like producing asbestos as your main product). The dividend yield of such stocks (which you will reinvest) is relatively attractive, and the company may increase its dividend to maintain an attractive yield when (and if) the P/E rises. But few stocks in today's market have a P/E as low as 7, and most stocks with 7 percent yields are too conservative for younger to middle-aged investors. Is "7 and 7" unrealistic in today's market and for your time horizon? Probably; even if you want to try a more conservative value-oriented strategy, a "12 and 5" strategy would probably suit you better.

9. *Buy stocks in companies which issue stock dividends:* Buying shares in companies which pay stock dividends in lieu of cash is another way to realize a profit since you can turn around and sell your newly issued shares. But watch out. Wall Street doesn't take kindly to overly large dividend payouts. In fact, such payouts reduce the stock's market price, meaning that your overall holdings will decline to the level where you don't really benefit from your dividend sales. Most nonretired investors shouldn't seek big dividends to cash out.

10. *Plan on dividend reinvestment plans (DRIPs):* Many companies offer investors who already own their shares a bonus for doing so —some in the form of a discount on the price you pay for new purchases of more of their shares, others by enabling you to eliminate brokerage fees when you use the automatic reinvestment of your dividends to purchase new shares of their stock.

Just because a company offers the DRIP option doesn't mean you should invest in it. You'll need to scrutinize such companies the same way you do any other company whose stock you're thinking of buying. However, among the hundreds of companies that offer DRIPs, some clearly stand out over time as top performers, including name brands that you know and most likely use on a daily basis: 3M, Caterpillar, Coca-Cola, General Electric, H. J. Heinz, Johnson & Johnson, McDonald's, Merck, Procter & Gamble, and Rubbermaid, to name a few.

How can you research DRIP companies? Get your hands on the Directory of Companies Offering Dividend Reinvestment Plans. To do so, call Evergreen Enterprises at (301)549-3939. There are also several books with this information; among them are *Buying Stocks Without a Broker* by Charles Carlson, the classic book on this type of investing strategy; and *Moody's Handbook of Dividend Achievers,* which rates over 300 companies that have increased their dividends over the past ten years. (Both are likely to be available at your local library or bookstore.) The National Association of Investors Corporation provides its members with a low-cost way to get started in DRIPs. (For more on the NAIC, see chapter 17.) Also, both Charles Schwab and Fidelity, among other leading brokers and fund managers, provide customers with dividend reinvestment plans for a modest fee.

There are drawbacks to DRIPs. The best DRIP companies are pricey, meaning it will be hard for you to accumulate a lot of shares in them. However, you are buying quality and, more important, doing so at a discount, which is the best way to buy quality I know. Record keeping can be a more lasting nightmare, since every dividend will mean another mailing to you. But more important, if you need to sell a DRIP, you won't be able to do it over the phone. When you sell a DRIP, you'll be required to present written authorization that it is in fact your intention to sell. Some DRIPs won't take any old written authorization—they'll require that your signature be notarized. One more DRIP drawback is that you'll have to pay income taxes on the reinvested dividends (as if you had cashed them), and you'll also have to pay taxes on the amount of the discount you received (the price per share that you paid minus the price you would have paid if you had bought it on the market). But these drawbacks are more than offset by the benefits of investing in a solid company which offers you the advantage of a DRIP.

11. Puts and calls: Investing in options may sound like a cool thing to do—but it's an essentially speculative way to bet on the direction of a stock's price. Think of it as being your own bookie and creating the spread. Most bookies know one thing very well: namely, how to make money off the suckers that use them. In this case, you're the sucker, and you're using yourself—unless you think you have suddenly acquired the ability to predict the near future of a stock's price (and if you think this, then you shouldn't have any trouble becoming the world's richest person in a matter of months).

Options can be "written" on individual stocks and more; for example: the NYSE Composite Index, Standard & Poor's 100-Stock and 500-Stock Indexes, the AMEX Index, the Nikkei 225 Index, as well as foreign currencies, U.S. Treasuries, and commodities futures contracts. In fact, one of the interesting figures to come out every morning ahead of the market's opening is the quantity and direction of people buying S&P futures. It's taken as a sign of the day's trend—and traders are trendy by nature. You, on the other hand, are not.

There are two things you need to know about options. First, there are two basic types of options: "puts" and "calls." Buying a put option gives you the right, but not the obligation, to sell shares of stock at a specified price at any time during the life of the option. Buying a call option gives you the right, but not the obligation, to purchase a set number of shares in a common stock at a specific price at any time during the life of the option. So buying a put is a bet the stock will go down, while buying a call is a bet that the stock will go up. Options are not written on all issues of common stock, only on the most popular ones. The second thing you need to know is that all options have a "strike price" (the price at which you may exercise the put or call) and an expiration date (the last day you may exercise the option to buy or sell the stock).

SCAMS AND SCHEMES

When it comes to money, scoundrels abound. And they come in all shapes and sizes—from the highfalutin' to the low-down, boiler-room, cold-call crush. But, fortunately, we are born with an innate warning system which can still alert us to the presence and dangers of predators in our midst. The problem is that, when it comes to investing, some us allow the cheese to mask the mousetrap.

The following scam alert is brought to you by your own brain— listen to it. If it sounds too good to be true, it probably is. If it sounds too simple to be believed, it probably is. If you feel you're being pressured, you are. If you think you are being misled, you are. If you think the investment opportunity is less compelling than the person trying to sell it to you, you're right. If you can't understand it, don't buy it. If the obvious isn't sufficient, steel yourself against the following MOs:

- You're asked for a little (or worse, a lot) of cash up front. If the investment was truly worth it, there wouldn't be the need for a lot of your cash, since other investors would also see the merits of the investment and flock to it.
- The pressure is on to close the deal immediately. Good investments always last longer than one week—as does the opportunity to invest in them.
- You have never heard of the company trying to sell you the investment.
- You have never heard of the company being invested in.
- The salesman is unwilling to send you information about his or her company in the mail (if they say it will take too long, tell 'em to FedEx it!).
- You can only deal with the firm over the phone. (Try finding their offices and find out how long they've been in business there.)
- You're told there's no way you can lose money in the deal.
- You're promised you'll get rich quickly.
- It's undeveloped land.

Most of us have probably been solicited by a scheme at least once in our lives. A chain letter is a scheme—promising untold riches that will materialize if only you participate and pass it on. Pass it up.

The Ponzi scheme is a classic investment scam which was recently replayed in the 1995 New Era scandal (which saw some of the world's wealthiest and smartest investors get burned to the tune of hundreds of millions of dollars). It's named after its most famous practitioner, Charles Ponzi, a 1920s scamster par excellence. In a Ponzi scheme, an investor is asked to invest a sum of money today with the promise of huge (above-market) returns. The scamster then apparently delivers the goods, with substantial "interest," just as he said he would. The same investor is then asked if he or she would like to invest in another project. Naturally, since the investor has just been given proof positive that this is a legitimate investment—after all, how else could the money have grown so quickly, and why else would this person have paid off—the investor consents. Filled with confidence, more money is often invested the second time around. However, how the money grows so quickly isn't discussed. (And here's where you can spot a Ponzi scheme from the outset: ask for specific details about how, when, and where the money will be invested, then track down the investment at its source. No luck? Walk.) How does the money grow so rapidly? Simple. The scam artist's ability to grow your money depends on his or her ability to recruit other investors whose money he or she then uses to pay you off. This can go on for many levels, until the scamster has accumulated enough dough to make it worth his or her while to move on (often to a country with rather lax extradition laws). You may have invested five or more times—but it's the one time the scamster doesn't make good that can make clear your financial folly.

Before you invest in anything, be sure you understand what you are investing in and more. For example, if it's a stock in a company you have never heard of before, track down the company's whereabouts, ask for its annual report, and call a few other brokers to ask what they might think about it. (Or ask other investors on-line.) Diligence in determining whether or not an investment is legitimate is as important as determining whether and to what extent it is appropriate for your objectives. Likewise, when it comes to those who would advise you about where to invest your money, you need to know who you are dealing with. Chapters 16 and 17 will help you do just that.

READY RESOURCES

- *Money*, (800) 633-9970.
- *Smart Money*, (800) 444-4204.
- *Worth*, (800) 777-1851, 800-278-5511.
- *Your Money*, (312) 275-3590.
- *Kiplinger's Personal Finance*, (800) 544-0155.
- *Fortune*, (800) 541-1000.
- *Barron's Guide to Making Investments*, by D. Sease, Prentice Hall.
- *101 Investment Decision Tools*, by J. Shim, Login Publishers.
- *Alchemy of Finance*, by G. Soros, John Wiley.
- *Standard & Poor's Sector Investing 95*, Standard & Poor, McGraw-Hill.

- *The Only Investment Guide You'll Ever Need,* Revised and Updated, by Andrew Tobias, Harvest Books.
- *Wall Street Journal Guide to Money and Investing,* by K. Morris, Simon & Schuster.
- *Investing on Your Own,* by D. Rankin, St. Martin's Press.

CHAPTER SIXTEEN

How to Buy Stocks, Bonds, and Mutual Funds

O K. You've got it. You want to invest. But you don't want to have to open up a Swiss bank account and establish residency offshore in order to shelter your $327 from fee-hungry brokers. But when you asked your best friend if he was investing, all he could do was smirk and tell you that thanks to Uncle Marcos, not only won't he ever have to work again, he won't have to worry about investing either—some guy in a pin-striped suit will do it for him. Your dad and mom are still arguing over whether or not they should purchase a new car or take advantage of the sale on twin cemetery plots (a guaranteed inflation-beating investment). You don't know where to turn.

GETTING STARTED

Talk is cheap. (Unless you're calling your psychic at her 900 number.) But while actions may speak louder than words, they can also—when it comes to actually investing your money—put you and your savings at risk. And I'm not talking about the risks associated with the various types of investment vehicles we've been exploring. I'm talking about the more subtle risks of the cost associated with investing. Whether it's a front-end load on a mutual fund, a commission charged by your broker on a stock or bond purchase, or a percentage charged for services rendered by your money manager, there are several ways in which you can lose money before a single dime gets invested.

As the markets and the types of investments offered have grown dramatically over the last decade, so too has the potential for complication and cost when it comes to the individual investor and his or her investing. Fortunately, today's individual investor has several cost-cutting advantages over our predecessors—thanks to keen competition among the brokerages for our business. Simple to learn. Easy to implement. You don't want to miss out on the following cost-cutting investing strategies. After all, the reward of learning what follows is that more of your hard-earned money goes directly to work for you.

Not surprisingly, buying stocks, bonds, and mutual funds isn't all that difficult. After all, what kind of a product would it be that failed to enable its buyer easy access to ownership? But there are some basic mechanics involved in the purchasing of each category of investment just mentioned (and real estate is another category with its own rules of buying and selling). How do you begin?

Opening a Brokerage Account

When it comes to buying stocks and most types of bonds you'll need to open up a brokerage account. While you don't have to go to the brokerage office in person, the process will probably be easier if you do. Like opening a bank account, opening a brokerage account is relatively easy once you know the ropes. And, as with a bank account, different types of brokerages will offer you more or less for your money, both in terms of the services they offer and the price you'll pay for those services.

Large or small, brokerage firms all charge you a fee for just about any service they perform for you. That's why you need to know the fees you will be charged for every service that your brokerage (or mutual fund company) offers—and periodically review those fees, comparing them what you were charged last year by your existing firm and with what other firms are charging now for similar services. That's the only way you can rest assured that your firm's fees aren't outlandishly high. (If they're outlandishly low, keep it quiet.)

There are three types of brokerages—full service, discount, and deep discount. As with a gas station, it's in your savings' favor to avoid full service. Full-service brokers cost you more money in fees and commissions every time you buy or sell (or even hold) a stock, bond, or mutual fund. You may like to pay more for the luxury of someone filling your own tank—but you get the same amount of gas in your tank for less money if you opt for self-service. Discount brokers offer you the opportunity to service your account yourself while at the same time providing you with many of the services that full-service brokers offer—from research to monthly account statements. Not only does opting for a discount broker make smart money sense—it also gives you a more direct involvement with your money and your investments.

If you're able to make reasonable investment choices, the more involved you are in your investment decisions, the better off you're likely to be in terms of making moves that relate to your objectives and goals. (You'll certainly never sell yourself a doggy stock just because the brokerage is sitting on a big pile of it.)

Before you choose a broker, be sure to contact the National Association of Security Dealers (NASD) at (800) 289-9999 to receive a background check on any broker you're thinking of hiring. The NASD will notify you whether or not the broker has a bad record —which is well worth knowing in advance. Failing to do so, after all, could have you singing the blues.

FULL SERVICE COSTS YOU MORE

Traditionally, full service offered you the most "service"—from fulfilling your requests for analyst reports on stocks you were interested in buying or selling to actively managing your account for you to making purchase and sale recommendations. But such services don't come cheap. Fees and commissions could run in the neighborhood of 3 percent or more for every purchase (or sale) of a stock, bond, or mutual fund.

While it's clearly in your savings' favor to avoid full-service brokers, there are some strengths that full-service brokerages feel should be noted—and scrutinized. Foremost among the strengths is the amount of research you'll be able to get your hands on by calling your broker. But there's a catch: this research will be done in-house, by the brokerage's team of analysts who, naturally enough, won't diverge dramatically from your broker's point of view—not to mention the broker's list of stocks he's under pressure to sell. Moreover, while this kind of research is among the best the Street has to offer, it's no longer as proprietary as it once was. In fact, thanks to the Internet (see chapter 20), you can set up your own hot list of investment sources for free, which can prove to be at least as useful to you in your investment decisions.

Don't Discount These Advantages

If you don't like to pay more for the luxury of someone doing a job that you can do for yourself, discount brokers are for you. Moreover, today's discount brokers provide many of the same services that full-service brokers offer—from research that's specific to your individual investments to monthly statements of your account and transactions. It costs you less primarily because you'll be making the investment decisions and calling them to make your trades, whereas a full-service broker will be calling you with suggested trades. Self-service gives you more direct involvement with and control of your investments to achieve your objectives. Discount brokers are user-friendly. Convenient. Reliable. Hey, they're the smart way to invest. So where's the catch? Not all discount brokers are created equal. In fact, the difference between some discount brokers (in particular, those who fall between the discount and deep-discount categories) can be as significant as the difference between a discount and full-service brokerage. In fact, where a discount brokerage firm can save you in excess of 50 percent on commissions (the fees charged to your account for buying or selling an investment), a deep discounter can save you as much as 90 percent on the same transaction, but there will be no service perks. And today, trading your account on-line can save you an additional 10 percent or more off regular full-service and discount brokerage commissions.

The following brokerages are among the leading discounters and they also offer you the convenience and cost advantage of on-line trading. Five of the largest discount brokerages, together with their toll-free numbers, are: Fidelity Broker Services, (800) 544-7272; Quick & Reilly, (800) 522-8712; T. Rowe Price Discount Brokerage, (800) 638-5660; Charles Schwab, (800) 648-5300; and Jack White & Co., (800) 323-3263.

COMPARING THE COSTS

The firms, services, and charges for everything from placing a phone call to placing an order differ widely from one full-service broker to the next—and from one discounter to the next. As a result, you'll need to do your own cost comparison, similar to the one described in chapter 5 when it came to selecting the best type of bank account and best type of bank for you and your needs. Create your own comparison using the following checklist as your guide:

* How long has the firm been in existence?
* Does it have an office in your area?
* How many offices does it have?
* How many brokers does it employ?
* How many institutional accounts does it manage?
* How many retail (individual investor) accounts does it have?
* How many retail (individual investor) accounts did it have two years ago?
* What commissions are charged for:
    1,000 shares @ $5
    1,000 shares @ $25
    500 shares @ $5
    500 shares @ $25
    100 shares @ $10
    10 shares @ $20
    1 share @ $50
* What is the minimum commission charged?
* Is there a dividend reinvestment plan you can participate in?
* Do they offer IRA accounts?
* What is the fee for starting, maintaining, and closing an IRA account?
* Can you buy no-load, no-transaction-fee funds?

Opening the Account

You don't need a brokerage account to invest. You can invest, for example, in mutual funds by directly contacting the fund company. But if you're going to buy individual stocks or bonds, or if you want to participate in one of the best innovations in the mutual fund industry in the last decade—namely, mutual fund networks (more about this later)—then you'll be better off with a brokerage account. With this in mind, selecting the best brokerage and type of account for you is obviously an important thing to do.

As previously mentioned, opening a brokerage account is mechanically as easy as opening up a checking account at your local bank. (For that matter, many banks offer you the option of buying stocks, bonds, and even mutual funds—for a fee. But chances are the performance record of your bank's mutual funds isn't nearly as great as their marketing is designed to have you believe.) But, opening a brokerage account is somewhat more intimidating. Not mechanically, but psychologically. After all, you're taking a giant step toward admitting that, at least in some sense, you've grown up. However, just because the mechanics of opening up a brokerage account are easy, it doesn't mean the task of selecting a suitable firm to meet your specific investment needs is a no-brainer. There are steps you'll need to take:

Step 1: Before you open a brokerage account, quiz yourself. When it comes to making a decision about what's best for you, you:

[ ] like to be in total control, even if it means having to spend extra time learning about the best avenues for getting you to where you ultimately want to be.

[ ] seek others' counsel when it comes to making decisions but ultimately make up your own mind as to what is best for you.

[ ] feel better listening to someone else's advice and judgment about what is best for you.

[ ] would rather pay someone to do a job that you could do yourself but don't have the time to learn to do it right now.

[ ] would rather learn some basic skills to ensure that you can at least judge whether or not the person you hired to do a job is, in fact, doing a good job.

[ ] have a bookshelf full of Time-Life do-it-yourself plumbing, home wiring, and roofing books, and all of them are dog-eared from overuse.

While these questions may seem unrelated to the simple step of opening a brokerage account, think again. If you're the type of person who likes to be in total control, then chances are you will fare well with a deep-discount brokerage. If, on the other hand, you would rather pay someone to do the job, then chances are a full-service brokerage is the road to take—at least until you get the hang of it. The bottom line is that deciding upon the type of investor you are planning to be—active, semiactive, or hands off—directly affects the type of brokerage you should select.

Step 2: You'll need to determine the type of ownership on the account:

1. Single Account: The account is solely in your name. You have sole authority to purchase and sell investments in your account.

2. Joint Account: This allows two signers to authorize the purchase and sale of investments in the account.

Step 3: Once you've decided who has access to your money, you'll need to establish the type of account that you want to open. You can choose from among the following:

1. Cash Account: In a cash account, all your transactions must be paid for in cash. When you open your account, you'll open a money market account or set up an automatic withdrawal through your existing checking account at your bank. Transfer of funds will be done electronically—so long as there are sufficient funds to cover your moves. The best way to cover your bets is to be able to pay them in full.

2. Margin Account: In contrast to a cash account, a margin account enables you to buy "on margin." Buying on margin is similar to taking out a loan to place a bet. Sound stupid? Well, some hotshots think they've got a sure thing—and margin their bet by as much as 50 percent of their brokerage account balance—to place their bet. But since none of us is infallible, it's clearly a risky way to invest. Not only that. As with a loan, you're charged interest on the margined amount (typically based on the prime rate plus 2 percent or more). What happens if the bet fails to materialize? Talk to Rocko.

3. Discretionary Account: What could be worse than you risking up to a 100 percent loss of your savings by investing on margin? Letting someone else do it for you! A discretionary account

allows your broker to invest your money at his or her discretion without getting your authority for each trade. Wrong!

Step 4: You need to match your investment plan with an account that can put your plan into action. Will you be making annual lump sum payments, monthly payments, or weekly payments into your account? How will your funds be allocated, when will they be disbursed, and at whose command? With these general facts and figures in mind, you can begin to examine what kind of brokerage account fits your unique situation.

Once you've figured out what type of brokerage and account is best for you, what amount you want to invest, and how you want to invest it, chances are you can do the rest of the work by simply picking up a phone and requesting the necessary paperwork. Or you can do it on-line in some instances (for more on this, see chapter 20). No matter what the sales pitch, however, don't lose sight of the fees you'll be charged. They add up—to no good.

Maintaining Your Account

You will need to keep tabs on your brokerage account much the way you do your bank account and loan statements. You should scrutinize every statement you receive from your broker to ensure the following:

[ ] Confirmation of all transactions (should be received within 24 hours since you have a maximum of five days to settle the trade)
[ ] Authorization of all transactions
[ ] Shares bought and sold at number and price agreed on
[ ] No unauthorized trades
[ ] (In any discretionary accounts) No excessive trading (known as "churning," which is, basically, one way a broker can generate more commissions for him- or herself by trading in your account often—too often)
[ ] What's in your account is what you expect to be there.

If there's any disagreement on one or more of the above, get a specific explanation from your broker. If you can't get satisfaction, try a higher level in the firm. Still no dice? You may have to contact the NASD for further advice.

How to Invest Without Opening a Brokerage Account

You can invest directly through the company or agency which issues the security or fund. Doing so can save you money, if not time. The following are some of the most straightforward ways to bypass the middleman and put more of your money to work for you.

STOCK PURCHASE PLANS: As discussed in the previous chapter, if you work for a company that is publicly traded, chances are you have the opportunity to participate in something called a stock purchase plan. Such plans offer you more than the convenience of buying the stock directly (no brokerage hassles whatsoever). For another, you can often purchase the stock at a discount to the listed purchase price of your company's stock. Such plans also provide you with an opportunity to reap some of the benefits of the future profitability of your firm—if, that is, you stay employed long enough to accumulate a sizeable stake in the company stock, and provided that your company is profitable. The last point should be your foremost concern when it comes to your participation in a stock purchase plan. If your company ceases to be profitable, or worse, goes belly-up, then you kiss all the advantages of this option good-bye. Is it worth the risk? You have the best inside track when it comes to being able to forecast your company's future worth. I think it's well worth considering, but I wouldn't let my investment in a stock purchase plan exceed 15 percent of my overall investment portfolio.

DIVIDEND REINVESTMENT PLANS (DRIPs): A DRIP is one of the best ways to purchase additional shares in a company whose stock you already own as it enables you to reinvest the dividends automatically in new shares of the stock. For more information on DRIPs, see page 192.

INVESTMENT CLUBS: Investment clubs are an increasingly popular way to invest—either as a group that meets on a regular basis and invests by consensus, or in a more informal way, through on-line groups which serve more as further resources (and plenty of opinion) about which way to invest in a market, industry, or stock. Strictly speaking, however, the former group is the one that most people think of. The definition is elastic, but an investment club, like the famous Beardstown Ladies, is a group of individuals (few if any professional investors among them) who meet regularly to review and revise their investments and investment strategies by pooling their knowledge and analytical resources to determine what to invest in. (See chapter 18 for more details).

How to Buy Mutual Funds

As we discussed earlier, for younger investors, mutual funds will probably be the way to go. So, for example, you will need to figure out which mutual fund companies offer you the best investment alternatives and low-fee deals. (Chapter 13 helps you sort this out.) Once you have accomplished this, you can simply dial the fund company and request an account application, the prospectuses for the funds you are interested in, and, if you believe in the company but don't know the names of specific funds they offer, you can also ask the investor representative to send you several fund prospectuses that relate to your investment interest and objectives. You can also ask if the fund company has any investing pamphlets or brochures that help explain mutual fund investing. Many do—and many are well written and objective when it comes to discussing the mechanics of mutual fund investing. You can do the same thing with brokerage firms for stocks and bonds. However, you need to be sure that such pamphlets aren't your only source of information about investing.

There are two great ways to purchase mutual funds: direct from the fund company, or through a fund network. There's also one lousy way: through a broker who will charge you for the privilege. Forget about it! Like purchasing stocks and bonds, buying shares in a mutual fund requires due diligence on your part. Some fund companies more closely resemble full-service brokerage accounts, with fees to match or best even the most greedy brokerage. Others provide you with ways to get more of your money working for you from day one. For now, let's look at the mechanics of buying shares in a fund.

One option is to buy directly from a fund company. All you need do is contact the fund company by phone and request the prospectuses and applications of the funds that match your needs and interests. The list that begins on page 171 will certainly speed up this process, but you can always dial up (800) 555-1212 and ask for the fund company's toll-free number if one isn't listed in the back of this book. Moreover, if you can get on-line and/or to the Web, there are a host of fund families which are hot-wired to your needs for prospectuses, annual reports, and investment guides. You'll simply need to fill in some blanks and let the fund company and the post office (or e-mail) do the legwork for you. Either way, once you receive the prospectuses and applications (which you'll be able to complete in short order), you can either take it to a branch office of the fund company or mail it back to them. Also, be sure to take advantage of setting up an automatic investment account, directly withdrawing from your checking account on a regularly scheduled basis so that your investing process is both specified and seamless.

It's easier to buy funds from several fund families today than it was just a few years ago, due to the introduction of fund networks. Fund networks are basically supermarkets of funds, offering hundreds of funds from over fifty fund families. While there are several fund networks that you can choose from, the three front-runners remain the three first-comers to this arena: Fidelity's Funds-Network, Charles Schwab's Mutual Fund Marketplace and One-Source, and Jack White's Mutual Fund Network. While opening up a fund network account is a great idea for most fund investors, in particular for you since the initial investment can be as low as $500 for an IRA account or $1,000 for a taxable account, there are differences between networks which you will need to know about in order to help you make the best selection for your specific fund investment needs and objectives.

Fund networks offer a menu of funds from different fund families, which, in turn, enables you to tailor-make your overall portfolio. Take a look at just some of the following fund families currently participating in the Fidelity, Schwab, and/or White networks:

American Heritage	Cohen & Steers	Janus
Ariel	Crabbe Huson	Kaufmann
Artisan	Dreyfus	Lexington
Babson	FAM	Merger
Baron	Fidelity	Montgomery
Benham	Founders	Neuberger & Berman
Berger	Gabelli	Oberweis
Blanchard	Guiness Flight	PBHG
Bramwell	Heartland	Rainier
Bull & Bear	Hotchkis & Wiley	Robertson Stephens
Cappiello-Rushmore	IAI	Royce

Rushmore	Strong	Wasatch
Schafer	United Services	Wright Equifunds
Skyline	Vontobel	Yacktman
SteinRoe	Warburg Pincus	

For a complete list of the specific mutual funds available through any of these networks, call them directly or visit them on-line for more details. Be sure to get and read the prospectus before investing in any fund, and research the fund relative to its peers and your own portfolio.

Why is investing in funds from different fund families advisable? Though many fund companies will deny it, groupthink is a pervasive and persuasive influence on fund managers under one family's roof. Also, some fund families have historically delivered better results in stock selection, others have surpassed their peers with bond selection, while still others have a better record abroad than at home. Participating in a fund network will enable you to select funds from those families which have delivered superior results in the past and enjoy access to lesser known and newer funds, as well as achieve the diverse portfolio that is key to your success.

With the advent of the networks came a new fee designation for mutual funds—the no-transaction-fee, or NTF, fund. Basically, an NTF fund has no up-front transaction fee associated with your purchase. Funds charging loads are not NTF funds, although some load funds may waive their loads for fund networks.

Take a look at the Network Review chart on page 210. This network snapshot will help you picture how the networks compare to one another. While the number of funds, fees, and minimums are subject to change, the chart will also help you create your own network checklist before you sign up.

You're sold on investing. Now you are also able to decide which is the best way for you to buy your investments. What's next? The next chapter will help you decide where to turn to for financial advice.

1995 Network Review

Network	NTF Fund Families	NTF Funds	Non-NTF Funds	Minimum Initial Investment	Transaction Fee on Sample Trade		Advantages	Disadvantages
Fidelity Funds Network	45	370+	1,600+	$2,500 or the minimum amount for the fund if higher	$5,000 $10,000 $25,000	$57.50 $69.50 $89.50	Comprehensive statements; Fidelity no-load funds are NTF; service	Highest minimum investment & minimum balance; highest transaction rates for trades below $9,800
Charles Schwab One Source & Mutual Fund Marketplace	45	300+	600+	The greater of $1,000 or the minimum amount for the fund	$5,000 $10,000 $25,000	$39 $70 $125	Service; on simultaneous sell & buy order you pay flat $25 fee for the less expensive side on non-NTF funds	Worst to buy low load funds (under 4%)—charges transaction fee & load; 90-day early redemption fee for NTF funds
Jack White Mutual Fund Network	100	680+	500+	The greater of $1,000 or the minimum amount for the fund	$5,000 $10,000 $25,000	$27 $35 $35	Lowest transaction fees; low minimum investment; largest selection of NTF funds	Lowest level of service

CHAPTER SEVENTEEN

What to Look For in a Financial Advisor

O K," he tells you, "I admit it. I sought counseling the other day to confront a side of myself I rarely like to see—the cold, hard, objective assessment of my real value as a human being. Here's what I learned. First, my technology fetish is now considered to be a sign of normality. Second, my desire for health care could leave me in critical condition. Third, I've been living in denial—clearly manifested by manic purchases like the BMW in the parking lot that I refused to admit was mine. What could my counselor do to help me? The answer, he claimed, lay somewhere in his shorts."

Even if you don't know much, chances are better than even that you know that selecting a financial advisor isn't as easy as changing your shorts. In fact, it's a difficult task and one whose difficulty is compounded by the obvious—few of us really know what we're looking for in an advisor, and few advisors are willing to get to know who we are (since we haven't yet made big money). Which points to one basic fact—that we ought to be able to do this for ourselves, at least in the beginning. But let's say you just have to have an advisor. Chances are you don't—but let's say you think you do. This chapter's for you.

PROFESSIONAL DESIGNATIONS

You could hang your shingle out tomorrow and be a financial advisor. Of course, a certificate won't guarantee investment success any more than past performance will. Anybody with a fairly good background in accounting, or even somebody who has taught themselves to read financial statements, can do value investing. Some think that when it comes to investing, a number of advanced degrees don't necessarily add a lot of value. But you'll want to know whether your advisor and firm are momentum-driven or strictly bottom-up stock pickers. Take a look:

CERTIFIED FINANCIAL PLANNER (CFP): This certificate, issued by the Institute of Certified Financial Planners, signifies that the individual who has earned it has passed a series of tests which attest to their ability to review and advise clients on a host of financial concerns, including banking, estate planning, insurance, investing, and taxes. Be advised that tests are no substitute for experience, intelligence, and integrity.

CERTIFIED PUBLIC ACCOUNTANT (CPA): A rigorous examination process, coupled with definable, relevant, and applicable experience and state licensing, yield one of the more meaningful professional designations for those whose career is focused on accounting, auditing, and tax preparation. This designation is an excellent indicator of a level of proficiency in the aforementioned fields, but is less indicative of the person's ability to advise you on non-tax-related investment matters.

CHARTERED FINANCIAL ANALYST (CFA): Like the CPA designation, this one denotes a person who has passed a rigorous three-year examination process, coupled with definable, relevant, and applicable experience in the fields of economics, ethics, financial accounting, portfolio management, and hardcore security analysis. Among those who would proclaim themselves qualified to analyze an investment's fundamental worth and appropriateness to particular portfolios, those with CFAs typically stand out.

CHARTERED FINANCIAL CONSULTANT (ChFC). An excellent addition to the CFP designation, this charter is offered to those who are CFPs and who have successfully passed a four-year program at the College of Bryn Mawr covering economics, insurance, investing, and taxes.

CHARTERED MUTUAL FUND COUNSELOR (CMFC): This new designation offered by the National Endowment for Financial Education enhances the ability of financial advisors to speak directly to their clients' mutual fund questions and concerns.

QUESTION THE "EXPERTS"

Don't get into bed with the first advisor you meet—or with an advisor you've just met. Remember, behind the vertical pinstripes lurks a horizontal interest—getting into your sack of money. A socio-anthropologist could tell you the ways in which investment advisors symbolize what car and real estate salespeople mimic every day. It's the deal of a lifetime, raised to a highbrow art form.

Typically, in under one hour, you'll be convinced that you have to make a decision which could dramatically affect the rest of your life. In a matter of a meeting or two, you'll need to assess your level of trust in the relationship with both the individual advisor and the firm, based on your general impression of their expertise and depth of knowledge. Select a firm for which the individual business is something to which they are dedicated and an area in which they have a great deal of experience. (Avoid those that don't.)

Don't be seduced by short-term performance but, for goodness sake, pay attention to it. While it's easy to be seduced by performance, it's also the quickest way to cast yourself in the financial equivalent of the "Crying Game"—the one where you wind up needing even more counseling. Surprisingly, however, when it comes to selecting a financial advisor, performance isn't the most important criterion. In fact, it's way down the list, according to Sanford Bernstein's *The Future of Money Management in America (1995 Edition)*, which provides an annual study of the investment management industry. His list of criteria is as follows:

1. Manager's overall expertise
2. Care manager takes to identify needs
3. Trusting the manager
4. Discretion of the manager
5. Attentiveness of the manager
6. Manager's desire to establish long-term relationship
7. Manager's reputation

Note that *nothing* has been said about performance. In fact, it's not until you get further down the list that investment track record gets a mention. (And it's not rated as being very important.)

As you interview several possible advisors, consider the following questions and issues:

Are you in it for yourself? Are you only representing yourself or a wider group? It could be your spouse, children, grandchildren—all of whom have separate needs but all of whose needs have to be satisfied. Your investment counselor must have the ability to work with a variety of generations and a variety of different investors with different needs.

Is your advisor commission based or fee based? You'll need to decide between fee-based investment counselors and those that charge a percentage of your money for their business. Here's a hint: fee-based is typically the best way to go. A fee-based counselor will charge you an hourly fee (typically $150 an hour), while a commission-based advisor charges a percentage of your investment return. The larger your account becomes, the more compelling is the fee-based structure.

Do they work for you? Is your advisor listening to you—or just lumping you into a computer model which, in turn, spits out a "personal" portfolio that bears all the family resemblance of a police composite sketch? How much quality time can he or she devote to you? Is the advisor you'll be working with experienced in your type of account? The better they can understand your needs, the better they can appreciate what is left unsaid by you, reading between the lines to better react to your changing circumstances and objectives.

Question the size of the firm. Is the firm too big to pay attention to you and your investment needs? Do you feel like Kafka's "K" outside *The Castle*—or Terry Gilliam in *Brazil*? (Run, don't walk, to the nearest exit.) Does the person answering the phone recognize who you are? No? How about your advisor?

Unfortunately, going with a smaller firm may not be a better bet. For one thing, the head of the firm—you know, the one who is going to run your account—will more than likely be doing many things besides managing your money. Chances are he's out pitching his business to prospective clients. You don't want to end up with a chief cook and bottle washer. No matter what the size of the firm, try to determine what the other diverting, distracting activities are that could potentially impinge on your advisor's overall workload.

Research the research. Know your firm's research capabilities. Resources clearly contribute to the quantification of overall expertise of management, so that the extent to which there are broad and deep resources would be a measure of potential expertise. However, a brokerage firm's research department, whose reports can be very good, have an ulterior purpose—to create transactions for the brokerage firm. Not so with an investment counselor who is fee based, i.e., not trying to sell you anything other than his or her service. (Think of your hair salon; they cut your hair for a flat fee—but do they try to sell you some overpriced styling gel?) Does your advisor do his or her own research? Are the facilities to do the research on the premises? Ask to be shown the research room of the firm—and ask to speak directly with the analysts. Even if you don't intend to invest globally, an knowledge of global competitors is useful. An advisor with a worldwide perspective understands the global competition that even domestically oriented companies now face.

WHY TENURE IS SIGNIFICANT. One of the least desirable characteristics you can face as a client is constant turnover in your representative. Is it going to be necessary to meet someone new every two to four years? Or will there be a continuity of relationship? Look for somebody who has at least a ten-year record. The reason for that is you can have five-year records that comprise a fairly attractive period in the market. Sometimes you don't get a full market cycle unless you go through ten years—a period in which you're more likely to see someone who has managed money in both a difficult market and a strong one. How did their portfolios fare on October 18, 1987 (the day after the crash)—and how did they finish up the year?

Find the person who is responsible for that ten-year record. In other words, if you're going to a firm and talking to them but the management of the firm has changed or the senior participants of the firm have changed, the ten-year record they're showing you may not be reflective of the current management. (When a mutual fund changes managers, it's a new fund.) Finally, the average tenure of a counselor at a firm establishes to some extent the firm's ability to provide a setting and an environment which keeps its good managers—and culls the bad.

Quality of the personnel and their experience is probably the most important single factor. But make sure that the advisor can describe in a commonsense, straightforward manner how he or she buys stocks and bonds. The explanation ought to be coherent, easy to understand, and they ought to be able to describe how they sell securities. Also, ask how much of that manager's marketable net worth is invested in the manner he or she is suggesting your money ought to be invested. If you're talking to a financial advisor who uses mutual funds as investment vehicles, for example, you would want to know that advisor had a significant portion of his or her marketable net worth invested in those same funds. That way, your financial advisor should ideally share your downside as well as your upside.

REFERENCES? Try asking your accountant and attorney. Ask your estate planning attorney. Even your divorce attorney.

DO YOU WANT ONE-STOP SHOPPING? Are you looking to find trusteeship services alongside investment counseling? Do you want your advisor to be able to counsel you in noninvestment areas like estate planning? If so, you'll want that expertise either within the actual counselor or the firm. But be forewarned that there are financial planners who hang out shingles as qualified advisors that can do everything and be all things to all people. If they sell insurance, or if they do wrap fees, they're doing it to you, all right.

DO YOU WANT SIGNIFICANT INPUT IN THE MANAGEMENT OF YOUR MONEY? Some firms will let you steer the ship, others won't take accounts unless they're on a fully discretionary basis. If you are you prepared to give up day-to-day control of your money, be sure that you ask for an investment memorandum outlining the advisor's understanding of your objectives and the general approach to be used in managing your account. You needn't go into specifics initially, but do set up the framework. Make the advisor understand what your objectives are, where the portfolio is now, and where you plan to go over the next six-month, year, five-year, and ten-year periods. Some kind of a written understanding of how the account is going to be managed makes good sense.

IS THE FIRM RESEARCH OR MARKETING DRIVEN? Is the firm built one investor at a time—or more than one successful investment over time? A long history of solid performance is more impressive than a long history of a company's existence. A marketing-driven firm will spend a lot of money on salespeople selling the firm and its products to you. A research-oriented firm will spend a lot of money on analysts in order to ferret out investment opportunities.

PERFORMANCE. Don't be seduced by it. In fact, you'd be better off resisting spectacular numbers. A reasonable range is a firm that achieves rates of return in the 8 to 12 percent compounded range on an annualized basis. Advisors producing returns in excess of 20 percent compounded should ring alarm bells in your head! Bottom line: if the pitch sounds too good to be true, step back from the plate. If, on the other hand, you think you have received satisfactory answers to your questions, try a short-term relationship on for size. It might fit your needs forever and a day—or just for this stage of your life.

READY RESOURCES

- Director of Arbitration, New York Stock Exchange, (212) 656-3000.
- Director of Arbitration, National Association of Security Dealers, (212) 480-4881.
- American Arbitration Association, (212) 484-4000.
- The Administrative List, North American Securities Administrators Association, (202) 737-0900.
- Broker/Planner Background Checks, (202) 737-0900.
- Institute of Certified Financial Planners, (800) 282-7526.
- International Association for Financial Planning, (800) 945-4237.
- International Board of Standards and Practices for Certified Financial Planners, (303) 830-7543.
- National Association of Personal Financial Advisers, (708) 537-7722.
- SEC-Registered Investment Advisors, (202) 272-3100.

CHAPTER EIGHTEEN

Investment Clubs

Remember how cool it was to create a club among your friends: secret passwords, ripped-out maps from your mom's *National Geographic*, the close attic air where you met to build model rockets—a world made woozy with model glue and chalk dust from the wall where you wrote out the day's agenda? Investment clubs aren't too different from the clubs we formed as children, although this time the goal isn't the moon—it's down-to-earth profit making. And profit making, as the Beardstown Ladies have so finely demonstrated, is within the grasp of a disciplined club. The flip side? A poorly managed investment club can be a great way to self-destruct both your friendships and your finances. However, as with investing itself, setting up a club can be done so that both the risks and the potential returns are managed in proportion to one another.

Starting an investment club is a smart move. Not only can you pool resources and so diversify a portfolio in stocks, bonds, and mutual funds, you can probably do so at a discount (relative to the size of the club's account and the brokerage service you jointly decide to use). Another benefit is knowledge. With several club members researching, analyzing, and sharing their insights in their specified industry or general market observations, you stand to learn and know more about both.

Investment clubs are an increasingly popular way to share friend-ship and profit. In fact, there are over 50,000 investment clubs in existence today, with more than a quarter of those clubs being active members of the National Association of Investors Corpora-tion (NAIC). The NAIC individual membership is over 250,000 in-vestors.

Does starting or joining an investment club make sense for you? While you may not have a lot of money or market know-how to your credit, you may be an asset to an existing club or, if you start your own, the source of inspiration. The following checklist will help you determine whether or not an investment club might make sense for you:

[ ] Do you like making decisions on your own, or do you find other opinions helpful to your overall decision-making process?

[ ] Will you be disciplined enough in your own research and analysis on a regular basis such that you will be able to say with certainty why you have selected, held, or sold every stock, bond, and mutual fund in your overall portfolio?

[ ] Do you enjoy talking with others about investment oppor-tunities?

[ ] Does the thought of sharing the management decisions that affect your money make you feel better or worse about investing?

If, after answering the above, you find that you are the type of person who likes to make decisions on your own, then have no fear, you're completely normal. In fact, it's probably better to at least start on your own in order to sort out the type of investor you are (i.e., determine through trial and error the investment style and investments that suit you and your objectives). If you decide that this is the path you will take, you will find that there's an association assigned for the individual investor—the American Association of Individual Investors.

HOW TO JOIN A CLUB

If you decide that joining a club would be worth a try, contact the NAIC for a list of clubs in your area. While club members are likely to be as suspicious about you as you are about them, you might find a familiar face or common ground (shared work history or schooling) that can help each of you feel more comfortable. Be sure you get to the bottom of the club's policies, procedures, and investment style and objectives before you overcommit yourself to it. Chances are that you will find most clubs are slanted toward a much older age group whose investment style and objectives, as well as the type of investments they select, simply don't relate to your own. Nevertheless, you can make good use of an existing club in terms of learning how they set it up—from membership to research to the brokerage account they use to what problems they had to overcome (which, knowing them in advance, you might be able to circumvent if you were to start your own club).

How to Start Your Own Club

Perhaps the best way to start your own club is to join the NAIC and pore over the materials they send you. These materials will help you decide between creating a club—which takes up-front time, and long-term (five-plus years) commitment—versus investing on your own. If, after due deliberation, you decide setting up a club works for you, then you'll need to begin the process of designing the club's investment principles and objectives, as well as to initiate your search for members.

You may already know who you want. If not, you can consider colleagues at work or among your friends and neighbors. (Faith in the almighty dollar has an interesting way of bonding people together.) But don't let anyone join for the asking. Be selective. Be up-front. Be prepared for questions concerning how the club works, what time and money commitments have to be made, who makes the ultimate investment decision (regarding what to buy, sell, hold), and much more.

The first meeting can be informal, but you'll need to ensure that it is also informative. You can, for example, bring your package of NAIC material to the meeting to show potential members what's in store. Open the meeting to discussion about the direction, operation, and objective of the club. Keep the mood light but the minds focused on the benefits of investing long term. If you have PowerPoint at home, create a little show on the beneficial effects of investing in stocks and stock mutual funds versus other types of investments. You'll set the tone for potential enjoyment and profit making. Investing is fun; losing money never is. It's up to you to make certain that each member has a seriously good time. To make certain everyone is on the same level, bring NAIC application forms with you to the first meeting, and basically insist that everyone become a member. (No, I don't work for NAIC. But I do think that if you are going to start a club, you and your potential members will benefit from this membership. I also strongly recommend that you purchase *The Investment Club Book*, by John Wasik—the best book on investment clubs on the shelf.) And, of course, don't forget to set the time and date of your next meeting (typically within two weeks' time).

You might even consider giving potential members a pop quiz—which you will take too—just to gauge how much (or little) each individual knows about investing. Don't make it too highbrow, but do point out the strength of knowing one's weaknesses. The following quiz might help you on your way:

1. What is the difference between value and growth investment styles?
2. How do you calculate the P/E of a stock?
3. What is a dividend yield? How is it calculated?
4. What is a growth stock?
5. What is the difference between a 12b-1 fee and a load?
6. What would you consider to be an adequate allocation among stocks and bonds for your age group (25 to 35)?
7. What is the advantage of a discount broker over a full-service broker?
8. How many individual stocks do you own?
9. How many mutual funds do you own?
10. What number of funds would you need to create a diversified portfolio?
11. How long have you been invested in the market?
12. When will you need the money you invest with the club?
    [ ] within 5 years   [ ] 5 or more years   [ ] 10-plus years

The results will help those individuals who are lacking to shift into high gear and prove to themselves and you that they're committed to working in the club's (as well as their own) best interest.

The first formal meeting will need to accomplish three things: establish operational procedures and roles, determine the initial investment amount as well as how you plan to take your initial plunge into the market as a club, and draft the partnership.

Setting up a club is serious business. Part of the sobering side of doing so is setting up the partnership, which will be the legal entity that represents the club in the real world—from its banking, brokerage, and investment accounts. Setting up a partnership will be explained in detail in the NAIC club kit, but the following pieces of the overall partnership puzzle should be in place before you advance the club from investing theory to investment practice.

[ ] Name and date of the partnership formation
[ ] Signature of partners
[ ] Contribution agreement
[ ] Disbursement of profits and losses to partners
[ ] Bank and brokerage accounts
[ ] Value of partnership share
[ ] Tax identification number of club

You will no doubt need to elect a scribe to take down notes about the meeting and to write a brief summary for ensuing meetings. This is necessary since, after all, agreements on the club's most valuable assets—money—are being made and transacted during this time. This can be rotational, since it's a bore. You will want to elect officials and a president as well as decide who will serve as a tiebreaker in case there are an even number of votes for and against a specific investment. As you go forward, the following agenda will help you on your way to running an efficient meeting:

[ ] Review minutes of previous meeting.
[·] Review company, industry, market, and economic news. You might want to assign members specific "beats" to report on. But every member ought to be vigilant in terms of the markets and the club's investments.
[ ] Review core (actual) investments and watch potential investments list. Creating a core list will no doubt be the order of many of your initial meetings. You can turn to chapter 14 for some details on how to build a successful investment portfolio. But be sure everyone is up to speed on basic economics, markets, and industries, too. And always keep your club's objective in mind.
[ ] Proceed to your portfolio; in the first year you'll be building

this portfolio. Portfolio building is a dynamic and fluid activity, but this doesn't mean it's unfocused. Be sure that members are in agreement from the outset as to what the portfolio's main investment objective is.

[ ] Ensure open-mindedness. New ideas, new industries or companies, the possibility of investing in international as well as domestic stocks and funds—you name it (or someone else nominates it) and, for the next meeting, prepare a brief analysis which will portend further research or the end of the idea.

INVESTING IN THE MARKET

Once you've got the basic agenda set and the partnership down, you will need to establish the club's reason for being—investing. How much should each member contribute on a monthly basis? Start small; $20 should do. And when should the club make its first investment? When you've built up $1,000, purchase shares in a money market mutual fund. From there, build into the market.

Of course, investing in the market requires that you select a brokerage, perhaps a broker, as well as the range of potential mutual fund investment opportunities. Chapters 14 and 16 examined the types and roles of brokerages in your overall investment process as an individual—and the rules generally apply here as well. Be sure that no matter what type of brokerage you select, you can invest in a wide range of securities, including DRIPs (see chapter 15) and no-load funds (chapter 13). Also, be sure that when you hire a broker, you keep tabs on him (or her). The following reminder of what to check for will help:

[ ] Confirmation of all transactions (should be received within 24 hours since you have a maximum of five days to settle the trade)
[ ] Authorization of all transactions
[ ] Shares bought, sold at number and price agreed on
[ ] Any unauthorized trades
[ ] Excessive trading (or "churning")
[ ] What's in your account is what you expect to be there

Remember: your broker works for you, so don't hesitate to make him or her explain and address any concerns you have about your account. If you are not satisfied with the answers you receive, try a higher level in the firm, or contact NASD for advice.

Clubs aren't for everyone. But, by the same token, there not just for the older set. In fact, the average monthly contribution from NAIC club members is under $45 per month. The advantages—from research to commitment—may help you stay invested and learn more about investments that you would otherwise not be inclined to do on your own. While there are drawbacks—the collapse of a club could wreak havoc on a friendship—you'll have to weigh them against the potential benefits.

READY RESOURCES

- National Association of Investors Corporation (investment club organization), (810) 583-6242.
- *The Beardstown Ladies' Stitch-in-Time Guide to Growing Your Nest Egg: Step-by-Step Planning for a Comfortable Financial Future,* by the Beardstown Ladies' Investment Club, Hyperion.
- *The Beardstown Ladies' Common-Sense Investment Guide: How We Beat the Stock Market—and How You Can, Too,* the Beardstown Ladies with Leslie Whitaker, Hyperion.
- *The Investment Club Book: Best Tips from Investment Clubs,* by John F. Wasik, Warner Books.
- *Investment Clubs: A Team Approach to the Stock Market,* by Kathryn Shaw, Dearborn.

CHAPTER NINETEEN

Ethical Investing

Perhaps the most controversial area of investing is the one that's supposed to do the most good—namely, ethical investing. The problem, in short, lies in the fact that few people can seem to agree on what constitutes an adequate definition of ethical investing. In fact, coming to ethical terms with investing is like trying to order dinner with a casual vegetarian who sometimes eats meat, a vegetarian who eats fish, and an ovalactarian who shies away from everything but a bean burrito (where the beans are definitely not fried in animal fat).

While ethical investing can mean several different things to several different investors, there are some recurring themes that most ethical investors share. Foremost among these is a concern over the role their invested dollars will play in terms of supporting companies and their products. Most ethical investors also focus on the way in which a company treats its employees. This focus typically examines whether or not a company exploits a labor force in order to minimize the expense of producing a product as well as what types of employee benefit plans are offered.

Ethical investors (as a group) also tend to see themselves in contrast with another group of investors—those who invest in "sin" stocks like tobacco and alcohol companies. Other ethical investors seek to impart their political as well as their ethical take on the world by avoiding stocks in companies that produce (in whole or in part) products for the defense industry.

If ethical investing sounds restrictive in nature, it should also by now be sounding restricted in scope. Surprisingly, however, there are many solid stock, bond, and mutual fund investment opportunities for the ethical investor to choose from. The trick is to select the best investment opportunities so that you can profit by doing good.

COMING TO TERMS WITH ETHICAL INVESTING

Take the following quiz to find out if you've got the right stuff to be an ethical investor. Note: Being an ethical investor doesn't guarantee that you're either a good investor or a good person.

1. Do you know the difference between "ethics" and "morals"?
    [ ] yes   [ ] no
2. Do you recycle?
    [ ] all   [ ] most   [ ] some   [ ] none
3. Do you know whether your bank is community
    [ ] active?   [ ] passive?   [ ] too global to act local?
4. Do you know where your clothes are made?
    [ ] all   [ ] most   [ ] some   [ ] none
5. Do you know where the materials from which your clothes are made come from?
    [ ] all   [ ] most   [ ] some   [ ] none
6. Do you know who makes the cans your soda sits in?
    [ ] yes   [ ] no
7. Did you look up the difference between "ethics" and "morals" yet?
    [ ] yes   [ ] no
8. Do you know where your over-the-counter drugs are made?
    [ ] all   [ ] most   [ ] some   [ ] none
9. Do you ever think about not buying a product because it is
    [ ] made out of a material from another (previously) living being?
    [ ] made from a natural resource as opposed to an available synthetic resource?

[ ] made by a company which also makes products designed to do harm to others?

[ ] made by a company you know nothing about?

[ ] made in a country where human rights violations are common?

[ ] made to further a cause that you wouldn't send a charitable donation to?

10. Have you ever discussed ethical investing with your
    [ ] friends?
    [ ] parents?
    [ ] colleagues?
    [ ] broker?
    [ ] investment advisor?

11. Have you ever felt remorse for purchasing a product which you found out was made by a country where freedom to invest as we do is limited or nonexistent?
    [ ] yes   [ ] no

12. Do you think the following are true?
    [ ] In China, laborers are often paid less in one week than you're paid in one hour.
    [ ] In Norway, hunting whales is celebrated.
    [ ] In Japan, ordinary investment clubs are illegal.
    [ ] In Mexico, exploiting cheap laborers threatens U.S. workers.
    [ ] In Thailand, prostitution is among the country's most profitable industries.

13. Would you ever invest in a company that either resides or does business in a place you would consider unsafe to visit?
    [ ] yes   [ ] no

14. Did you ever buy something at a local corner store (not a national chain) where you knowingly paid more for a product which you could just as easily and more cheaply have purchased from a national chain store?
    [ ] yes   [ ] no

15. Have you looked up the difference between "ethics" and "morals" yet?
    [ ] yes   [ ] no

16. Did you just look up the difference between "ethics" and "morals"?
    [ ] yes   [ ] no

17. Would you knowingly buy a product which was made by child

labor—aside from the roadside glass of lemonade for 50 cents?

[ ] yes   [ ] no

18. Do you know which companies your mutual fund(s) invest(s) in?

[ ] all   [ ] most   [ ] some   [ ] none

19. Do you know in which countries the companies you invest in do business?

[ ] all   [ ] most   [ ] some   [ ] none

20. Have you ever exercised your shareholder rights?

[ ] yes   [ ] no

21. Is the sole goal of your investments to make more money?

[ ] yes   [ ] no

22. Would you consider an investment which would make less money but would, in return, more closely match your own personal values?

[ ] yes   [ ] no

23. If you could, would you ever invest in a company which produces a product that is illegal?

[ ] yes [ ] no

24. Would you ever invest in a company which promoted a product to a specific age group, even though that product would cause health problems for that age group?

[ ] yes   [ ] no

25. Have you ever volunteered to work for a political campaign?

[ ] yes   [ ] no

26. Have you ever volunteered to work on a project where money was no object?

[ ] yes   [ ] no

27. If you could own the house of your dreams by investing in one company whose only product was the detonator for a neutron bomb, would you?

[ ] yes   [ ] no

28. Would you consider investing in a company which produced substances essential to the manufacture of chemical weapons if doing so meant you could amass a sizeable enough fortune to successfully lobby against all such weapons?

[ ] yes   [ ] no

29. Do you use chemicals that are poisonous to you or the environment to clean your house and car?

[ ] yes   [ ] no

30. If you could only get a mortgage from a bank which is known to provide little or no minority lending, would you
     [ ] wait for a few months and try to requalify at bank with a better record?
     [ ] take the mortgage, no questions asked?
     [ ] take the mortgage, but ask to speak with the bank's president about their restrictive lending record?

31. Do you give change to people on the street?
     [ ] often   [ ] sometimes   [ ] never

32. Do you send a small charitable donation to a local shelter for homeless people or battered women?
     [ ] often   [ ] sometimes   [ ] never

33. Are you a registered voter?
     [ ] yes   [ ] no

34. What type of bag do you ask for at the grocery store?
     [ ] paper   [ ] plastic

35. Do you recycle your wire hangers?
     [ ] yes   [ ] no

36. Would you consider taking one week of your vacation time to volunteer in an urban renewal project?
     [ ] yes   [ ] no

37. Would you be more inclined to invest in a company which provided solid medical and retirement benefits for its employees even if doing so meant cutting into its profit margins?
     [ ] yes   [ ] no

38. Do you consider yourself to be an ethical person?
     [ ] yes   [ ] no

39. Do you consider yourself to be an ethical investor?
     [ ] yes   [ ] no

40. Would you consider ethics as a viable investment consideration when thinking about buying or selling stocks, bonds, and mutual funds?
     [ ] every time   [ ] sometimes   [ ] never

SCORECARD

Answering the above questions may have (a) heightened your sense of your potential role in responsible investing, (b) increased your ire concerning those who would tell you how you go about your own business, (c) made you more inclined to read the rest of this chapter, and/or (d) made you less inclined to read on. Reading on is strongly suggested, since, after all, you took the time to fill out the above and now might want to know just how well you scored. Not that scoring well means anything—especially if you're a cynical quiz taker (you know the type—they think about which answer is most likely to score well regardless of their true first response). If you fall into this camp, the following won't do you much good. If, however, you answered the questions about ethical investing honestly (i.e., ethically), then you might benefit from the following scorecard.

To begin the process of rating yourself, total the number of yeses and nos, oftens and nevers, alls and nones, and somes and sometimes from the above list.

Total number of **yes** responses   _____
Total number of **often** responses   _____
Total number of **all** responses   _____
Total number of **most** responses   _____
Total of **yes**, **often**, **all**, and **most** responses   _____

Total number of **no** responses   _____
Total number of **never** responses   _____
Total number of **none** responses   _____
Total of **no**, **never**, and **none** answers   _____

Total number of **some** responses   _____
Total number of **sometimes** responses   _____
Total number of **some** and **sometimes** responses   _____

50+ yes, often, all, and most responses: You're good. You're real good. I bet you don't even cross a sandbox without checking for ants (which you then sidestep). Chances are you won't be shaken from your path of living and investing well within your definition of ethical means. Since this is the path you've chosen, you should pay particular attention to the remainder of this chapter since it will help you review your current investment portfolio in light of your ethical and investment objectives as well as present you with some of the best ethical investment strategies and opportunities in the market today.

40+: You tend to be better at being good than you give yourself credit for. You might not have ever considered yourself to be an ethical investor but, in effect, that's what you are. After all, look at the way you steer yourself from products and companies which participate in doing harm (to the environment or to other living beings), and steer yourself toward those that help raise the standard of good business practices. Since this participation is, on some level, unconscious when it comes to your actual investments, you can benefit from this chapter's explanation of how to discern the level of ethical intent and action on the part of a company or mutual fund (which invests your money in several companies). You'll also learn how to be more proactive in your future investment decision making so that you can wed your profit with your own well-developed ethical practices.

30+: So you never really thought about investing and ethics in the same boat. Relax. It's a big boat—and one in which most of us find ourselves. As a result, your investment portfolio might be jam-packed with companies which exhibit characteristics that, were they to be present in a friend or colleague, would give you reason enough to reevaluate your feelings and estimation of them. Ignorance used to be bliss, but now that you've taken the above quiz the only way to return to the state of bliss is to actively turn your back on the question of ethical investing. Reading this chapter will help you come to terms with your own quandary, as well as demonstrate that being an ethical investor isn't nearly as constricting as you might think. After all, the definition of ethical investing is, in reality, a question of morality and not ethics at all (as you would know by now if you had checked the definitions of "ethics" and "morals"). Morals are socially defined, malleable, flexible, open to interpretation and challenge. This chapter will help you stretch your thinking about investing to the point of returning to your existing portfolio with some potential changes in mind.

Fewer than 30: OK. Maybe the devil made you do it. Chances are you could care less whether you are even reading this blurb. You invest to make money—period.

A MORAL DECISION

Most people confuse ethics with morals. This gets in their way of their being able to determine between questions concerning what is basically good and evil and what the majority interprets to be acceptable and unacceptable. That's why, aside from the financial

merits, when it comes to investing in companies that are solid cit-
izens, it's easy to find yourself questioning whether or not the company is a good company. For one thing, it may have just donated
a new playing field to your town, while at the same time its manufacturing plant is located in an area where pollution controls and
labor regulations are virtually nonexistent. While a company may
be a good citizen, it can also be a bad neighbor. By the same token,
if you're investing a company which itself participates in actions that
you don't find acceptable, the company still may not be unethical.

The decision as to how great or little a role the question of ethics
will play in your overall investment decision-making process isn't
up to you—the way we'd all like to think that it is. If ethics were
up to us, we'd have to rename it morals. The reality is that ethical
investing is really a form of social responsibility made manifest
through investing. Sound confusing? Well, in a sense, it's a good
thing that it is—since it makes you think twice about the kind of
company you've invested in from a wider angle than a profit
perspective alone. In short, asking yourself more questions about a
company's business practice is a great way to be more diligent and
vigilant about your research and investments.

There are those who argue that ethics and investing shouldn't
be in the same equation. I advocate a more profitable middle
ground—one which seeks companies based on their financial and
business ethic merits together. But what exactly does this mean?
The following might be a likely conversation with yourself: "Do I
invest in tobacco companies (or in mutual funds that do)?" Your
response might be, "Not knowingly, although I do invest in funds
that could easily do so since, as far as I know, there's nothing written in the prospectus about not doing so." Does this make you an
unethical investor? I don't think so.

Ask yourself the following:

- Am I conscious of what companies I invest in are up to in terms
  of their labor and business practices? Not necessarily, but I can
  find out more.
- Do I want to take the time and effort to do this? Not really.
  But a quick glance at my funds' holdings should help me answer, in general, whether the overall investment picture is good
  or bad. Besides, I know I own a company like IBM, which has
  to manufacture some its parts in some fairly questionable
  regions in the world.

- Does that make IBM a bad company—or me an unethical investor? I don't think so. By the same token, I don't own RJR/Nabisco since I do believe the product they produce is harmful to the health of those who use it—and to those who are around those who do.
- Does that make me an ethical investor? To a certain extent, I guess it does.

Figuring out the ethical intent of a single company can be simple, as in the case of a tobacco company. Figuring out the ethical makeup of a large, diversified company requires that you dig deeper. For example, IBM makes parts for defense systems, and the parts themselves may be manufactured in areas where human rights violations and labor regulations are lax. But does this make IBM a bad company? It has one of the better employee-benefit structures going in corporate America. It's an excellent, tax-paying citizen. It does the right thing by its employees and shareholders. You'll have to think about it. The same negatives hold true for most manufacturers, while the same positives don't. So, on a relative basis, IBM wins. On an absolute basis, it's your call.

Mutual funds pose a particularly difficult problem for the ethically inclined investor, since your qualitative concerns can be overwhelmed by the quantitative reality that there are more companies in a fund's portfolio than you can shake a stick at. In fact, some funds invest in hundreds of companies. Getting to know each one up close and personal may not be in the cards—and the fact is that some funds sell and buy faster than you can get to know the companies they hold. Solution: determine the top five industry weightings of the fund's current portfolio. This can be done by glancing at the most recent semiannual report or prospectus. (For more on dissecting a fund, turn to chapter 13.) Figuring out which industries your fund factors can give you an essential clue as to the fund's overall ethical intent. For example, the following industries might be considered dubious by a peace-loving, animal-rights-oriented, vegetarian: agriculture, biotech, chemicals, defense/aerospace, and energy.

You also can determine the top fifteen company holdings in terms of the percentage of your fund's overall assets. Not only will that give you an idea of which companies the fund manager has bought, it will also serve as an indication of the types of companies he or she will be willing to buy.

AN ETHICAL INDEX

There is an index comprised of companies which meet specific, ethically minded and socially practicable criteria. Created in 1990, it is designed as a competitive standard to the S&P 500. Known as the Domini Social Index 400 (DSI 400), it's named for the woman who invented it, Ami Domini; she also manages some "ethical" funds. This market-capitalization-weighted common stock index monitors the performance of 400 companies which successfully passed the following screens: positive record on the environment; employee benefits; community action; and safety and usefulness of the products. Companies which won't pass muster on this index are those concentrating in significant military contracts; significant involvement with the nuclear industry; or commitment to the tobacco, alcohol, and/or gambling industries.

Ethical Investment Opportunities

How has the DSI compared performancewise to the S&P 500? Let's take a look (opposite).

Bottom line: You can make good money investing ethically.

Socially Responsible Investment Funds

One of the great ways to build a list of companies you might consider investing in is to request a prospectus and semiannual report from a socially responsible fund. Request these items from three or more of the following table of "socially responsible" funds and you'll accomplish two things at once: First, you'll build a large list that will take some time to research for those companies you deem acceptable—and those you don't. And this leads to the second accomplishment—namely, coming to see that there are different interpretations of what ethical investing is, and which companies count. Or, you could cut to the end of this chapter and take a look at a list of socially responsible funds put together by the Washington, DC–based nonprofit Co-op America (a group dedicated to wedding the goal of profit with the ideal of a better world).

Some funds focus on one specific industry in order to provide investors the opportunity to concentrate their assets in a focused, as opposed to diversified, investment vehicle. While doing so can set you on a collision course with risk, it can also serve as a bene-

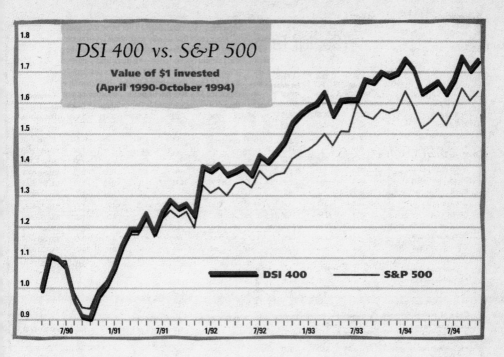

ficial piece of an overall portfolio's pie. The environment is an area in which many ethical investors concentrate. Take a look at the table of environmental funds that invest in companies that are directly involved in cleaning up the environment or have a solid environmental record, on page 236. But keep in mind that investing in a fund which concentrates its assets in one theme can be as messy as investing in only one that concentrates in a single industry. You'd be well advised to consider a more diversified approach to your ethical investing. But if you think you'll clean up by investing in the environment, try limiting your commitment to under 10 percent of your overall portfolio.

There are also responsible parking places for your cash. Money market mutual funds are a great place to temporarily park your cash and, for the ethical investor, the list of money market funds provides some ethically sound funds.

Social Investment Funds

	9/94 Assets (millions)	Year To Date	1 Year (or since incept.*)	3 Year Average Annual	5 Year Average Annual	10 Year Average Annual	Annual Avg. Since Inception	Max. Load	Expenses	Telephone
Equity										
Ariel Appreciation	$162.0	-8.39%	-8.39%	3.85%	7.90%	n/a	7.98%	0.00%	1.50%	800/725-0140
Ariel Growth	149.5	-4.22	-4.22	5.22	5.37	n/a	12.42	0.00	1.30	800/725-0140
Calvert Social Equity Portfolio	92.8	-12.18	-12.18	-0.94	2.43	n/a	4.86	4.75	1.17	800/368-2748
▶ Calvert Strategic Growth Fund	60.0	n/a	18.55*	n/a	n/a	n/a	n/a	4.75	2.60	800/368-2748
Covenant Portfolio	4.3	2.88	2.88	n/a	n/a	n/a	5.86	4.50	2.50	800/275-2683
Domini Social Equity Fund	33.4	-0.36	-0.36	5.97	n/a	n/a	7.21	0.00	0.80	800/762-6814
Dreyfus Third Century	368.5	-7.45	-7.45	-0.23	7.27	11.11	11.01	0.00	1.10	800/645-6561
Neuberger & Berman Soc. Resp.	67.2	n/a	-2.21*	n/a	n/a	n/a	n/a	0.00	1.50	800/877-9700
New Alternatives	29.8	-3.71	-3.71	1.30	3.80	10.72	10.59	4.75	1.11	800/423-8383
Parnassus Fund	141.4	11.98	11.98	21.58	16.67	13.47	13.46	3.50	1.50	800/999-3505
Progressive Environmental Fund	1.8	-23.99	-23.99	-3.66	n/a	n/a	-3.29	4.50	2.50	800/422-7284
Rightime Social Awareness	7.4	1.55	1.55	3.77	n/a	n/a	5.27	4.75	0.75	800/242-1421
Women's Equity Mutual Fund	n/a	n/a	n/a	n/a	n/a	n/a	n/a	0.00	0.50	800/424-2295
Working Assets Cit Growth	52.7	-0.67	-0.67	n/a	n/a	n/a	6.02	4.00	1.70	800/223-7010
• Domini Social Index		0.18	0.18	6.81	n/a	n/a				
• NASDAQ Composite		-3.20	-3.20	8.65	10.58	11.76				
• S&P 500 Reinvested		1.31	1.31	6.27	8.70	14.38				
• Lipper Growth Fund Average		-2.17	-2.17	5.39	8.59	12.55				
Global										
Calvert World Values	175.0	-2.73	-2.73	n/a	n/a	n/a	6.66	4.75	1.10	800/368-2748
• Lipper Global Fund Average		-3.03	-3.03	8.18	5.88	14.31				
• MSCI World Index		5.08	5.08	6.85	3.67	14.84				
Fixed Income										
Calvert Social Bond Portfolio	61.6	-5.34	-5.34	4.10	7.18	n/a	8.29	4.75	0.80	800/368-2748
Muir CA Tax-Free	17.3	-7.16	-7.16	4.13	n/a	n/a	5.71	4.50	0.46	800/648-3448
Parnassus Fixed Income	4.6	-6.76	-6.76	n/a	n/a	n/a	2.56	0.00	1.00	800/999-3505
Parnassus CA Tax-Free	4.0	-6.36	-6.36	n/a	n/a	n/a	3.21	0.00	n/a	800/999-3505
Working Assets Cit Income	25.2	-3.08	-3.08	n/a	n/a	n/a	4.18	4.00	1.70	800/223-7010
• Corporate Debt A Rated		-4.64	-4.64	4.35	7.21	9.34				
• Lehman Aggregate Bond Index		-4.24	-4.24	5.29	8.26	10.55				
Balanced										
Calvert Social Managed Growth	512.0	-4.74	-4.74	2.75	5.40	10.39	10.08	4.75	1.30	800/368-2748
Green Century Balanced	3.0	-4.10	-4.10	n/a	n/a	n/a	-0.05	0.00	2.50	800/934-7336
Parnassus Balanced	17.6	-5.39	-5.39	n/a	n/a	n/a	7.78	0.00	0.94	800/999-3505
Pax World Fund	397.0	2.65	2.65	0.73	6.40	10.27	8.65	0.00	1.20	800/767-1729
Working Assets Cit Balanced	44.0	-2.31	-2.31	n/a	n/a	n/a	4.54	4.00	1.70	800/223-7010
• Lipper Balanced Average		-2.50	-2.50	5.22	7.82	11.59				
Money Market										
Calvert Social Money Market Fund	143.9	3.69	3.69	3.16	4.54	5.83	6.51	0.00	0.90	800/368-2748
Green Century Money Market Fund	3.1	3.75	3.75	n/a	n/a	n/a	2.77	0.00	0.50	800/934-7336
Working Assets Money Fund	102.2	3.24	3.24	2.82	4.26	5.57	5.97	0.00	1.20	800/223-7010
• Lipper Money Market Average		3.65	3.65	3.19	4.59	5.88				

Bank Money Market

(FDIC Insured)	Current Yield	Account Mission	Telephone
Alternatives Federal Credit Union	2.27%	Loans for affordable housing/community	607/273-4611
Community Capital Bank	2.53	Community Development	800/827-6699
South Shore Bank	5.17	Supports low income urban development and environmentally stable businesses	800/669-7725
Vermont National Bank	5.63	Supports housing, agriculture, education, environmental projects and small businesses in Vermont	800/772-3863

You're a Shareholder, You Have the Right to Try to Correct a Wrong

There are two ways in which you can apply your social investing inclinations—avoidance and engagement. With avoidance, either you never invest in or you sell stock in companies whose ethics you come to question. But is there a better way? Well, it's an age-old problem—to avoid or to work from within. If you think that you can make change happen (and you can at least try), then you should become familiar with your shareholder rights and exercise them.

Shareholder rights are not just for the big fat-cats. As a shareholder (in a stock, or mutual fund) you own a piece of the corporation. In doing so, you create the opportunity for yourself to stand up and be counted. Granted, you may be the only one standing, but at least you can begin to raise the level of consciousness in the room. Becoming an active shareholder is easier than you might think. In fact, one way to start becoming an active shareholder is through the mail—sending letters to the CEO, chief financial officer, chief financial advisor, and board members to let them know where you stand on your belief that the company, while good, could become much better. Of course, it's only your personal opinion. And there is no guarantee your letter will be read by the person you sent it to. Is there a way around this problem? Of course. It's called a proxy.

Always vote your common stock proxies. They come in the mail and you simply fill them out. If you don't, the board will vote for you. Do you let other people vote for you in other spheres? I thought not. So get involved and fill out the proxy. Want to take it to the next level? As long as you have owned $1,000 worth of stock in the company for more than twelve months prior to the company's annual shareholders' meeting, you can stand up and be counted—directly, by sponsoring a resolution for a vote on a subject near and dear to you.

There's more that you can do. You can also submit a proposal for changing corporate policy. You'll need to do this by the book, however, since a proposal of this kind is strictly regulated by the SEC. The best way to proceed on this front is to get a copy of *The Shareholder Proposal Process*, a sixteen-page guide that's put together by the National Shareholders Association and it's available at no cost to you. (See Ready Resources at the end of this chapter for phone number.) In a matter of minutes, you learn how to propose change.

Another way is to transfer your proxy to an organization that you believe in. The drawback to doing this is that it takes your vote out of your hands. If you want to pursue this course of action but don't know where to turn, contact the First Affirmative Financial Network. FAFN will help you unite with institutions or coalitions which are sponsoring resolutions on issues that match your own agenda.

AN END IN ITSELF?

Some people view money as the root of all evil—but it would be hard to build a church or temple without it, just as it would be hard to keep a roof over your own head and food on the table. But the flip side is that you can do well by doing good (to a greater or lesser extent). And, perhaps more important, if you invest in accordance with your conscience, you just might be more inclined to stay fully invested—no matter what temporary tempest the market is tossing your way.

READY RESOURCES

- *The Clean Yield Newsletter,* (802) 533-7178.
- *The Social Investment Forum,* (617) 723-7171, (202) 833-5522 (membership).
- Co-op America's Socially Responsible Financial Planning Handbook, (800) 424-2667.

CHAPTER TWENTY

On-Line Investing

The world of investments hasn't changed all that dramatically in the last few years—but the realm of investment research, as well as your ability to access it, is changing minute by minute. In addition, the ways of requesting and receiving annual reports, prospectuses, and applications for brokerage accounts, mutual funds, and more is changing daily. Investing has become a dynamic, interactive, on-line event for individual investors like yourself.

Unplugged? Let's start with a basic distinction between on-line services and the World Wide Web. On-line services differ from Web sites in that they offer you a range of sites to browse and members to converse with, whereas the Web is open to anyone with access to a server—either through an on-line service or a lower-cost server. Generally, an on-line service will cost more but will provide a larger menu of services. The Web will cost less to access but, by the same token, takes some knowledge to navigate and to separate the investment wheat from the chaff.

On-line investing isn't the wave of the future. It's here and now. And while many people may use a paid on-line service or server to participate in areas of interest to them, the truth is there's one area which can return the favor in a more rewarding manner than idle chat; it's the virtual world of investing. There are dynamic links between on-line services and the World Wide Web that enable you to cruise back and forth on a superhighway of real-time information and data. If you prefer, you can pull off the info-bahn and park at hundreds of repositories of historical investment data, charts, and commentary. No matter which way you turn, however, one thing is clear. When it comes to investing, there's no need to take a back seat. In fact, your keyboard can put you in the driver's seat when it comes to researching your own investments.

How to Get There

There's a catch with the info highway. It's hard to find a map that's (a) written in English, (b) current, and (c) accurate. New sites are built every day. Paths to familiar sites change. There's also the increasing number of free sites changing into paid services. No matter.

Chances are, some of the sites that you'll find listed in this chapter may no longer exist by the time you read this. However, there are several main sites which will be around for a long time to come. The point is to get used to feeling your way around the Web to locate the sites that are most useful to you and your investment decisions. When it comes to the on-line services, the process is even more streamlined.

ON-LINE SERVICES: On-line services continue to grow, some faster than others—and some better than others. America Online, CompuServe, and Prodigy are the big three. Fortunately, you can test-drive each site, typically for ten free hours, in order to select the service that best suits your needs. Use the free ten hours to your advantage and cut to the chase—the one that will inevitably help you build a better level of understanding about your current investments, established objectives, and potential opportunities you may have overlooked.

If your Mac or PC didn't come equipped with preloaded trial runs of every major on-line service, it's not hard to come by them. For one thing, they're in the mail or the plastic-wrapped issues of *PC Week* or other computer-related magazines—or even one of the growing number of on-line and Web-specific magazines on the shelf. And, if you still can't get your hands on a disk, simply pick up the phone and request a trial disk.

- America Online, (800) 827-6364
- CompuServe, (800) 543-4616
- Prodigy, (800) 776-3449

They're a snap to install and work since there are prompts along the way that tell you what to do next. In fact, they're kind of fun and, more important, they add value to any investor's research capabilities.

THE WEB: People talk about the Web as if it's free. The truth is, for most of us it isn't since we at least pay for the modem time. However, while there are costs involved, exclusive use of the Web can result in lowering the overall cost of on-line investing—in some cases substantially so. In fact the average cost of twenty hours per week through a Web server is under $20, whereas for the on-line services the same twenty hours can cost you over $40.

Are the savings worth it? Well, as with your decision between a full-service broker and a discounter (which weighed in favor of the discounter), you need to assess your level of literacy with the medium, as well as your desire and need for service. On-line services, like America Online, provide comprehensive market coverage, research libraries, real-time quotes, and discussions of the market and every category and type of investment, as well as the ability to tap into areas of interest to investors who are like-minded (and contrary). The on-line services provide excellent investment resources plus the ability to link to Web sites. They're the best of both worlds but you'll pay a premium price for them. True, by themselves, the on-line services would pale in comparison to the volume of information available on the Web. Also true: Web sites are becoming increasingly dynamic in terms of being interactive, useful, user-friendly, and easy to find.

On-line services have an increasingly generous menu of investment sources and market commentaries. Their menus are, for the most part, easy to understand and check out. The World Wide Web, on the other hand, is both wild and wonderful—easy to get lost in, refind yourself, discover a new investment opportunity, or run into a scam artist. (If you run into a scamster, or want to learn more about how to avoid them, go to the Center for Abused Investors— http://www.investoraid.com.) Since you can't jump onto the Web with a six-gun at your side, you'll have to learn to tame it in more peaceable ways. The following advice should help you do just that:

- Be patient.
- Don't be intimidated.
- Be persistent.
- Don't allow yourself to get sidetracked.
- Know why you're going on-line and where you're heading.
- Keep an accurate list of the pathways to sites you like (create a hot-list, and save that hot-list in a hard-drive file so that you can retrieve it if your on-line file gets corrupted).
- Review your research process for possible streamlining.
- Don't give out your name and address willy-nilly.
- Never reveal your account password (and change it often).
- Avoid giving any information about yourself—most Web sites are set up to get such information since the site can then sell your name and address to other businesses.
- Avoid hot investment tips.
- Always scrutinize everything you read or are told on-line.
- When it comes to on-line banking and investing, review the security discussion on page 55.
- View the Web as a wide net which yields potential for fun—and profit.

MAJOR PLAYERS AND NICHE SOURCES

Nothing new under the sun? Check out "sun" using your Web browser and you will see there's plenty that's new. But don't stare at the sun too long. You've come this far; the next level is up to you. And that's learning where some of the most significant investment sources on the World Wide Web are located. You can always start a search by using a popular engine like Web Crawler (http://www.webcrawler.com) or Yahoo (http://www.yahoo.com) and typing in the name of the subject matter (e.g., economy, stocks, mutual funds) or specific name (i.e., the name of a company, security, or mutual fund) in which you are interested. Or you can review the following hot-list of sites that shouldn't be missed.

- Stock investors should first go to The Syndicate, which lists over 1,000 financial sites on the Web. But you need to get beyond The Syndicate's main page to the stock-specific listings. To do so, type: http://www.moneypages.com/syndicate/ and, once there, type: misc.stocks and misc.invest newsgroups. This site will keep you busy.

- Fund investors go directly to NETWORTH for a free and searchable database on over 7,000 funds, and to receive prospectuses on several of them electronically. Type: http//networth.galt.com/www/home/navigator.html
- Fund investors should also go to the Mutual Fund Home Page which links you to a vast menu of fund related sites. Type: http://www.chanel1.com/users/fund/
- The *Wall Street Journal*'s money and investing site is a must-see. Modeled after its most meaningful "C" section, you'll find the top finance news and investment stories, as well as the next day's "C" section hours before your neighbor gets his hard copy (and it won't smudge). Type: http://update.wsj.com

Stocks, Bonds, and Mutual Funds

Use your browser to help locate any sites that are exchange-specific. As of this writing, not one of the three major U.S. stock exchanges (NYSE, AMEX, Nasdaq) was on the Web. However, by the time you read this, chances are all the major exchanges will be out there—in virtual space awaiting your cursory glance. Fortunately, the Web isn't all that constrained by what it lacks—since it offers so much. Take a look at one or more of the following:

- Stock Source is a unique Web site that offers investors the ability to track initial public offerings—plus a searchable database of those IPOs going back two years. Address: http://www.catalog.com/cgibin/var/war/ssource/ss-home.html
- Although bonds shouldn't be a large part of your portfolio (see chapter 10), if you want information about them, be sure to visit the Federal Reserve Bank of New York site for quotes on U.S. Treasuries and bonds at: http://www.ny.frb.org/.../mktrates/qsheet.shtml
- Some leading full-service brokerages offer free sites worth visiting, but you might have to yield your name to enter, which could translate into never having an uninterrupted dinner again in your lifetime—since brokers love to call when you're home. Still, the information available on the following is first-rate:

- Gruntal   http://www.gruntal.com
- Wertheim Schroder   http://www.hyrda.com/
                                wertheim/
- Merrill Lynch   http://www.ml.com
- Prudential
  Securities   http://www.prusec.com

- Many fund companies have jumped on-line as well as into the Web. Easily accessed on-line, and through NETWORTH on the World Wide Web, this is one investment group that has done its Web work. Some of these sites offer full-blown financial and investment resource centers, while others provide fund-specific details and prospectuses. The following list is by no means all-inclusive, but the following fund families have done a better-than-average job at providing investors with some serious investment tools and information:

- Fidelity   http://www.fid-inv.com
- Fidelity On-Line   America Online
- Vanguard On-Line   America Online

Company Research

If you're thinking about buying stock in a company, and you want to know some deeper details than its name, check out EDGAR, Electronic Data Gathering and Retrieval. This is the SEC's database of electronic corporate filings. Here you'll find filings from most publicly traded companies—from large-caps to small-caps. EDGAR provides customized company reports as well as bulk data. To get there, type: http://edgar.stern.nyu.edu

Markets and Economy

The following sites will yield a bountiful crop of hard data on the overall market economy. Each on-line service has a market center with updated market statistics, commentary, and related news. In the Web, you can quickly locate current news of investment note by heading directly to the *Wall Street Journal* site (see page 247). You can also move to one or more of the following sites for further information:

- Bank of America Capital Markets (economic news and data): http://bankamerica.com:80/cap_markets2.html
- Bloomberg (economic and market statistics): http://www.bloomberg.com/
- Economics and Statistics Administration (economic news and industry research): http://www.doc.gov:80/resources/ESA_info.html
- Economics and Statistics Resources (economics and market statistics): http://www.lib.lsu.edu:80/bus/economic.html
- Census Bureau (demographic stats and studies): http://www.census.gov/
- Chicago Fed (economic statistics and studies): gopher://gopher.great-lakes.net:2200/00/partners/Chicago Fed/finance/forex_c.prn
- Commerce Department Statistics (news and numbers from various industry groups and trade sectors): gopher://una.hh.lib.umich.edu.70/11/ebb

Investment Zines

What is a "zine"? It's a live magazine—live on the Web, that is. Most of the major finance magazines, from *Fortune* to *Mutual Fund Magazine*, are available on the Web as well as through the several on-line services. Ferreting them out is easy: just type their name in your browser and go. Zines are worth looking at—even if you've never cracked their hard-copy cover. Which ones? For starters, try one or more of the following:

- *The Economist*   http://www.economist.com/
- *Fortune*   http://www.pathfinder.com
- *Mutual Fund Magazine*   http://www.mfmag.com

Trading On-Line

More than any other investment-related area, trading on-line has transformed itself from a poor relation of the traditional method of investing to a user-friendly, resourceful way to invest. The oldest sites (they've been around for at least one year!) are still the leaders of the pack:

- Fidelity   http://www.fid-inv.com
- Schwab   http://www.schwab.com
- Quick & Reilly   http://www.quick-reilly.com

Setting up an on-line trading account is similar to opening a regular brokerage account—except you can do it from the comfort of your laptop rather than trekking downtown, paying for parking, waiting for an elevator, etc., all to get to someone else's desktop. Trading on-line is exactly like trading by phone—except that you have a written record of your buy or sell order.

You can reach me at **Lowellinc@AOL.com.**

PART V

Your Future Is in Your Hands

CHAPTER TWENTY-ONE

Your Best Retirement Investing Options

When the discussion shifts from the latest "Friends" show re-run to retirement-oriented investments (and if it hasn't happened to you yet, wait a month or two and I guarantee it will), most people start talking in codes: "My IRA's so much more efficient than the SEP I used to participate in, but I've lost the tax-deductible status ever since my husband started to participate in his company's 403(b), since a 457 was out of the question. But, my company is offering a 401(k), with matching funds . . ." You could be sitting there counting sheep or the unopened Zima bottles in the fridge, for all you care.

Well, it may surprise you to learn that, when it comes to investing for retirement, so-called slackers do a better (that's right, *better*) job than their parents. This fact would probably surprise your parents even more! The facts are as follows: over 40 percent of twenty-somethings have a savings account and invest in mutual funds; over 60 percent of Gen Xers already participate in a retirement investing plan; over 75 percent set retirement savings as a priority in the field of their financial-related focus. About 60 percent already participate in a 401(k) plan, compared to around 50 percent for boomers.

This good news is most likely the result of four main factors: The job market is tight, meaning you're well aware of the hardships you face in making ends meet today which, in turn, doesn't exactly bode well for tomorrow—so you're looking to safeguard yourself from financial collapse in more concrete ways. Second, you see how many of the boomers before you—the glamour-pusses of the 1980s—are having to downsize in order to keep a roof over their heads. Third, you don't believe Social Security will be around when you retire. And fourth, there's much greater media coverage of issues relating to retirement and the need to create your own cash reserves for it.

Now, you and I know that our retirement days are far, far away. You're not sitting in some bar bemoaning the fact that you have thirteen more years to go before you can hang up your mailbag and retire to Tampa. You're sitting in the bar thinking about tequila sunrises, not the sunset years which are twenty-five-plus years down the road. But don't kid yourself. A comprehensive survey of "retirement confidence" completed by the Employee Benefit Research Institute (http://www.ebri.org) revealed some interesting facts about our preparedness for and confidence in retiring. Seventy-five percent of those surveyed said they were confident regarding their retirement income prospects, but 30 percent of the same group admitted to having nothing saved for their own retirement—and 60 percent hadn't even attempted to calculate how much they would need to save to fund a comfortable retirement (one which enabled them to maintain a similar lifestyle). Now, of course you don't want to be stuck in the lifestyle you're living today—since you're young and working toward a better one.

The respondents of this survey were workers in your age group as well as far beyond; the study thus provides an interesting lens through which you can view the potential pitfall of being overconfident when it comes to investing today for that distant tomorrow. In fact, in contrast to the rosy scenario pictured above, this survey reveals that among those aged 26 to 34 who responded that they were very confident about their retirement income, 30 percent had no money set aside. (The survey didn't ask about debt levels, which, as you can imagine, are likely to be very high.)

Our Changing Future

Things are not what they used to be. It used to be that planning for retirement was a fairly straightforward proposition—one which entailed tallying your pension and Social Security benefits to ensure that you could maintain a modest lifestyle. Nowadays, neither pensions nor Social Security are sure things. Today, there are seventeen taxpayers for every Social Security recipient. By the year 2030, there will be only two taxpayers for every Social Security recipient! Add to this troubling news the fact that inflation has to be factored into the mix—an inflation rate of 4.5 percent means that the cost of living will double every fifteen years. No wonder so many people are discouraged rather than encouraged about becoming more knowledgeable and active in terms of funding their own retirement.

For example, do you know why 401(k) plans and other self-funded retirement plans have become so popular? Increasingly, employers and the federal government expect you to be responsible for the lion's share of your retirement income. While for your employer this is a good thing (it reduces the expense and liability of funding traditional pension plans), for you it means that there's no guaranteed amount of income that you can rely on for your retirement.

There are attractive retirement investment alternatives available to you—but it's up to you to understand and select the most appropriate one(s) for yourself. And while it is difficult to predict the level of retirement income you'll need (since it's hard to know how to predict the level of living and sundry expenses you'll encounter when you join the pink flamingo, shuffleboard set in thirty-plus years), now is the best time to start taking advantage of a tax-advantaged investment plan, as well as determining an appropriate investment strategy so that your retirement years will be truly golden ones.

Chances are that you haven't yet accumulated a substantial nest egg for retirement. If you are like most people, you have experienced more pressing and immediate concerns, such as buying a home and raising and educating children. Whatever your circumstances, however, you should regularly direct some attention to planning for your retirement—and then some of your resources.

INVEST FOR A BETTER TOMORROW, TODAY

You can develop a sound retirement plan today. True, there are many details that need to be worked out—and worked on. But the sooner you start, the better—and the sooner you review the plan you've got, the sooner you can rest assured that it is the best one for you. If you have neither plans nor savings nor retirement investments in the works, relax. You've got time—so long as you begin right now—to develop a plan that will work for you. And remember that with no plan, you're only working against yourself.

TAKE STOCK OF YOUR PROGRESS IN MEETING YOUR RETIREMENT NEEDS: Estimating how much you will need to accumulate by the time you reach retirement age can be startling. If you are still young, this amount may seem more like the gross national product of a small country, but it is attainable. Caveat: Don't include the value of your home in your retirement-related assets unless you plan to sell the house and become a renter when you retire.

Gauging your retirement expenses in order to establish an overall investment goal isn't as hard to do as you might think. In fact, it easier (and less painful) to do than to create a livable budget! The tricky part is that your current lifestyle is probably not the lifestyle you'll rise to in the next five to ten years. Given that you're just starting out, the old rule of thumb: current gross annual income – amount of annual savings × 80 percent = an adequate amount of income that your investments will have to provide for up to thirty years or more, simply doesn't work. For example, if your current income is $30,000, and you save $1,500, that means you spend, including taxes, $28,500. To calculate the annual income in current dollars necessary to maintain this living standard during retirement years you would multiply the amount you spend, or $28,500, by 80 percent, to get $22,800. Not exactly living high on the hog. To project your necessary retirement income when you reach retirement age, adjust the results of this calculation upward to 100 percent of your current income, assuming that, in the next five to ten years you will increase your gross income by 20 to 25 percent. When that happens, scale back to the more conservative 80 percent.

Figuring out the amount of income your total retirement package (including pension, investments, and, yes, Social Security) will have to generate on an annual basis for a span of at least two decades is perhaps the simplest part of the overall equation. The more difficult part is to estimate what you need to save today in order to achieve your very distant objective. Fortunately, worksheets with this in mind are plentiful—and most are accurate and easy to implement. (My favorite worksheet is found on America Online and is produced by Fidelity.) Interactive worksheets will help you determine what you need to save today in order to reach a more financially secure tomorrow—based on your changing fortunes. But there's also a basic rule which you should invest by: you will need to invest a minimum of 10 percent of your gross income in a portfolio which delivers an annualized return of at least 8 percent in order to maintain your current lifestyle.

TAKE ACTION TO CLOSE THE GAP BETWEEN THE RESOURCES YOU NOW HAVE AND THE RESOURCES YOU WILL NEED TO RETIRE: Figuring out how much you need to retire in comfort usually leads to the realization that you don't yet have enough money to meet your needs. If misery does love company, then there is some solace in the fact that very few people achieve financial independence until they are very near retirement. But what is most important is to make sure you take action today to provide for your financial needs throughout your retirement.

- Get started on planning your retirement investment strategy today.
- Learn about the available retirement-oriented investment plans as well as the types of investments which are best suited to your objective.
- Regularly review your retirement investment strategy and investments' performance.
- Revise your retirement investment strategy and investments to keep pace with the benchmarks you establish.

That's it. You now know what you need to save today to brighten your financial future. Don't worry if you can't muster the money immediately. Chances are you do have some significant debts to pay off and a home's down payment to save for, too. But, on the other hand, don't postpone your retirement planning—or investing. Start small. Start today. Don't delay.

CHAPTER TWENTY-TWO

Retirement Investment Strategies

Those 401(k)s are here to stay. Whether you participate in a 401(k) or another type of employer-sponsored retirement plan (or are about to), you need to know how to make the best moves within the plan. To do so, you'll need to learn more than the mechanics of investing in them. This chapter is divided into two sections—401(k)s, and other types of pension plans. While there are similarities and differences among each type of plan discussed in detail below, there is one basic truth you can't afford to forget: no matter how good the plan is, it's up to you to select the best way to invest in it.

401(K) PLANS

Participating in a 401(k) couldn't be easier. If you already do so, or if you don't currently participate but have the opportunity to do so, read on. If, on the other hand, you don't currently have the option of investing in a 401(k), don't feel too left out. For one thing, you may be able to participate in a 403(b) plan. And if that isn't an option, you still have a host of retirement investment plans to choose from—from company-sponsored pension plans (also detailed below) to individually sponsored ones (described in the next chapter). Still feel left out? Well, even though you can't open a 401(k) the way you can an IRA (i.e., by picking up the phone and calling a mutual fund company), you can certainly suggest that your company create a 401(k) plan. It's worth a shot.

An increasing number of companies—large and small—are offering 401(k) plans. To participate in a 401(k) plan, you designate a fixed portion of your pretax salary to be deducted from your salary to be invested in your company-sponsored investment plan. It's a great start—especially if your employer matches part of your contribution to the plan. How great? Let's take a look.

A 401(K) IS TAX-ADVANTAGED: Participating in a 401(k) saves you federal (and most likely state) income taxes in several ways. First, the money in your 401(k) is known as deferred compensation, meaning it doesn't appear on your W-2 form and thereby escapes both federal income tax and Social Security taxes (unless your gross income after the 401(k) contribution exceeds the maximum income for which Social Security is withheld). The money you invest in your 401(k) also grows tax-free until you begin making withdrawals. Dividends, interest, and capital gains won't be taxed as long as you reinvest them in the plan. And depending on where you reside, your 401(k) contribution may escape state and local income taxes. Say you earn a taxable $30,000, and contribute 8 percent ($2,400) of that to your 401(k). As you'll note on your W-2 form next year, your earnings subject to federal (and most state) tax will be $27,600. Second, reducing your federal income taxes means that the $2,400 you contribute goes directly to work for you. Moreover (assuming you're in the 28 percent bracket with a 5.5 percent state tax), your doing so reduces the amount you pay to Uncle Sam by $672 (federal) and $132 (state)—a savings of 33.5 percent on money you earned and put to work for yourself. Now that's a bargain!

Naturally, if your employer matches your funds (in whole, or, as is far more likely, in part) it's an even better deal—perhaps the only source of found money for those without a silver spoon. And participating in a 401(k) plan is easy and convenient; as with a regular investment account, the automatic withdrawal of a specified sum from your paycheck will help you remain steadfast on your self-funded retirement course. But, that said, don't make the common mistake of thinking that investing in a 401(k) is a no-brainer. While opening an account is clearly the right thing to do—and while it couldn't be easier—that's the bare beginning of your 401(k) planning. Like any potential portfolio of investments, the vehicles you select in your 401(k) portfolio can get you where you want to go or set you on a collision course.

When the cherubic human resources department guy or gal knocks on your cube inviting you to attend an informational meeting about 401(k) plans, attend—even if you already have one. Why? Chances are you'll be brought up to speed on a number of issues that affect you and your money! Examples? The rules and contribution limits governing your 401(k) change. Your company may change the number and types of investments that you can select for your 401(k). Your company may change the way in which you can participate in managing your 401(k) fund by changing either its matching amount or the frequency with which you can make trades.

How to Invest in Your 401(k)

When it comes to constructing your 401(k), you may be surprised to find that you're either limited in terms of the types and number of investment vehicles you can choose from, or presented with a dizzying menu of choices. Most plans offer stock, bond, and money market funds. Others may offer guaranteed investment contracts (GICs) and the option of purchasing shares of the company's stock. No matter which camp you fall into, the fact is that, when it comes to selecting the best way to construct your 401(k) portfolio, you're the boss. You decide how you want to invest your 401(k) funds, and you select from the available menu the best way to satisfy your appetite for a financially secure retirement.

Treat your 401(k) like you would any other long-term investment plan (for further discussion on creating portfolio strategies that work, turn to chapter 14). Since you've got a long time before you retire, you can take on some added risk in order to potentially increase your returns. Doing so will entail building a portfolio of predominantly small-cap value, large-cap growth, and international stock funds. Forget about cash or bonds for now—they're too conservative and, in the case of cash, the stock funds you select will already have a small position in cash (meaning that your overall portfolio will have a cash position—a position which you need to watch to ensure that it doesn't ramp up, leaving you out of the market when you thought you were fully invested in it).

Remember: diversifying across industries, stocks, and countries is one of the best ways to deliver solid returns. How can you ensure that your portfolio is well diversified? Well, forget about the fund names—they'll lead you down a primrose path but reveal little about their actual objectives. (For a thorough review of mutual funds, turn to chapter 13.) Instead, get thee to a library, which will likely have recent issues of *Morningstar* or *Value Line* wherein you'll find a host of information about the funds that reside in your 401(k) plan. You can also request (from your employer or human resource person, or the funds themselves) copies of prospectuses which will describe the various investments and overall objective of each fund.

Chances are, your plan offers some growth, balanced, bond (income), and cash reserve options. Which should you concentrate on? Growth and more growth. You're young, and you're in the business of growing your capital—not trying to preserve it (yet). Moreover, since this money is earmarked for your retirement—i.e., an event that's twenty or more years away—you can afford to take on some additional risk in the form of an aggressive small-cap value or large-cap growth concentration with some foreign exposure added to your mix. Remember that the risk of taking no risk (i.e., putting your 401(k) money into a money market account) is that, over the long run, you're likely lose to inflation.

Note: Preretirement needs also should be provided for outside of your 401(k) plan. Funds invested outside the 401(k), particularly those salted away for your current or potential children's' college education, should be invested much like your 401(k) plan investments—aggressively at the starting gate for maximum growth.

REVIEWING IS ESSENTIAL: Some people will go out and buy the *Star Wars* trilogy—and watch it over and over again. But when it comes to reviewing their 401(k) statement (which typically arrives on a quarterly basis) do they even view it once? Many don't—and that's a mistake. Every time you receive a statement involving your finances you should review it to ensure that its: (1) your account, (2) the right amount of initial investment, and (3) reflects any trades that you authorized or that you did not authorize. I also keep a running portfolio of my 401(k) funds, checking their performance on a daily basis by turning to the fund section of my local paper. I like to know how the funds I have selected are performing relative to certain meaningful benchmarks—like the S&P 500 for my large-cap growth funds and the Russell 2000 for my small-cap growth funds and the EAFE for my international funds.

This is a great way to stay up to speed on the overall market as well—after all, the stocks each fund invests in come from different industries. By keeping track of each fund's performance, I can follow wider industry and economic trends in terms of how they affect my own financial well-being. If the performance of a particular fund or stock is steadily deteriorating over several quarters relative to similar funds or stocks (i.e., within the same industry), then it's probably time to consider an alternative fund.

Of course, you should not trade in and out of funds on a regular basis. In fact, market timing (trying to time the best time to buy and sell, and frequently trading in and out of the market) doesn't work. What does work is selecting the best funds available for the long haul; these may well not be the funds with the best short-term performance. Since some 401(k) plans provide a limited menu of investment possibilities, this may prove to be very difficult indeed. What you'll need to do is to look for investment style (value versus growth—and small-cap value versus all else) and country allocation (established versus emerging market) in order to cull the best from your limited lot. If, on the other hand, you've got a menu that's a mile long, you'll need to sift the wheat from the chaff. And once that's done, you'll need to establish a way to determine (on a regular basis) whether and when to readjust your 401(k) portfolio. Look at the long-term portfolio allocation in chapter 14 to see how a typical 401(k) might be arranged at your stage in life.

Some employers may restrict your ability to actively manage your own 401(k) investments, while others encourage it. The more you know about your plan's rules, the more likely your 401(k) will perform in accordance with your expectations and objectives. You have the right to trade the investments within your 401(k) up to four times per year. Of course, you're restricted to the preset menu offered by your employer. The rules regarding such trades are specific to your company's plan. Your employee benefits department is the best place to go for all the details.

WHAT NOT TO INVEST IN YOUR 401(k): Avoid tax-free investment vehicles (like a muni bond fund) since the 401(k)'s tax-advantages render the other null and void. Nix also on GICs—there's nothing truly guaranteed about them (insurance companies which offer these products can fail, just like S&Ls but without the $100,000 federal guarantee), and they are not the best investment alternative for you (rarely delivering a better performance than a conservative stock fund). True, when you buy a GIC, the insurance company promises to pay a specified interest rate over a specified period of time. Don't believe everything you hear.

I would also avoid placing shares of your own company's stock in your 401(k). As one of my personal finance mentors was fond of saying, as optimistic as you might be about your company's financial future and fortunes, you never know what's going to happen to its stock price. Instead, hold those shares in a separate account—and don't let them account for more than 20 percent of your overall retirement portfolio. The last thing you want to have happen is have the bottom fall out of the company's stock price and your 401(k), too.

WHEN NOT TO INVEST IN A 401(K): Not all 401(k)s are created equal—and some are downright dangerous. For one thing, many 401(k)s don't provide you with a menu of potential investments that are suitable to your age, income, and objectives. So, for example, your plan might not offer an aggressive growth fund or an international fund—or it may provide funds with poor performance records in those market areas or, worse, load funds. If you think that your plan is too restrictive, don't be afraid to just say no. True, 401(k)s are addictive—and, if the menu of investment choices is solid, then it's worth getting in the habit of contributing. But just because everyone says 401(k)s are the best thing to invest in doesn't mean that you particular plan is. Scrutinize the plan the way you would any menu of potential investments. If there isn't a way to build a portfolio you can live with and prosper by, consider opening an IRA.

WHEN TO QUESTION YOUR 401(K): Fraud happens. And where large sums of money are involved, fraud happens more. In 1995, the U.S. Labor Department investigated over 300 cases of possible 401(k) fraud—out of the more than 250,000 401(k) plans that were up and running at the time. While the 300 problem cases represent a thin .01 percent of all plans, the increase in plans may bring about an increase in the number of employers who might dip into this retirement pool. Here are some clear warning signs that can alert you to potential problems with your 401(k):

- You notice a steep drop in the value of your account that can't be explained by the market activity of the last quarter or the performance of the funds (or other types of investments which you hold).

- The deductions from your paycheck don't match the contributions on your 401(k) statements.
- Your 401(k) statements should arrive on a regularly scheduled date, four times per year. If your quarterly statement arrives late or at irregular times during the year, get an explanation from your benefits administrator—and be on guard.
- You have heard of former employees having difficulty when it came to receiving their benefits.

If any of the above problems seem to be occurring in your plan, and you can't get a reasonable (and understandable) explanation form your plan administrator, then by all means contact the Pension and Welfare Benefit Administration at (202) 219-8776. They'll return your call within 24 hours—so they say. Be discreet, since you don't want to be in the position of angering a thief or wrongly accusing someone for an honest mistake.

Borrowing from Your 401(k)

There's a key fact that you need to keep in mind when determining how much of your salary you want to go to your 401(k). That fact is that early withdrawal of funds in your 401(k) is not simply frowned upon—it's punished. There's a 10 percent penalty tax for early withdrawal. As a result, you need to be sure that your investing budget doesn't collide with your living budget. Plan ahead so that the amount you slate for your 401(k) won't impact your current lifestyle.

If you absolutely, positively have to access the money in your 401(k) plan, there are ways to do so without incurring the penalty tax; they are:

1. You retire
2. You die
3. You become disabled
4. You leave or lose your job
5. Your plan is terminated and no successor plan is established
6. You demonstrate extreme need
7. Other unusual situations

You must demonstrate both an immediate and substantial financial need as well as your inability to meet that need with any other resources. Purchasing your principal residence, meeting deductible medical expenses which exceed 7.5 percent of your adjusted gross income, and paying post-secondary tuition are demonstrations of such need, as is demonstrating need related to the imminent foreclosure of your principal residence. But think of your 401(k) as a last resort. If you have planned well, you shouldn't have to use it until you retire—which is what it is for!

Loans from 401(k) funds are permitted for up to 50 percent of your account balance up to $50,000, though loans of less than $10,000 may exceed 50 percent of your balance. Such loans must be for a stated interest rate and have a predetermined repayment schedule. Except for home loans, the maximum loan period is five years. If you don't repay the loan within the specified time period, the outstanding balance is taxable and subject to the 10 percent penalty (if you are under age 59½). Interest on such loans is not tax deductible.

Rolling Funds Over into an IRA

If you leave your job for any reason, you can take your 401(k) with you. But, if you don't reinvest the money in a similar tax-advantaged plan, you'll be taxed and, most likely, spend your retirement money. For some of us, the sum can be downright tempting—in the $10,000-plus range. Just enough for a year off in Europe. For others, with smaller amounts, the thought may be that the amount is incidental. But don't forget about the long-term benefits of compounding. Spending your retirement money is a huge mistake which can take years to recover from! So, play it smart, avoid paying the penalty tax—and avoid spending your retirement resources prematurely; rollover your 401(k) money into an IRA within sixty days. You can do this so as long as you rollover at least 50 percent of your balance. But if you don't rollover 100 percent, you're just cheating yourself. Also, be sure that the IRA you open is a new IRA, so that your tax-advantaged investments aren't commingled with your taxable investments—a paperwork nightmare. Moreover, if you commingle your funds with an existing IRA, you may not be able to re-rollover the funds into a new 401(k) down the road. (For more on IRAs, see the following chapter.)

PENSION PLANS

Some people don't have the option of investing in a 401(k)—but do have the choice of participating in a pension plan. If you work for a company that has its own pension plan, and you plan on being there for the duration (or at least ten years), and the company itself lasts through your tenure, then you may be able to retire with a pension that provides for the lion's share of your retirement needs. But be aware of the fact that fewer and fewer employees can rely on their place of employment either for their career or to still be there ten or more years down the road. While pension plans used to be the parachute most employees counted on for their golden years, we face a new corporate climate in which the top level is provided with golden parachutes while middle managers and below are often asked to jump ship with little or no parachute.

Company pension plans usually require you to make after-tax contributions, which are either wholly or partially matched by your employer's contributions. And while this means that there are no immediate tax benefits as there are with 401(k) plans, you are getting your employer's contribution, and your investments will enjoy the benefit of tax deferral.

Is a pension plan your only option? Well, chances are good that if you answer yes, you're thinking about it being the only option with the potential for matching funds, since you *are* free to open an IRA (which won't be deductible if you or your spouse currently participates in a retirement plan at work) or, if you're self-employed, you can consider a SEP or Keogh (all of which are explained in detail in the following chapter). In fact, I would recommend doing both, so that your retirement money isn't restricted to what could be a narrowly defined stable of investment opportunities through your pension at work, and so that you can take advantage of opening an IRA through Fidelity, Charles Schwab, or Jack White, wherein you can buy funds from over forty different fund families.

Most pension plans provide the following: defined rights, benefits, eligibility standards, and predetermined formulas to calculate your benefits. You'll need to get a handle on all the above by contacting your employee benefits administrator.

There are two basic types of pension plans: defined benefit and defined contribution plans. A *defined benefit plan* establishes a predetermined retirement sum. While this may sound like a dream come true, the results are less than spectacular, even risky. For one thing, your employer sets the amount and while it may seem like a generous amount to you today, remember that you've got another thirty years to go—thirty years that are prone to the toll inflation takes. Moreover, expecting a specific amount of benefits is a far cry from actually receiving them. You're putting a lot of faith in your employer who could, like so many businesses before them, fail to last as long as you—taking your pension plans down the tubes with them.

A *defined contribution plan* is even less secure. Here, your employer makes a certain contribution to the pension fund each and every year. When you retire, you receive a monthly amount based on whatever happens to be in the fund at the time.

If I sound fairly skeptical about such pension plans, then you're hearing me loud and clear—but it is only my opinion. Many current pensioners would chase me down with their walkers and club me into silence with their four-pronged aluminum canes. But things change—and nowhere is this more evident than in corporate America, where downsizing has been (and is likely to continue to be) the rule—not exactly the kind of playing field I'd want to be playing on with my retirement funding! Nevertheless, there's one solid benefit to a pension plan—and it's called being vested in one.

Vesting

Simply put, vesting is the rate at which your pension contributions permanently accrue to your account. A typical vesting schedule: 100 percent vesting upon completion of five years of service. An alternative: a seven-year, graduated vesting schedule of usually 20 percent after three years of service and 20 percent for each year thereafter. If you are out of work because of a prolonged illness or disability, your vesting will most likely be affected. In fact, you can lose all benefits accrued to a certain point.

Should you terminate your employment with a company and receive vested benefits, the benefits must be put into a rollover IRA within sixty days, or they will be regarded as taxable income for that year, and they will usually be subject to a 10 percent penalty tax for distributions received before age 59½. You may also have the option of keeping your vested pension benefits in the company until you reach retirement age, at which time you can draw a small pension. But don't let someone else have control over your retirement money or even a portion of it. Again, you should go for a roll-over IRA.

Of course, if you have suffered an unplanned layoff, you may need to use some or all of these retirement benefits to meet living expenses—which means you didn't have a sufficient emergency account set aside. As with using any money earmarked for retirement, do it as a last resort, if at all.

Plan Benefits

Unlike a 401(k) or an IRA where you designate your spouse as your beneficiary, your pension plan probably won't include an option that will pay your spouse in the event of your untimely death. Why? Such benefits typically are available only if you have become eligible for early retirement or are within ten years of normal retirement age—neither of which is likely to be the case for you.

Permanent disability could impose severe financial hardship on you and your family. Some pension plans provide for disability by allowing for the distribution of a reduced income previously slated for your retirement. Others provide a disability plan that's separate from the retirement plan. Another option to prepare for the un-expected accident is to take out a disability insurance policy on your own. If you are the sole or primary source of revenue—this is a must.

Chances are that you will have the ability to invest in one or more of the company-sponsored retirement investment plans. Chances are that doing so will be beneficial. However, you need to ensure that the benefits are there in terms of the merits of the investments offered. The merits of the tax advantages are clear and present, but what happens if you don't have any of the above retirement investment plans at your present place of employment? Consider the next chapter as your immediate future's source of retirement investment plans.

Ready Resources

- *401(k): Take Charge of Your Future,* by E. Schurenberg, Warner Books.
- *401(k) Book,* by R. Sasanow, Henry Holt.
- *Keys to Investing in Your 401K,* by W. Boroson, Barron's.

- *Your Retirement Benefits,* by P. Gaudio, John Wiley.
- *Standard & Poor's 401(k) Planning,* by A. Miller, McGraw-Hill.
- "What You Should Know About the Pension Law," Consumer Information Center, P.O. Box 100, Pueblo, CO 81002.
- "A Guide to Understanding Your Pension Plan," Pension Rights Center, 1346 Connecticut Ave., NW, Washington, DC 20036.

Chapter Twenty-Three

Retirement Plans for the Self-Employed

We're an entrepreneurial crowd. We like to be in control of our present way of living. But, if you aren't also salting away money for retirement, you not only won't be able to enjoy your present lifestyle for too much longer (since you'll be forced to save more), but you will also fail in the single most important entrepreneurial test of all: securing an independent life for yourself.

Whether you are an entrepreneur or not, you need to take matters into your own hands when it comes to saving for your retirement. But, if you don't have a 401(k) or other type of employer-sponsored retirement plan at your disposal, you'll need to figure out a tax-advantaged way to build your own retirement savings war chest. The best way is to create a tax-advantaged plan which enables you to invest in a range of investment vehicles—specifically, a range of stock mutual funds from different fund families. The following plans fit the bill.

IRAs—Individual Retirement Accounts

More than just an old standby, an IRA is an excellent investment vehicle. What exactly is an IRA? An IRA is a type of investment account, not an investment in and of itself. Like a 401(k), an IRA can be a tax-advantaged investment account which can help you achieve your objective of a financially secure retirement.

IRAs used to be the best-known form of tax-advantaged investment accounts. Today, 401(k) plans may be more talked about. But there's no denying that millions of Americans have invested billions in IRAs. Should you invest in one? What are the advantages and disadvantages of doing so for you? How can you make the most of your IRA account, if that's what you've got—or where you're headed?

There are three main aspects to participating in an IRA: (1) opening the account, (2) selecting and managing the funds you invest in it, and (3) (way down the road) planning how you will withdraw from it. Bottom line: the benefits of tax-deductible and tax-deferred IRAs versus non-tax-advantaged or tax-deferred investments is that more of your money goes to work for you—and more of your money reaps the rewards of compounding.

Is an IRA right for you? Basically, if you are employed but don't have the ability to participate in a 401(k), 403(b), or other type of pension plan at your place of employment, and you are not self-employed (either full- or part-time), then, yes, by all means, open an IRA. If, however, you have other options (most of them were just listed) to invest in your retirement, then you'll need to weigh their strengths and weaknesses against those of an IRA.

While all IRAs are tax-deferred accounts, not all IRA accounts are tax-deductible. Anyone with job-related income (i.e., not that hefty trust fund you've got) can contribute to an IRA. You can contribute up to $2,000 of this income to an IRA each year. Married couples can contribute up to $4,000, if each spouse is making at least $2,000. If one spouse has no income, then the couple can contribute up to $2,250; and, no, you can't get around this limit by paying your spouse to do housekeeping.

There are two types of IRA accounts: *tax-deductible* and *tax-deferred*. IRA profits are always deferred until you make withdrawals. But your IRA contributions may or may not be tax-deductible as you make them. What determines your ability to deduct your IRA investment? If you and/or your spouse participate in a company's retirement plan, AND your combined income exceeds $40,000 ($25,000 for singles), the IRA contribution is not fully deductible. The deductibility phases out evenly over the next $10,000 of income, so if you or your spouse participate in a company's retirement plan, AND your income exceeds $50,000 ($35,000 for singles), the IRA contribution isn't deductible at all.

Even if you can't deduct your IRA contributions, it can still make sense to put as much money as you can afford into an IRA. Regardless of deductibility, IRA money still grows tax-free, and this keeps more of your money at work for you.

However, don't make the common mistake of thinking that tax-advantaged, tax-deductible, or tax-deferred means "tax-free." They don't. When it comes time to withdraw the money you've stowed away in your IRA, as with most investments, you will be taxed. But, by that time, you will have no doubt read all about the best ways to minimize such taxes and have established dozens of trust accounts for you, your children, your children's children, and so on. For now, let's focus on how you can build the chest that you'll put your treasure in.

OPENING YOUR IRA ACCOUNT: Like the types of investments we've talked about in previous chapters, getting started opening your IRA account is easy. To do so, you can call or walk into your local bank, brokerage, mutual fund investor center, or insurance company and request an application. (If you call, ask that the application be sent to you at home; no one in your office needs to know your personal business.) Note: Where you open your IRA affects the range and type of investment options available to you. If no-load mutual funds from several different fund families aren't an option, move on to an account which does offer them.

If opening an IRA account is as easy as opening a brokerage account or purchasing shares in a mutual fund, so choosing the holder of your IRA account (bank, brokerage, fund company, etc.), and selecting the types of investments that will comprise your IRA portfolio, is as complex a task as selecting the best brokerage, stocks, bonds, and mutual funds for your actual portfolio.

TIMING: If you decide that you will be best served by opening up an IRA account, the sooner you do so, the better—literally. Waiting until the last minute is rarely a good way to do anything with your money (unless you're feeding a parking meter). And when it comes to investing in an IRA, the benefits of doing so earlier in the year —as opposed to at the tax-time deadline of April 15th the next year—are substantial. If you make your $2,000 1995 IRA contribution in April 1996, and also make your 1996 contribution in April 1996, that is from an investment standpoint just like making two contributions in one year; you've effectively doubled your $2,000 annual contribution to $4,000.

Looked at another way, you'll get an extra year of tax-deferred growth out of your 1996 contribution. Either way, moving up your $2,000 annual contributions by twelve months can mean more than $20,000 extra when you retire (at 8 percent annual growth over thirty years). This effective "extra payment" is all perfectly legal; in fact, you could make your 1996 contribution as early as January 1996, or as late as filing time in April 1997.

PERFORMANCE AND YOUR IRA PORTFOLIO: After setting up your IRA account, you'll need to figure out what types of investments you want to put in it. In doing so, you'll need to create one portfolio that can accomplish two things. First, you'll need to ensure that your IRA performs in accordance with your return objective. Ensuring that this is the case will require you to relate your IRA's performance to your other retirement-oriented investments. Second, you'll want to be certain that the investments you've selected for your IRA portfolio are the best possible choice.

You can put just about any type of investment in your IRA portfolio, among them: CDs, U.S. bonds (bills or notes), money market funds, stocks, corporate bonds, mutual funds, zero coupon securities, unit investment trusts, limited partnerships, options (for self-directed IRAs only), and U.S. gold and silver coins. My preferences: taxable stocks, bonds, and mutual funds. (There's no sense putting a tax-free investment, like a municipal bond or muni bond fund, in a tax-free account!)

As with your other investment portfolios, you will be best served by actively managing your IRA portfolio. What does active management mean? Among other things, it means reviewing the investments in your IRA's performance as compared to other available investments. Doing so isn't all that difficult. For one thing, most banks, mutual fund, and insurance companies issue monthly or quarterly statements which allow you to track the performance of your IRA account in terms of its total return. And tracking the constituent parts of your IRA portfolio has never been easier, thanks to the increased coverage in even local papers of mutual funds—which, I repeat, are the best way to build your investment portfolio from scratch.

CHANGING YOUR MIX: Making changes to particular parts of your overall portfolio in order to account for changes in the overall market is a good idea. But don't confuse this with making changes to your overall portfolio. If you've done the job right, you shouldn't have to make dramatic changes to the overall objective that your portfolio was originally designed for. Also, be careful of chasing after this year's winning stocks, bonds, and mutual funds. While there are legitimate reasons for selling and buying new stocks, bonds, and mutual funds to enhance your IRA portfolio's return, buying a highflier is *not* one of them.

What parts of your IRA portfolio might need to be adjusted? If you want to increase your exposure to international markets, for example, you may want to add an additional international fund or up the ante in the one you've got. (For optimal portfolio allocations, return to chapter 14.) How do you do this? If you haven't exceeded the contribution limit for the year, you can purchase the fund for your account outright, or, if you have reached the maximum, you can consider selling another investment or reducing your money market amount in order to purchase the international fund with the proceeds. Some plans restrict the number of trades you can do in a given time frame—per quarter or per year. You'll need to be sure that your IRA account enables you to make at least one trade per quarter. Not that I'm advocating active trading. Far from it. Instead, I'm advocating your right to react to changes in the market.

Do you need to shift money from another retirement plan—a 401(k) from a previous employer, for example—into a new or existing IRA? There are two ways to do so: direct transfer and rollover. In order to pursue a direct transfer, you will need to lend the custodian of your old account the right to transfer those assets directly into your new account. Typically, this entails having to physically sign a specific form (so it won't happen overnight). Once the form has been signed, the old custodian can then transfer your money and whatever investments it's invested in into your new account. You may encounter some delay between the time you sign the form and when the money gets transferred. Stay on top of your old custodian to ensure that they are working on your behalf (rather than their own—after all, the longer your account stays with them, the more fees they receive).

When it comes to rollovers, be sure that you are in charge. Rollovers typically happen when you transfer your investments from an existing retirement plan or when your existing IRA funds are transferred from one account to a new IRA. For example, if you decide to change jobs from a company which currently provides a 401(k) plan, and you're taking a job at a company which doesn't offer any retirement plan, you'll need to roll the funds in your old 401(k) plan into an IRA (within sixty days—or a 10 percent penalty will be incurred). Note: Do not place money from an existing retirement plan into an existing IRA. Why? If you do, you will be "comingling" your tax-advantaged retirement money with your taxable investments—making the transfer a confusing proposition. Instead, set up a new IRA account as the repository for your accumulated 401(k) savings. Should you become employed by a company which offers a 401(k) in your future—and chances are great that you will work for a company which offers a pension, 401(k), or 403(b) plan before your toes turn up—then it's in your best interest to safeguard the savings you've already accumulated. Also, if you're a job hopper, keep in mind that you're entitled to one personal rollover per each 12-month period (whereas direct transfers may be made as often as you want).

Withdrawal Penalty!

If you withdraw before your time, you'll get the hangover without the wine. That's because withdrawing funds from your IRA before you reach age 59½ makes them subject to a 10 percent penalty tax in addition to being fully taxed as regular income. (On the other hand, you will have to begin IRA withdrawals by April 1 or the year after turning age 70½ or you'll be subject to a whopping 50 percent penalty from the IRS.) Exceptions? One is noted below. But be careful. This is your retirement money—nothing, save a dire emergency, should push you into using it. Of course, once you near retirement age—59½ at the earliest, unless you become permanently disabled—you will need to plan on the best way to withdraw funds.

You can make personal use of your IRA funds for up to sixty days per year while rolling over your account. Don't do it. It's simply too easy to fritter away the money, leaving you holding less than zero (since the IRS will want that 10 percent penalty!).

Retirement Plans for the Entrepreneur

If you are self-employed and earning income—i.e., you're getting paid to play your guitar in the bar on Thursday nights and not just toting it around for the Antonio Banderas look—then you can create your own self-employment retirement plan, even if you currently participate in your full-time employer's pension plan. The benefits of doing so are threefold: your contributions may be fully or partially tax deductible, you'll enjoy the benefits of tax-deferred growth of your investments, and you'll build a better retirement stash for yourself. Even if you stop playing at being a musician later in life, you'll have established an additional source of retirement revenue for yourself.

We'll look at two types of plans, the **Keogh** and the **SEP** (simplified employee pension). Like other retirement plans, the threefold benefits of these plans come with some strings attached. There are specific maximum contributions and deadlines for those contributions, and the money you invest won't be available to you (without severe penalties) until you reach 59½. But, since this is part of your retirement savings, these shouldn't be drawbacks. Just don't look to these plans as a source of funds for preretirement financial expenses, like college tuition or the down payment for that vacation home on the Vineyard.

You can set up a self-employed retirement plan if you are self-employed (full- or part-time). That's it. No big character check or profitability analysis. You work for yourself. You get paid. You can participate. (And chances are you should.) Even if you are a full-time employee and participating in a pension plan, as long as you have income from one source of self-employment, chances are you'll qualify for one of the following self-employed retirement plans.

SEPs—Simplified Employee Pension

Simplified employee pension plans (called SEPs) are a non-CPAs answer to self-funding a retirement plan. Why? Ease. Instead of maintaining a separate pension plan (as is required with a Keogh, detailed on pages 274–77), your SEP contributions are deposited directly into your IRA account. If you have employees, consider a salary reduction SEP—detailed below—to enable your employees and you to fund your own retirement plans at lower cost.

IF YOU OWN THE SHOP: As with the Keogh plans described later, you have to offer a SEP to your employees if you provide one for yourself. In order to start a SEP, an employer must file IRS Form 5305-SEP.

HOW SEPs WORK: First, you'll need to set up an IRA account (see page 267) into which your contributions can be placed—or your employer can establish one in which you can deposit your contributions. Your employer can then make contributions in accordance with specified limits. Once a SEP is established, your employer must contribute to the accounts of each employee who is over age 21 who has performed services in at least three of the five proceeding calendar years.

TAX ADVANTAGES: Like regular qualified retirement plans, your contributions to a SEP are tax deductible up to the lesser of $30,000 or 15 percent of your compensation, although your employer may set the percentage at less than 15 percent. (The percentage will be the same for all employees.) Contributions made within three and one-half months after the close of a calendar year are treated as if they are made on the last day of the calendar year. If you're an employer, your contributions to your employees' SEPs are not subject to FICA or the Federal Unemployment Tax Act (FUTA) tax withholdings, although state income tax usually will have to be paid on your contribution amount.

HOW MUCH: For your own (not employer-sponsored) SEP, you can contribute 15 percent of your gross self-employment income, up to $9,500 in 1996. You can also contribute to a separate IRA on top of the SEP contribution.

DEADLINE: Like an IRA, you can set up a SEP after the end of the tax year in which you want to begin taking the deduction as long as you fund it before April 15th. The deductible SEP contributions can be made at any time until the April 15th deadline.

WITHDRAWAL PENALTY: Premature withdrawals from a SEP are subject to a 10 percent penalty. Age 59½, death, or disability are the thresholds you must cross if you want to avoid this punitive loss.

Salary Reduction SEPs

If you own a small business, you may qualify for a special form of SEP known as a "salary reduction SEP." As with a 401(k) plan (described in detail in the previous chapter), employees elect to have their contributions deducted from their pay (rather than employers' making the SEP payments in addition to their salary). If you have twenty-five or fewer employees at any time during the preceding year and at least 50 percent of them agree to participate in the salary reduction SEP, this is probably the best route for you to take.

Is what's good for your employer good for you? If you work for a small business with twenty-five or fewer employees, you may be called upon to vote this option in or out of your own retirement funding future. Employee-funded SEPs contain a salary reduction provision allowing employees to reduce their salaries and to have the reduction amount (called "elective contributions") deposited in the plan. Doing so provides you with two advantages: your taxable salary base is lowered (meaning less of what you earn goes to Uncle Sam), and you retirement funding is increased (meaning more of your money goes to work for you). True, there are limitations on the total amount of annual elective contributions you, as an employee, can make. But while the percentage of your income that can be set aside is lower, SEPs have the advantage of being easier to set up and maintain—especially when compared to a Keogh.

Keogh Plans

Keoghs are designed to provide *unincorporated* self-employeds the opportunity to set up a personal pension fund. Modeled after a large-company pension plan, Keoghs can be set up by self-employeds for themselves and their employees. If you are not self-employed, but work in a company through which you participate in a pension plan, you may also set up a Keogh plan if you earn income from another line of work.

Keoghs aren't all that easy to set up if you're trying to go it alone. They're subject to changing, complex, confusing rules. Fortunately, many financial institutions offer an easy way to open a Keogh (since they do most of the technical work for you). Banks, brokerage firms, and mutual fund companies can help you understand and open a Keogh. But as with most things in life, the more you know about a Keogh before you start asking questions, the more meaningful your inquiry will be. The following Keogh primer should help you cover the basics and then some. That way, you can help yourself determine if a Keogh is for you and, if so, you can proceed.

WHAT IS A KEOGH? A Keogh is a retirement plan designed for incorporated self-employeds to provide tax-deferred retirement benefits to themselves as owners or partners in their company, as well as to provide such for any eligible employees.

HOW DOES A KEOGH WORK? You make contributions to the account which are tax-deductible, and all interest accumulates tax free until the time such funds are withdrawn. You can contribute, and deduct, up to 25 percent of your net income—or a specified sum set by the federal government each year, whichever is less. Of course, you don't have to participate to the maximum. You can instead invest an amount that is appropriate relative to your other retirement savings plans.

TYPES OF KEOGHS: The most common form of a Keogh is a *defined-contribution* plan. The second type of Keogh provides a *defined-benefit* plan. If your business is booming and your income stream is strong and well in excess of what your lifestyle expenditures absorb, a defined-benefit plan can allow among the highest annual tax deductible contributions, well in excess of the cap on a defined-contribution Keoghs.

DETAILS: If you have a Keogh plan, you can also open, or continue to contribute to, an IRA (see the following chapter for the scoop on IRAs). Or, in addition to the regular tax-deductible Keogh contribution, you can place the $2,000 tax-deductible contribution you would make to your IRA in your Keogh account and still deduct it from your tax return. However, the amount of your additional Keogh contribution reduces, dollar for dollar, the yearly amount that you may contribute to your IRA. And if you are having a particularly good year, you may also make voluntary contributions to your Keogh account of up to 10 percent of your earned income on top of what is normally contributed; these contributions are not tax-deductible, but the earnings are tax-deferred.

DEADLINES: Whichever Keogh plan you choose, you must set it up by December 31st of the year in which you want to begin taking the deduction. However, once you have set up the account, you don't have to make the actual contribution until your tax return is filed (including extensions) in the following year. (Of course, the sooner you contribute, the sooner the positive effect of compounding can begin to work for you.) Note: if you want to set up a retirement plan but missed the Keogh deadline for last year, and it is not yet April 15th, you can consider setting up a SEP, detailed above.

The amount you contribute to your defined-contribution Keogh and the amount you can legitimately deduct are not always equal to each other, although the deduction can't exceed the contribution—ever. The amount of your deductible contribution is directly related to which type of defined-contribution Keogh you select: money-purchase or profit-sharing. (If you're running a solo venture, there probably won't be much of a difference between the two plans, but if you have employees, consult your accountant before making a move into a Keogh.) With a money-purchase plan, your contribution amount is a fixed percentage of your income; no matter how little or how much you make, you're obligated to provide the specified percentage. A profit-sharing plan is by far the more flexible. You can contribute as much (approximately 15 percent of your income) or as little as you want. This means that when things are going boffo for you, you can contribute to the max—and when a lean year comes (as they always do, even for Netscape or Snapple!), you can scale way back or even not make a contribution.

MORE DETAILS: Deductible contributions to a money-purchase Keogh plan are limited to 25 percent of your net income after your Keogh deductions are accounted for. Deductible contributions to a profit-sharing plan are limited to 15 percent of your net income after your Keogh deductions are accounted for.

How can you calculate the amount of deductible contributions you can make? For money-purchase plans, your deduction percentage is determined by dividing 25 percent by 125 percent of your total income plus the Keogh deduction divided by the maximum percentage to arrive at 20 percent. For profit-sharing plans, the deduction percentage is determined by dividing 15 percent by 115 percent to arrive at 13.0435 percent. You can use both plans together to obtain the maximum percentage deduction permitted by the law. This part's a snap. You can contribute 10 percent to money-purchase and 15 percent to profit-sharing and get the full 25 percent.

LONE SHARK: As with an IRA, there are stiff penalties associated with early withdrawal of funds. Nevertheless, and also similar to an IRA, you can loan yourself money from your Keogh nest egg—you can, that is, if you're an employee of a business which offers such a plan. Owners can't. An employee is defined as an individual who owns less than 10 percent of the business. An owner is defined as, you guessed it, an individual who owns more than 10 percent of the business.

OWNERS FIRST: If you own the business, you're prohibited from loaning funds to yourself from the Keogh kitty. If you do so you'll be subject to a 5 percent penalty assessed in the year you make the prohibited loan; and 5 percent each following year until the entire loan is repaid with interest. Failure to repay the loan will net you a *100 percent fine.*

EMPLOYEES NEXT: If you are employed by the next Bill Gates, and you own 10 percent or less of the business, you can loan yourself a sum which either can't exceed a specified sum or up to 50 percent of the vested Keogh plan benefits (with a specific contribution ceiling), whichever is greater. You have five years to repay the loan unless you use it to buy your residence, in which case the repayment period can be longer. But note the penalty attached to failing to repay the loan: you'll be taxed on the outstanding balance and, if you're under 59½, you'll pay an additional 10 percent penalty.

TAXING NOTE: If your Keogh plan covers only yourself, or you and your spouse, you must file IRS Form 5500 EZ by the end of the seventh month following the end of the plan's fiscal year (July 31st if your plan year is the calendar year), if the assets you have in your Keogh plan at the end of the plan year exceed $100,000.

As you can clearly see, SEPs and Keoghs make investing in IRAs look easy. There are distinct advantages to each plan—beyond the ease with which one can or can't participate in them. For the successful entrepreneur, saving the maximum tax-advantaged amount (i.e., the SEP or Keogh route) may make the most sense. On the other hand, for those just starting out, an IRA is the best place to start.

READY RESOURCES

- *IRA Investing Made Easy,* by A. Hutchinson, Globe Pequot.

CHAPTER TWENTY-FOUR

Tax-Wise Investing Moves

O K. Nothing, not even the Brady Bunch ice capades, could be as mind-numbing as taxes. Forms and more forms. Numbers that don't add up. Annual, quarterly, monthly statements from hell. You might as well give up, move to a place where taxes don't exist. If only such a place did exist—but then, how would they be able to afford to build roads, finance schools, foster religious freedom, not to mention paying for all those haircuts and parking spaces at airports that our politicians make such good use of.

Knowledge versus legwork—that's what tax strategizing is all about. But who has the time to do either? Not you. I mean, let's face it—there are movies to be seen and coffee bars you've yet to blow the froth from. And while I can't offer you individual tax advice, I can make sure that you are up to speed on some of the more essential areas relating to taxes and your investments. Reading the following can help you both save a bundle and maximize the earning power of your hard-earned money. Now we're speaking a language that isn't dead. Let's take a look.

Basically there are a few definitions you need to know, and several sources and several strategies that can help you master the tax-related issues of your overall investment plan. First, always evaluate the tax consequences of your investing (and financial-related) moves. But never invest in something solely for the tax benefits of doing so. Instead, weigh the merits of the investment in light of several factors—from your personal objective to the inherent quality of the investment to the potential tax ramifications of it.

DEFINING MOMENTS

When it comes to investing, there's a defining moment at year-end. It's the moment when you determine just how well your investments have done over the year. If they've done well, then chances are you have *capital gains* to account for. If they have done poorly, you may have *capital losses* which, once accounted for, can help you reduce the overall tax burden of your capital gains.

CAPITAL GAIN: The difference between an asset's (for example, a stock's) purchased price and selling price, when that difference is positive. Taxes must be paid when that asset is sold. Selling an asset which has capital gains is known as selling the gains that have, through their sale, become *realized*. As long as you hold onto your investments, you don't pay any capital gains taxes on the increase in value these investments. That's one benefit of buying and holding—although, eventually, you will have to learn some fancy estate-planning footwork.

CAPITAL LOSS: The difference between an asset's (for example, a stock's) purchased price and selling price, when that difference is negative. In this case, a negative can be a positive come tax time. That's because of your ability to take advantage of a "tax loss." Doing so is relatively easy: you simply exchange shares in a losing stock or fund into a similar stock or fund. This method of exchange is known as a "tax swap." You can apply the loss against any capital gains plus $3,000 of your personal income. (Moreover, if you have suffered more loss than your swap can swallow in a given year, you can carry the excess loss over to future years.)

WASH SALE RULE: If you want to buy the stock or fund back—and just use the loss to your advantage—you can sell the original stock or fund, but be sure to *wait* thirty-one days before switching back into it. If you do it sooner, the IRS will consider it a "wash sale" and disallow the loss.

DISTRIBUTIONS: When it comes to investing in mutual funds, you lose the ability to control your capital gains, since the fund manager will be the one who is buying and selling shares in the securities which comprise his or her portfolio. Distributions are comprised of long-term capital gains, short-term capital gains, and dividend income. Since 1991, taxes on long-term capital gains have been capped at 28 percent, while if you're in a higher tax bracket (31, 36, or 39.6 percent), you'll pay that higher rate on short-term gains and income. Distributions do not affect tax-deferred retirement accounts. The whole point of an IRA, 401(k), SEP, annuity, or other tax-advantaged account is to allow for tax-free compounding of interest and capital gains.

INVESTOR'S TAX PLANNING CHECKLIST

You will need to coordinate your investment tax planning with other important personal financial planning areas, including investments and retirement planning. As you do so, keep the following items in mind:

- Keep meticulous tax records. (See chapter 4 for details.) It's the only way to stay ahead of the flood of forms—on your investments and more.
- Don't be sold on an investment solely on the merits of its tax advantage. Do be sold on the merits of investing in a tax-advantaged investment plan like a 401(k) or 403(b).
- Hold the stocks you buy—and let the capital gains work in your favor.
- If you're owed a refund, send in your tax return early. Filing late means you lose the ability to receive and invest the refund—meaning you lose interest on money you could have had sooner.
- If you owe the IRS money, don't send in your tax return early. Paying early means you lose interest you could have earned.
- Amend your return if you overpaid taxes the previous year and get a refund.
- Donate stocks, not cash. If you are looking for a way to avoid capital gains tax and benefit a cause you believe in (and one that the IRS believes in, too), donate the appreciated stock and, in return, get a deduction for its current market price.
- Donate your clothing (not all of it) and other personal items —furniture, radio, scale, or toaster oven, or other property you don't need or use—to a charitable organization. (Sorry, your best friend who was just fired from that cool software company

doesn't rate as a charity in the eyes of the IRS.) You can deduct the fair market value of the items—which can translate into a great inverse investment.

- Delay buying a fund until after its distribution is made. (Call your fund company to find out if and when it will be making a distribution—typically, toward year-end.) That's because income and capital gain distributions create an immediate tax liability in taxable accounts.

- Note that you should receive 1099-DIV forms by the end of January. You should record "Ordinary Dividends" (box 1B) on Schedule B of your federal tax return as dividends. Naturally, capital gains distributions (box 1C) are recorded as part of your calculation of capital gains (or losses) on Schedule D.

INVESTOR TAX STRATEGIES

If you don't like paying the government more of your hard-earned money, and you dislike putting less of your savings to work for you, this section is for you.

MAXIMIZE YOUR 401(K), 403(B), IRA, OR OTHER TAX-ADVANTAGED OR TAX-DEFERRED CONTRIBUTION: This is a winner—and a no-brainer. Chances are you will qualify for one tax-advantaged retirement-oriented investment plan—and so much the better. It's especially advantageous if you can participate in a company-sponsored 401(k) or 403(b), since contributions are made with pre-tax dollars and you may receive the added benefit of matching funds from your employer. The maximum contribution ceiling is also higher in some plans—for example, a 401(k) versus an IRA. Bottom line: participate to the maximum—but realize that the maximum for you isn't necessary the maximum allowable contribution. You need to ensure that your other living expenses are accounted for, too. Otherwise, you run the risk of dipping into your retirement fund for current living expenses. There is a substantial penalty for doing so.

CONTRIBUTE TO AN IRA IF YOU HAVE MAXED OUT ON YOUR 401(K) CONTRIBUTION: Even if the IRA contribution is nondeductible, it's a good deal since your money grows tax deferred until withdrawal. Also, plan ahead so that you can contribute to your IRA as early in the year as possible. The earlier you begin, the more time your money has to compound tax-deferred.

REQUEST AND REVIEW YOUR BROKERAGE OR FUND COMPANY'S TAX REPORTS: Full-service brokerages and even most major discount shops, as well as some mutual fund companies and many leading fund networks, provide you with most of the necessary tax information you'll need.

MUNI BOND FUNDS: These funds (see chapter 10) are potentially an excellent tax-exempt investment since buying municipal bonds directly is expensive and risky in terms of you inability to invest in several and research all. Be sure, however, that the munis are issued in your state (or Puerto Rico), in order to ensure exemption from both federal and state income taxes.

READY RESOURCES

The following IRS publications (free for the asking) can help you consider, evaluate, and file your investment-related taxable transactions. Ask for them by number and title.

PUBLICATION NUMBER	TITLE
1	Your Rights as a Taxpayer
17	Your Federal Income Tax
334	Tax Guide for Small Businesses
448	Federal Estate and Gift Taxes
463	Travel, Entertainment, and Gift Expenses
501	Exemptions, Standard Deduction, and Filing Information
505	Tax Withholding and Estimated Tax
523	Tax Information on Selling Your Home
525	Taxable and Nontaxable Income
526	Charitable Contributions
527	Residential Rental Property
529	Miscellaneous Deductions
530	Tax Information for Homeowners (including Owners of Condominiums and Cooperative Apartments)
533	Self-Employment Tax
534	Depreciation
535	Business Expenses

CONCLUSION

The Most Important Investment You'll Ever Make

When it comes to living life on your terms, you're the only person who can decide what those terms are. Failure to do so will result in a compromise that can, sooner or later, become unlivable or, worse, tolerable. Why is living a tolerable life worse than an unlivable situation? Because when something is unlivable, you move on. When it is tolerable, you stay put and suffer the consequences.

We'll be able to see the majority of those one generation ahead of us living a tolerable retirement lifestyle—one they wouldn't have chosen for themselves from a lifestyle catalog, but one which their lack of investing forced them to accept. If they had broken their backs sending their children to private school, encouraging learning and self-advancement, and investing in their own offspring, then, yes, give them the benefit of the doubt. This small subsector at least invested in *someone's* future. But don't feel too terribly sad for the majority, at least not for those who charged their way through life, never saving enough. It's no wonder this group ate their way through their savings, since they probably blew at least one quarter of their disposable income dining out. They probably spent over $150,000 on uselessly expensive cars, too. Self-indulgence, not self-discipline, was the rule. Make your life an exception to it.

While many of us know that life is what we make of it, the siren call of spending what you earn now (rather than investing it in a distant future) can be overwhelming. And it's not just temptation of what we desire that can drive us to the poorhouse. It's also fear of the unknown. And when it comes to investing—the best way to ensure a better life for ourselves now and in the future—fear of the unknown can set us way back in terms of being able to reap the rewards which long-term investing can bestow.

In working your way through this book, you began on one side of what may have appeared to be an unscalable mountain. If you have read every chapter contained in this book, then you have scaled the peak and seen the world of investing for what it is—a bountiful landscape with some treacherous slopes which can be avoided or managed within reason. If you tunneled from the introduction straight through to the final section, you still know the core theme of investing: to provide a financially secure future for yourself. No one else can climb a mountain for you. No one else can get you to prove to yourself that you have the stamina to invest regularly and often. But that's the only way you'll be able to overcome the most troublesome obstacle between you and living life on your own terms—call it the object of money.

Money won't make your life more meaningful. Nor should your life be bent by the pursuit of money alone—or by merely the things that money can buy. There's far more to life than what money can buy. But, by the same token, a life lived in the quiet desperation of debts owed is unsettling. You know it is. By the time you retire, you'll not only need to have paid off all your debts, you will also need to have a war chest of easily $1 million—just to maintain your current $45,000 lifestyle of today. You've known it. You can't get around it. But you can achieve it—so long as you begin to invest in your future today.

There are more immediate financial hurdles. Saving for a down payment on a home. Paying off your college or grad school loans. Your car is on its last rounds. There's always something in the here and now which can steer you away from your longer-term goals. There's no easy answer to any of the hurdles you face. But there is

a significant advantage in knowing what they are, and what strategies you can use to win the race. That's what this book has been
all about—winning the race of your own financial independence.
Doing so opens up a world of opportunities that extend far beyond
the horizon of making, saving, and investing. Taking care of your
financial life (in the here and now, as well as for the future) will
enable you to invest more meaningful time in yourself as well as in
those who mean the most to you. (A capital idea!)

As you have learned, the recipe for investment success is a simple
one. You have the ability to invest wisely and well. You have the
resources. You understand why it's in your best interest to invest,
and to do so consistently and long term. There's no artificial substitute or minute method available. You need to make it on your
own. In fact, the only way you can rest assured that you'll have your
cake and eat it too is by investing from scratch.

GLOSSARY

Coming to Terms
with Your Investments

Use this glossary to help you on your way to building a basic investment vocabulary.

Advance/Decline Ratio. The number of stocks whose prices have advanced versus those that have declined over a given day. Typically calculated at the close of market, this ratio is used to represent the general direction of the market.

Annual Report. Yearly report of a company's overall financial condition (from operations to balance sheet) which, by law, must be sent to all shareholders.

Asked Price. A security's (or commodity's) price as offered for sale on an exchange or OTC (over-the-counter) market. (See *bid price*.)

Asset. Value attributed to stocks, bonds, real estate, mutual funds, or, in terms of a company, the value of owned equipment or plants.

Asset Allocation. A strategy for diversifying money in major investment categories as well as particular types of investments within each category.

Automatic Investment. A method for investing in mutual funds which enables you to select a specific amount to be withdrawn from your bank savings or checking account on a regular, scheduled basis and invested in a mutual fund. It's a good low-cost way to start investing in mutual funds, since many funds are willing to waive their minimum in order to get what they hope will be your long-term participation in their fund.

Automatic Reinvestment. Typically, the automatic reinvestment of dividends in new shares of a company's stock or a mutual fund. Some companies and almost all mutual funds allow automatic reinvestment. A smart move, even though you will have to pay taxes on the dividend amount (whether you reinvest or receive it in cash).

Average Annual Return. A measure of historical return; the amount per year you would have had to earn to achieve the same total return over the time period in question.

Average Maturity. The average maturity is the weighted average of the maturities of all of a fund's bond holdings. (The maturity of a bond is the date the debt is due and payable.) Typically, the longer a fund's average maturity, the greater its interest rate risk. Not as meaningful as a bond fund's *duration*.

Balance Sheet. Company's accounting of its current assets, liabilities, and owner's equity at a specified point in time. Found in the company's *annual report*.

Balanced Fund. A fund that invests substantial portions in both stocks and bonds.

Bear Market. A sustained period of falling stock or bond prices. In the stock market, fear of economic downturn, and proof of it, tends to bring the bear out of hibernation. In the bond market, rising interest rates bring on the feared animal.

Beta. The extent to which a fund's or stock's value tends to go up or down as the market goes up or down. A growth fund with a beta of 1.5 would most likely go up 15 percent when the market as a whole is up 10 percent. (Or down 15 percent when the market is down 10 percent.)

Bid Price. The highest price a prospective investor (or market maker) is prepared to pay for a security, usually just under the *asked price*, the lowest price a seller is willing to accept.

Blue Chip. Large, well-known, established companies whose stock is considered to be a solid investment and safer than other companies' stocks, since a blue chip is unlikely to go bankrupt.

Bond. An IOU issued by a corporate or government entity in return for a pledge of repayment of the original face value invested, plus interest payments to be paid on specified dates.

Bond Fund. A mutual fund that invests primarily in bonds.

Capital Gain. Profit made on the sale of securities or property. Federal capital gains taxes are currently capped at 28 percent, even for investors whose income is taxed in a higher bracket.

Capital Gains Distribution. A mutual fund's distribution to shareholders of gains realized on the sale of securities within the fund's portfolio.

Typically, the distributions are made once per year, and can affect the optimal timing of your own purchase or sale of the fund.

Capital Loss. When the amount realized on the sale of an asset is less than the amount originally paid for it.

Capital Preservation. The objective of ensuring that the amount of capital doesn't become reduced over time, which in turn means that risks are avoided in favor of a defensive portfolio. Nevertheless, some growth of capital must ensue, if only to be able to safeguard the capital from inflation's toll, and some income is also usually sought, to allow periodic withdrawals without depleting principal.

Cash. The most liquid asset, typically thought of in the form of negotiable currency, but inclusive of cash equivalents: interest-bearing short-term instruments like a money market fund or Treasury bill.

Cash Cow. A business that generates a continuous cash flow which, in terms of companies that issue publicly traded stocks, typically results in reliable dividends.

Cash Dividend. Taxable cash payments made to shareholders from a corporation's earnings. Some companies issue a stock dividend in lieu of a cash payout.

Cash Flow. A company's net income after expenses but before accounting for abstract costs such as depreciation. Cash flow is one indicator used by stock analysts to evaluate a company's ability to pay off debt and keep paying dividends.

Certificate of Deposit. Better known as a CD, a specified-term, fixed-interest-earning debt instrument issued by a bank or savings and loan. A good temporary parking place for cash you will need at a specified date in the near future (CD maturities can range from three months to five years). Penalties apply for early withdrawal. Most are FDIC insured.

Certified Financial Planner (CFP). A certificate, issued by the Institute of Certified Financial Planners, that signifies that the holder has passed a series of tests showing the ability to advise clients on a host of financial concerns, including banking, estate planning, insurance, investing, and taxes.

Certified Public Accountant (CPA). One of the more meaningful professional designations for those whose career is focused on accounting, auditing, and tax preparation. A rigorous examination process, coupled with relevant experience and state licensing, combine in this certification process.

Chartered Financial Analyst (CFA). A designation given to a person who has passed a rigorous (three-year) examination process, coupled with relevant experience in the fields of economics, ethics, financial accounting, portfolio management, and hard-core security analysis.

Chartered Financial Consultant (ChFC). A charter offered to CFPs who have also passed a four-year program at the College of Bryn Mawr, which covers economics, insurance, investing, and taxes.

Chartered Mutual Fund Counselor (ChMFC). A new designation offered by the National Endowment for Financial Education, showing a financial advisor's enhanced ability to advise clients on their mutual fund questions and concerns.

Closed-End Investment Fund. A fund that sells a fixed number of shares in its portfolio of securities, contrasted with an open-end fund which issues new shares per new purchase. Closed-end fund shares trade on the major U.S. exchanges and the over-the-counter market. Their market value is determined by supply and demand, which leads to shares being sold at either a *premium* or a *discount* to the actual *net asset value* of the fund's portfolio.

Commission. Percentage (based on selling price, amount managed, or service rendered) charged by a brokerage firm—be it real estate or investment.

Commodities. Goods, from foodstuffs to metals, traded on several exchanges by traders speculating on supply and demand's effect on the goods' prices.

Common Stock. Share of ownership in a company. Stock prices can rise or fall with the company's fortunes, or even with stock market supply and demand fluctuations (which may or may not be entirely rational).

Compound Interest. Interest earned on previously paid interest as well as on original principal amount. Example: $500 principal at 10 percent annual interest would become $550 in one year, but going forward, that $550 at 10 percent would become $605, after realizing $55 in interest during the second year ($50 on the original principal, plus $5 on the first year's interest).

Contrarian. An investor who examines the investments and trends that consensus wisdom is buying into, and invests in their opposite.

Corporate Bond. Debt instrument (IOU) issued by a private or public corporation, as opposed to a government entity. Corporate bonds typically share the following characteristics: their income is taxable; they have a *par* value of $1,000; they have a specified maturity; and they're traded on one of the major exchanges.

Correlation. The extent to which a fund and the stock market (usually as measured by the S&P 500 index) tend to move together.

Coupon. The original interest rate paid on a bond's face (or *par*) value. A $1,000 par bond paying $50 per year has a 5 percent coupon.

Credit Rating (bond). A letter grading of potential risk. Standard & Poor's (S&P) and Moody's are the top rating agencies, and both rate companies based on their ability to repay bondholders' interest and principal. Standard & Poor's ratings of AAA (Moody's highest rating is Aaa), to BBB (Baa), signify a range of "investment grade" bonds, while ratings of BB (Ba) or lower denote "below investment grade" bonds, more commonly referred to as "junk bonds." A rating of D signifies the bond is in default.

Credit Rating (consumer). A report of a consumer's history of timely (and untimely) bill paying, used to determine potential credit risk for mortgages, new credit cards, and other loans.

Current Yield (bond). Determined by dividing a bond's annual interest by its current market price. It differs from the coupon rate in that it accounts for the price paid for the bond (as opposed to its *par* value). For example, while the coupon rate of a $1,000 *par* bond paying $50 per year is 5 percent, the current yield of a bond bought at $950 with a $50 income would be 5.26 percent.

Cyclical Stock. A stock whose performance is closely tied to the health of the economy. In tough times, these stocks falter. In good times, they typically rise rapidly. Housing, cars, and "deep cyclicals" like steel manufacturers are directly affected by the consumer's (and industry's) willingness and ability to purchase goods.

Debt-to-Equity. A ratio which is calculated by dividing a company's total liabilities by total shareholder's stock in the company, and which is used to help measure a company's ability to pay its creditors if the company itself fails.

Default. Failure of a company or other debtor to make principal and/or interest payments on schedule.

Defensive Stocks. The antonym of cyclical stocks, since the company's products tend to be staples (like food) that consumers can't or won't do without (unlike a new car). As a result, their performance is less affected by economic downturns.

Derivative. A bet on the direction of interest rates or the price of some other security or commodity. Some funds and investors use derivatives aggressively to enhance the yield or potential return of their portfolio, while others use them in an attempt to reduce the risk of their portfolio. Derivatives aren't all bad—but the excessive proliferation of them is a potential warning sign.

Discount. The reflection of a price reduction in the product or security you're buying at market. For example, relating to bonds, a discount is the difference between the bond's *par* value and its current market price where that price is lower than the *par* value. (In contrast, buying a bond at a premium would mean the current market price is higher than the *par* value.) For a closed-end fund, a discount is the amount by which the purchase price is less than net asset value.

Discount Broker. A broker who typically charges less (in comparison to full-service brokers) for services rendered—from trades transacted to reports and recommendations issued. There's a wide variance in such costs and services among discounters and deep discounters.

Discount Rate. The interest rate the Federal Reserve Board charges member banks on loans. This rate in turn affects the interest rates on loans consumers will pay, since banks use the discount rate as the benchmark from which they mark up the rate on their loans.

Distribution. A payment made to a shareholder. Except for income from municipal funds, distributions are taxable.

Diversification. A strategy for reducing investment risk by investing in different categories and types of investments as well as (within the stock market) different industries and company market capitalizations.

Dividend. A distribution of earnings to shareholders, either by an individual company or by a mutual fund.

Dividend Reinvestment Plan. Like *automatic reinvestment,* the reinvestment of dividends in new shares of the stock or fund. You will have to pay taxes on the dividend amount (even if you don't receive it in cash).

Dollar-Cost Averaging. Investment method in which a specific, equal amount of money is regularly invested on a scheduled basis. This method can reward the investor who employs it with more shares bought at lower prices than at higher prices.

Dow Jones Industrial Average (DJIA, or "The Dow"). A stock market index which has withstood the test of time by adequately reflecting the movement of the market as a whole. It's calculated by adding up the prices of thirty large-cap stocks, which results in a potential flaw (according to some critics)—namely, its narrow definition and exclusion of newer industries and companies. Nevertheless, this index is the most widely used measure of the market.

Duration. A measure of a bond fund's interest rate sensitivity, based on the maturities of the bonds in the portfolio. A fund with an effective duration of 4 should lose 4 percent if interest rates rise 1 percent, or gain 4 percent if interest rates fall 1 percent.

Earnings per Share (EPS). Portion of a company's profit allocated to each outstanding share of common stock. (Total profits divided by number of shares of common stock.)

Economic Indicators. Statistics used to represent the current state of the economy and also to predict (with a meteorologist's accuracy) the direction of the economy.

Efficient Market Theory. A theory which suggests that market price reflects market value, meaning that dart throwers and analysts have an equal chance of selecting the best stocks.

Equity. A fancy name for common stock.

Ex-Dividend Date. The date on which stocks (or mutual funds) effectively pay out their dividends. Shareholders who own the fund on this date receive the dividend, the share price tends to fall by the amount of the dividend on this date, and automatic reinvestments are made on this date. (However, actual dividend checks may be delayed by several days.)

Expense Ratio. The amount investors in a fund pay for expenses incurred in the operation and management of the fund during the year. This expense may be 1 percent or more.

Face Value. Worth of the bond or other security as stated on it.

Family of Funds. Group of funds "owned" (that is, managed and operated) by the same investment management company. (Technically, each fund is owned by its shareholders, who could vote to move the fund to another fund family.)

Fixed-Income Fund. A mutual fund which invests in fixed-income securities such as corporate bonds or Ginnie Maes.

401(k) Plan. Employer-sponsored tax-advantaged retirement plan which enables contributors to put pretax dollars in the investment vehicles offered by the plan. The employer often matches the contributions of participating employees.

403(b) Plan. Equivalent to 401(k) plans, but for nonprofit employers.

Fundamental Analysis. Analysis of a company and its securities based on hard data from its balance sheet and income statements, sales, earnings, and management, as well as extrinsic economic factors which affect the company's ability to operate profitably. Such analysis can be used as a predictor of future potential. Contrast with *technical analysis.*

Fund of Funds. A mutual fund whose portfolio consists of other mutual funds.

Futures Contract. Written agreement to buy or sell a commodity or security for a specified price at a specified future date.

Growth Fund. A mutual fund which invests in growth stocks. In doing so, this type of fund seeks to deliver *capital appreciation* to its shareholders, rather than income. As a result, a stock's earnings growth is favored over its actual or potential dividends.

Growth and Income Fund (G&I fund). A mutual fund which typically combines the objective of *capital appreciation* with the generation of some *income.* Note: Some G&I funds are very close to growth funds, offering virtually no income; others look almost like bond funds, with little room for capital appreciation.

Growth Stock. A stock in a company characterized by above-average growth in earnings or sales. Growth stocks tend to have a high price relative to earnings, and provide little if any dividend. Growth stocks also tend to have a high *beta* (or risk), but can offer long-term investors the potential for solid capital appreciation. Contrast with *cyclical stock* and *value stock.*

Hedge. A strategy used to neutralize the risk inherent in an investment. The phrase, "hedging one's bets," accurately reflects the objective: to break even whether the hedged assets move up or down. Hedging, which is often accomplished with the use of *derivatives,* sometimes fails to protect against risks as planned.

Index. A standard or benchmark against which the performance of a market, industry, company, or security (stock, bond, real estate, mutual fund, and more) is measured.

Index Fund. A fund whose objective is to match a specific market index, most commonly the S&P 500 stock index. Since most funds fail to beat their relevant index benchmark, an index fund is likely to perform slightly better than most funds in the long term.

Inefficient Market Theory. A theory that holds that an informed investor stands a better-than-even chance of outperforming a chimp and a dartboard. Contrasted with the *efficient market theory,* this one encourages research, analysis, and the ability to beat a fellow investor to the punch—finding hidden profits or pitfalls in a given company.

Inflation. The rise in the prices of goods and services as reflected in the consumer price index (CPI), which tracks consumer goods, and the producer price index (PPI), which focuses on industrial goods and materials. Inflation decreases the purchasing power of your dollar in the long run. The cause is usually attributed to an increase in the money supply.

Investment Company. An arrangement whereby investors pool their assets into a corporation or trust which then employs professional management to invest the assets according to a stated objective. Mutual funds are one form of investment company. See *Unit Trust, Mutual Fund,* and *Closed-End Investment Fund.*

Investment Objective. A fund's aim, as stated in its prospectus. Investors should choose a fund whose objectives match their own—although they need to go beyond the stated objective and examine the fund's history of actually hitting what it says it's aiming at.

Individual Retirement Account (IRA). A tax-deductible retirement investment plan—or, at least, a tax-deferred one. Penalties apply for early withdrawal.

Load. A mutual fund's sales charge. See chapter 13 for a list of the ways a mutual fund can take a bite out of your investment.

Mutual Fund. A professionally managed portfolio of securities (one or a combination of stocks, bonds, cash, real estate investment trusts) which enables investors to pool their money and reap the potential rewards (or suffer the possible consequences).

Net Asset Value (NAV). The market price of a fund, derived at the close of market every day by determining the value of the fund's total assets (the value of each security as well as cash and cash equivalents) less its liabilities divided by the total number of its outstanding shares.

No-Load Fund. A mutual fund whose shares can be bought and sold at NAV without any sales charge. There may, however, be redemption fees (a fee charged for selling the fund, generally within a specified time of purchase).

Offering Price. The Net Asset Value per share, plus the sales charge. Also called the "asked price." For no-load funds, the NAV and offering price are the same.

Open-End Fund. See *mutual fund.*

OTC (over-the-counter). Stocks not listed on any exchange but bought and sold through a computerized network of traders. The Nasdaq is the leading over-the-counter market in the U.S.

Par. The face value of a bond; the principal amount that should be paid when the bond matures.

Portfolio. Term used to describe an investor's or fund manager's investment holdings.

Premium. The opposite of *discount.*

Prospectus. The fund's equivalent to a company's annual report. The Securities and Exchange Commission (SEC) requires every fund to provide each shareholder a prospectus wherein the fund describes its investment objectives, investments, past performance, fees, and services.

Sector. The constituent parts of an overall industry. For example, pharmaceutical companies and semiconductor manufacturers as distinct from health and technology.

Sector Fund. Fund which invests in companies in one defined sector or related group of sectors.

Technical Analysis. Means by which technical analysts look for trends (and other more abstract symbols) to tip them to an investment's future prospects, primarily using charts of a security's past price performance. Contrast with *fundamental analysis.*

Tenure. A fund manager's time at the helm.

Total Return. The annual appreciation of an investment (including its capital appreciation, dividends, and/or interest) and thus a clear marker as to how much your investment has grown since you bought it.

Turnover Rate. Calculated by taking the value of all the fund's trades (buys and sells) and dividing it by twice the net assets of the portfolio, indicating how aggressive a manager is being with regard to trading in and out of (or within) the market. A turnover rate in excess of 100 percent generally means a pretty aggressive manager. If the manager's good, that's not a problem; but excessive turnover can drive up fund expenses and hurt returns.

Value Stock. A stock that is considered cheap relative to earnings or assets. Value stocks tend to be stodgier players in slower-growing, defensive, or cyclical areas. Contrast with *growth stock.*

Yield. The rate of interest payments on a bond. The current yield on a bond is the amount of yearly interest divided by the current value of the bond. A more useful measure of yield is the yield to maturity, which takes into account the fact that bonds selling at a discount or premium to their *par* value will get closer to *par* value as they near maturity. The SEC now requires that funds report yield to maturity.

Yield Spread. The difference between the yield on one kind of income investment and the yield on a standard investment, usually U.S. Treasury bonds. The yield spread between a bond and the benchmark U.S. Treasury would tend to indicate the degree of credit risk expected for the bond.

INDEX